Great Australian Pubs

YOUNG & JACKSON

Great Australian Pubs

LEE MYLNE

EXPLORE AUSTRALIA

Contents

Introduction

THE DOOR TO the bar opens in a burst of cool air, admitting a gaggle of merry-makers. Soon we are doubled up with laughter, shamelessly eavesdropping on the conversation and good-natured antics of a group of race-goers who have dropped into the pub we're in. It's hilarious and unexpected; a few minutes' earlier, all has been quiet but the sudden burst of frivolity and banter has added life to our surroundings and we catch the mood instantly. It's a cold night outside, but the sudden influx of a new crowd of drinkers has brought warmth and new energy into the bar. The noise level rises, laughter rings out around the room, the barman throws a grin our way, and the fire burning in the grate seems to glow a bit brighter. Just another night in an Aussie pub, with an atmosphere all its own that's hard to beat.

'There is nothing which has yet been contrived by man, by which so much happiness is produced as by a good tavern or inn.'

– Samuel Johnson, 1776.

It's a scene that is played out over and over around the country. Head to the pub and you're almost guaranteed there'll be someone looking for a chat on any topic you care to choose. Go solo, with a book perhaps, and you'll find somewhere to while away time in a cosy corner. Order a drink, a counter meal (or something more elaborate) and you're set. Whatever your mood, you'll find a pub somewhere to match it.

'Writing a book about pubs? What do I do to get your job?' That was a common reaction during the course of my research for this book. A lengthy pub crawl around Australia to check out and select 100 pubs worthy of recommending was right up the alley of almost everyone I talked to.

But as there are around 4000 pubs, taverns and bars in Australia, how was I to choose only 100? Everyone has their favourite, often their 'local', which is considered incomparably better than any other pub! Starting with some of the most famous and obvious contenders – like Melbourne's Young & Jackson and Sydney's trio of the 'oldest' – the Lord Nelson, the Fortune of War and the Hero of Waterloo – I added some outback icons, like South Australia's Prairie Hotel at Parachilna and the Daly Waters Pub in the Northern Territory, and started building my list from there.

What I was looking for, more than anything, was pubs that had a story to tell. And the best ones were those with tales that linked them to Australia's wider history or important events. In many ways it was easy, as pubs have been at the heart of Australian communities since they first began trading. They have been forums for political events and social change, have hosted some of Australia's top musicians and strangest events, and have evolved into so much more than simply a place to drink, eat or stay.

And everywhere I went, I asked around the bar for other recommendations. There were some beauties. My route map criss-crossed with new 'finds', I doubled back here and there if something cropped up that seemed unmissable. Sometimes there were disappointments. The pub where the licensee welcomed me in his bathrobe missed being included in the book (not only for that reason); the few where I was greeted with suspicion or rudeness did too. Racist and offensive comments from an almost exclusively male clientele struck another from my list. But for the most part I found friendly, welcoming conversation and congenial company, good food, comfortable beds that ranged from the ultimate in luxury to budget/basic, and great atmosphere.

This book aims to give a guide to what great Australian pubs can offer. They differ widely in style and atmosphere and in the services they provide. Some have poker machines; others most adamantly point out that they do not. Many no longer provide rooms, others have just a few or have added accommodation to their original buildings. Most of the pubs featured in this book have been part of their communities for a century or more, but there are a few that have been rebuilt or largely modernised. The variety is enormous and adds to the fun of discovering what makes a place tick.

Along with information about the pubs themselves, you'll find ideas about things to do in whatever town you are in. Bear in mind that this is a guide only; things change. Owners or licensees move on, as do chefs. Some of the beer on tap is likely to be different by the time you get there, and the room rates or prices on the menu may have increased. Hours of opening also vary; most pubs open for drinking at around 10am or 11am and stay open until 'late'. Many are licensed until later than they actually stay open, especially in country areas where the hours may be determined by demand.

Depending on the day of the week, or the time of the day, you may find your visit to any pub in this book is quite a different experience to mine. Nevertheless, I hope it's still a good one. Some publicans talk of hard economic times and – in country areas particularly – nights when the bar is all but empty. They battle on, fortified by the camaraderie that comes when the customers walk through the door.

Australia's pubs have welcomed everyone from royalty to riff-raff. Movie stars and miners have supped in their bars and slept in their beds, as have bushrangers and bards, soldiers and sailors, saints (yes, literally) and sinners, farmers and feminists, explorers, politicians, surfers, writers, and more. Some of them still linger ... it's a rare pub that can't rustle up a ghost story or two, and you'll find some of them in these pages.

I hope you enjoy reading about them, and visiting them, as much as I did.

Lee Mylne

September 2011

New South Wales

and Australian Capital Territory

Opposite (clockwise from top): The Newport Arms; The Lord Nelson Brewery Hotel, The Rocks; The Australian Hotel, The Rocks; Wig & Pen, Canberra.

The AUSTRALIAN *Hotel*

THE ROCKS

> ...comfortable, full of atmosphere and close to everything that Sydney has to offer.

The Australian Hotel, The Rocks

'LIKE STAYING AT my granny's house,' a visitor has written in the guest book at the Australian Hotel. Well ... in a way it is, if that means slightly dated but comfortable rooms, with some chintz and floral decoration, sash windows and a few things a bit frayed around the edges – plus a decanter of port on a silver tray in the corner of the lounge.

The rooms above the Australian have not been citified or modernised, a refreshing change when so many inner-city hotel rooms look as if they've been designed by the same person. But granny's house (hopefully) hasn't been the scene of one of Sydney's most notorious unsolved murders, and probably doesn't attract such a big Friday night crowd.

The Australian is in the heart of The Rocks, at the corner of Cumberland and Gloucester streets. It is the area where Australia's first European settlers – British convicts and their overseers – claimed the land and built their camp on the sandstone cliffs in 1788. Those were rough and unruly days, but the murder happened at the hotel in the 1950s.

Shocked patrons were witnesses to the gangland-style killing of 27-year-old John William Manners outside the hotel on 8 June 1956. A married man with two children, Manners was also a one-time professional boxer, thief, stand-over man and gangster. Witnesses described how he had been drunk that afternoon, falling asleep on a bar

The Australian Wine Emporium, adjacent to the hotel

stool and waking up frightened and anxious. He stepped out of the pub's saloon doors on to Gloucester Street and was felled by three bullets. George Joseph Hacket was charged with his murder but was acquitted of the crime in October 1956, and the case has never been solved.

The original Australian Hotel was located on George Street, next to where the Museum of Contemporary Art now stands. The *Sydney Gazette* announced its opening on 12 August 1824, making it the oldest continuously licensed hotel in Sydney. When the city was gripped by plague in the early 1900s, many buildings were torn down, including the Australian. The licence was transferred to a new building at 116 Cumberland Street, near the site of today's hotel.

The guest lounge, 'like granny's house'

In 1913 the existing hotel opened and is now a well-preserved example of Edwardian-style architecture, retaining many period features including metal awnings, etched signage, split-level bars and saloon-style doors. The hotel is listed on the State Heritage Register and the Conservation and Heritage Register for Sydney Harbour Foreshore Authority, as well as by the National Estate, the National Trust of Australia (NSW), and the Royal Australian Institute of Architects Register of 20th Century Buildings of Significance.

THE AUSTRALIAN HOTEL

ADDRESS
100 Cumberland St, The Rocks

TELEPHONE
(02) 9247 2229

WEBSITE
www.australianheritagehotel.com

RATES
$99 double Sun–Thurs, $119 Fri–Sat, including self-serve continental breakfast in the guest lounge.

HOURS
Mon–Sat 10.30–12am; Sun 10.30am–10pm.

GRUB
Mon–Sat 11.30am–10pm; Sun 11.30am–9pm.

TOP DROP
There are more than 130 boutique beers to choose from. One of the most popular is Scharer's (reputed to give no hangover, because of its lack of preservatives).

NEARBY ATTRACTIONS
Almost directly across the road on Gloucester St is the historic Susannah Place Museum, in a working-class terrace built in 1844 (www.hht.net.au). The pub is also a 100 m walk to the departure point for Sydney's Bridgeclimb (www.bridgeclimb.com).

MORE INFO
www.sydney.com

Cumberland Street bar

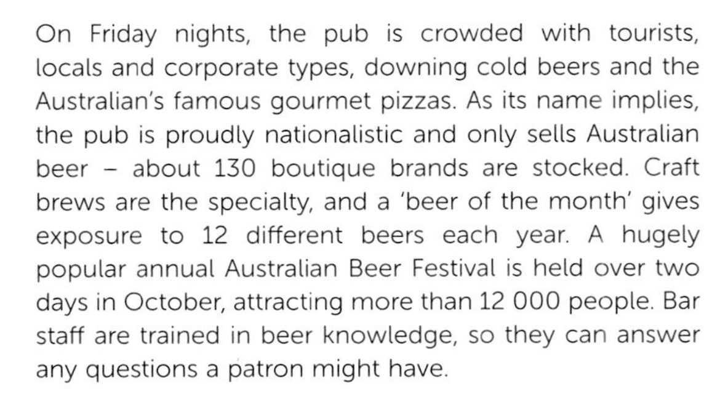

On Friday nights, the pub is crowded with tourists, locals and corporate types, downing cold beers and the Australian's famous gourmet pizzas. As its name implies, the pub is proudly nationalistic and only sells Australian beer – about 130 boutique brands are stocked. Craft brews are the specialty, and a 'beer of the month' gives exposure to 12 different beers each year. A hugely popular annual Australian Beer Festival is held over two days in October, attracting more than 12 000 people. Bar staff are trained in beer knowledge, so they can answer any questions a patron might have.

Big nights on the calendar are New Year's Eve, Australia Day and Anzac Day (the pub is the biggest two-up arena in Sydney), when 6000 people throng here for a street party and the pub serves a barbecue, as well as meat pies, and cheese and Vegemite pizzas. The Australian is renowned for its pizza toppings, and its gourmet range includes kangaroo, crocodile and emu (just to name a few).

You can sit outside at a table on the footpath, but there are also lots of choices inside. Apart from the main bar, you can tuck yourself away in the Alcove, part of the Bottom Bar on the Gloucester Street side of the hotel, where there are long tables and old wooden church pews. For a quieter spot, try the cosy Ladies Parlour – the first place in Sydney where women were allowed to drink in a hotel – with its Federation-style high ceilings and warm atmosphere.

The casual Snug Kitchen & Cafe, which has been a cafe since 1880, is next door on Cumberland Street, and on Thursday, Friday and Saturday nights you can head to the Australian Wine Emporium, adjacent on Gloucester Street. With pressed-metal ceilings but a modern vibe, this is another spot to visit if the noise outside is too much for you. There's always the roof terrace, too: climb up to it for a view of the Sydney Opera House and Harbour Bridge, or just to enjoy a different perspective on the city in the fresh air.

Guest room

A door off Gloucester Street takes you upstairs to the pub's nine guest rooms, which have queen, double or twin beds, and share five bathrooms. There are two corridors of rooms, meeting at the main guest lounge, at the triangular corner overlooking the junction. The lounge has a television, video, a few books and magazines, tea and coffee available all day, and other complementary little touches, such as bowls of fruit and the decanter of port. There's another, quieter, lounge at the far end of the second hallway.

Just like granny's house? Perhaps not, but clean, comfortable, full of atmosphere and close to everything that Sydney has to offer.

THE ROCKS

SOLDIERS, SPORTING HEROES and stars of the stage and screen have all sunk beers in the Fortune of War – it's had a long history as one of Sydney's most popular watering holes. Pull up a stool in the George Street Bar and you're becoming part of its colourful history.

One of Sydney's oldest pubs, the Fortune of War has always been a 'first and last stop ashore' for Australian troops as they set out to experience their own 'fortunes of war'. During World War II the hotel was a favourite haunt of sailors from the Royal Australian Navy, Royal Navy and Merchant Navy when their ships were berthed at nearby Circular Quay.

> ANZAC Day sees veterans making their way to the Fortune of War to reunite and reminisce about their time of service, the walls of the old bar ringing with war stories.

These days, ANZAC Day still sees veterans from World War II and Vietnam making their way to the Fortune of War, to reunite and reminisce about their time of service, the walls of the old bar ringing with their war stories. But if you head upstairs to the quieter First Fleet Bar you'll find a tribute to Sydney's convict roots; the walls are hung with colourful sketches of the 12 First Fleet ships which sailed into Sydney Cove in 1788, and their passenger lists.

Fortune of War's George Street Bar

In fact, it was a convict who built the Fortune of War. The hotel's licence dates back to 1828, making it Sydney's oldest continuously licensed pub, but its origins go back to the earliest years of the colony. In 1801, Samuel Terry arrived in New South Wales after being transported for seven years for theft. Making the most of this new life, by the time his sentence was over Terry had established himself as a merchant in Parramatta. In 1810 he moved to Sydney Cove and opened a public house. He soon became one of the most prominent and successful men in Sydney, and a major landholder.

In 1828, Terry built a new hotel and public house which he called the Fortune of War, and the first recorded liquor licence for the Fortune of War was received that year. Terry's wealth earned him the nickname 'the Rothschild of Botany Bay', and when he

Fortune of War sign

The Russell Hotel provides accommodation adjacent to the Fortune of War

died in 1838, he left an estate of £250 000 – an immense fortune. The pub was owned by his family until 1860, when it was sold to Robert Moore, who had been the licensee since 1840.

Since the Fortune of War's licence was first granted in 1828, all the pubs from the same era have been de-licensed or demolished, and thus it is the oldest pub in today's bustling tourist hub of The Rocks. It has survived changes in ownership, the bubonic plague of 1900, natural disasters and wars, and has had a cast of colourful characters lean up against the bar.

The Moore family continued to own and run the hotel until the turn of the century. The original hotel was demolished in 1921–22 and a new building erected in its place, in the then fashionable Federation arts and crafts style.

Fortune of War's entrance

The licensee since 1987 has been well-known Sydney sportsman Bob Keyes. A former rugby league player of note, Keyes not only holds the licence for Sydney's oldest pub, he also played with the oldest Australian Rugby League club in the country. The Newtown Bluebags was formed in January 1908, the first of the league's foundation clubs. During his career with Newtown from 1962 to 1970, Keyes played 163 games and scored 37 tries.

The George Street Bar has a heritage-listed hamper-style bar, and its walls are hung with memorabilia. There's a photographic history of the Sydney Cricket Ground, images of the 1908 world heavyweight title fight between Tommy Burns and Jack Johnson, and a great photo of boxer Les Darcy sparring on Balmoral Beach just before he sailed to the United States in 1916, where he died suddenly the following year. The bar-fight scene in the 1981 television mini-series *A Town Like Alice*, starring actor Bryan Brown, was filmed in the George Street Bar, and there's a framed newspaper clipping recording the action.

Upstairs, the bistro in the First Fleet Bar serves homemade lunch favourites such as gourmet pies, smoked salmon on a potato patty with avocado sauce, beef goulash, asparagus and bacon quiche, or a roast of the day. In the bar, you can get burgers, a BLT, chips or wedges from lunchtime till late. On Sundays, kick back and listen to trad jazz with the Robbers Dogs from 3–6pm, and there's also live entertainment every Friday and Saturday 8pm–12am.

FORTUNE OF WAR

ADDRESS
137 George St, The Rocks

TELEPHONE
(02) 9247 2714

WEBSITE
www.fortuneofwar.com.au

HOURS
Daily 9am–late.

GRUB
The bistro in the First Fleet Bar is open weekdays 12–2.30pm; barfood available all day until late.

TOP DROP
The George Street Bar has 15 beers on tap, both local and imported.

WHERE TO STAY
There's internal access from the Fortune of War to the adjacent hotel, the Russell, built in 1887. This recently refurbished 29-room hotel has a wine bar, sitting room overlooking George St and a rooftop garden. Rates start from $159 double for standard room with shared bathroom or $249 double with ensuite (extra person $30 per night).
www.therussell.com.au

NEARBY ATTRACTIONS
It's a short walk to Circular Quay, the Sydney Opera House, Sydney Harbour Bridge, and The Rocks historic precinct. Almost directly across the street is the Museum of Contemporary Art.

MORE INFO
www.sydneyvisitorcentre.com
www.sydney.com
www.visitnsw.com

The Hero of Waterloo

The HERO *of* WATERLOO

MILLERS POINT

TALL TALES OF Sydney's rough-and-ready early days abound, and none are more vivid than those you may hear across the bar at one of the city's oldest pubs, the Hero of Waterloo. Perched on a corner block in historic Millers Point, adjacent to The Rocks, the sandstone walls of this pub have many a story to tell. Enter under the swinging portrait of the hero, England's Duke of Wellington, who defeated Napoleon at the Battle of Waterloo in 1815. Inside you'll find more pictures of the Duke and Bonaparte, but the hotel's own history is almost more fascinating.

In 1842, George Paton, who had helped build the nearby Garrison Church, bought the triangular parcel of land from Johnathon Clarke, the first owner of the adjacent Shipwrights Arms. The Arms had been built from sandstone blocks used as ballast on ships from England, but Paton, a stonemason, built the Hero from sandstone brought up from the Argyle Cut (which you will walk through on your way to the harbour). He used convict labour, every man working to a quota of blocks and marking each with his own symbol – look closely and you can see them carved into the stones.

The licence was granted two years later, in 1844, and the Hero became a favoured drinking spot for the garrison troops of the colonial days, who manned the forts at each end of the street (the 'upper' and 'lower' forts gave the streets their names). The Hero was in good company, as opposite was the Whalers Arms (then called the Little Princess).

Under the floor of the bar is a maze of stone-walled cellars and a secret tunnel which runs from the cellars to the former Shipwrights Arms and the harbour.

Many stories and rumours swirl through the history of the Hero of Waterloo, now an historic landmark classified by the Heritage Council of New South Wales and the National Trust. Under the floor of the bar is a maze of stone-walled cellars and a secret tunnel which runs from the cellars to the former Shipwrights Arms and the harbour. What was it for? The best guesses are rum smuggling and press-ganging – where a young man might find himself at one moment drunk at the bar, the next dropped through a trapdoor into the cellar, bundled through the tunnel and waking the next day at sea, shanghaied and aboard a ship bound for strange, faraway shores.

In these subterranean corridors, beneath ceilings of wattle and daub, there are also cells, still hung with chains. 'We think it's a place where – like in the old days in England – the local police might have asked the publican to keep troublemakers overnight,' says current owner of the Hero, Ivan Nelson, as he points out the various notable features of this extraordinary place.

The Hero no longer takes overnight guests, but that doesn't mean all is quiet in the dark hours. Nelson and his wife Kazuko, who live upstairs, were woken one night soon after

Tunnel entrance in the cellar

moving in by the sound of the piano being played in the bar.

'My wife woke me up, thinking that someone had broken in,' says Nelson. 'I went downstairs, and when I got to the door of the bar, the music stopped. There was no-one there, but the lid of the piano had been left up when we always left it closed.'

After doing some research, they believe the spirit is Anne Kirkman, a woman who died in 1849, in her thirties. 'She is a poltergeist, which means she moves things around,' says Nelson. 'Other people have also told us they have seen a strange woman.' But he says a visiting Buddhist monk told him that the several ghosts who haunt the Hero are all happy presences – and they don't want to leave the pub.

More earthly piano music can be heard in the bar on Wednesdays and Thursdays from 7pm and on Fridays and Saturdays from 8pm. The Hero is famous for its live music, and has regular performers including Irish band Green Jam, who have been playing there every Sunday for more than a decade. With a repertoire of 'rousing Celtic foot stampers' as well as pop and rock, they know how to work a crowd and the infectious atmosphere keeps Sydneysiders coming back for more.

'The Jammies' are now almost legendary and jamming with them at the Hero is popular with other musicians – even the occasional international star who might pop in! Irish jam sessions run from 7pm on Sundays, while if old-time jazz is more your style, Saturday and Sunday afternoons are the time to be there.

Lunch and dinner are served in the restaurant, or you can order from a bar menu. A Hero burger is made on a damper roll, with salad, beetroot, tomato, Spanish onion, mustard-seed mayo and chips. Other dishes include lamb shanks, a salmon curry, fish and chips, or a fisherman's platter, with most plates priced at less than $20. Daily specials are also available.

There are open fires in the restaurant and the bar, especially welcome in winter. With such a warm and inviting atmosphere, it's no wonder those friendly ghosts don't want to leave.

Dining room

THE HERO OF WATERLOO

ADDRESS
81 Lower Fort St, Millers Point

TELEPHONE
(02) 9252 4553

WEBSITE
www.heroofwaterloo.com.au

HOURS
Daily 11am–10pm.

GRUB
The restaurant is open daily for lunch, 11am–3pm, and dinner, 5–10pm.

TOP DROP
The bestselling beers are James Squire Pilsener and James Squire Amber Ale. The wine list is exclusively Australian and New Zealand labels.

WHERE TO STAY
Nearby is the equally historic Observatory Hotel (but it's definitely not a pub), a great choice if you're looking for 5-star luxury. Rates start at around $300 double. www.observatoryhotel.com.au

NEARBY ATTRACTIONS
Observatory Hill is just a street away, where you can visit the Sydney Observatory. You can look around by yourself, or take a $7 guided tour that gives access to the telescope towers, telescope viewings and 3D theatre sessions. The best time to visit is at night, when tours cost $17 (bookings essential) and include the chance to look at the sky with astronomer guides. www.sydneyobservatory.com.au

MORE INFO
www.sydney.com

THE LORD NELSON BREWERY HOTEL

THE ROCKS

The Lord Nelson Brewery Hotel

WHEN BLAIR HAYDEN and his partners bought Sydney's oldest continuously licensed hotel in 1985 and turned it into a brewery hotel, they became the latest in a long line of owners to create their own piece of history in The Rocks. It was, says Hayden, 'a run-down, dirty hole' with very few patrons. But he had a vision to create Australia's first brewery in a pub and to emulate the traditional English pubs that he admired.

Today, the old stone walls and wooden floors welcome people from all walks of life, and it's a far cry from the establishment on the north-east corner of Kent and Argyle streets that was first granted the liquor licence, known then as the Shipwright Arms, on 29 June 1831. It was owned by Richard Phillips, who soon changed its name to the Sailor's Return, because of the patronage of the seafarers and workers on Observatory Hill.

In 1838 Phillips sold the pub to a former convict and sly-grog trader, William Wells, who lived on the opposite corner in a two-storey colonial home he had built using sandstone blocks quarried from the area at the base of Observatory Hill. Wells continued to operate the pub opposite his home firstly as the Sailor's Return, but in 1840 he too changed the name, this time to the Quarryman's Arms.

A year later, Wells sold the Arms and transferred the liquor licence to his home, which he extended along Kent Street, adding the second and top floors to create the Lord Nelson. The Wells family owned the hotel for the next 48 years, also operating other hotels around Sydney, including the Wynyard Hotel, the Star Hotel in Balmain and the Quarryman's Arms in Pyrmont.

The walls are now hung with pieces of interest, including an original page of *The Times* newspaper of 7 November 1805, with details of the Battle of Trafalgar and Lord Nelson's death, and a copy of the hotel's first licence. Today the hotel is heritage listed by the National Trust.

The Lord Nelson became the first pub in Australia to have its own micro-brewery on the premises. Patrons can watch part of the brewing process through large windows that separate the brewery from the main bar.

New Zealander Blair Hayden bought the pub – after looking at about 200 premises, he laughs – with the intention of putting in a brewery. He loved the Australian colonial architecture and aimed to produce an ambience similar to that of English pubs that he had visited while living and working in the UK.

The bar has large screens for watching big sporting events – but there are no poker machines. 'I wanted to create a place that was in the true tradition of pubs, a place of conviviality,' Hayden says. 'There's no gaming here. We never wanted that because it disrupts conversation; a pub is a place for people to meet, eat and enjoy themselves.'

Today, the pub attracts an eclectic group. On weekdays you'll be in the company of business workers from the city, regulars and some tourists; on weekends there are more tourists, but also 'regulars' who may have come from outside the city, perhaps Newcastle or the Blue Mountains, specifically for a day at the Lord.

Part of the appeal is the beer. In 1985, the Lord Nelson became the first pub in Australia to have its own micro-brewery on the premises. Patrons can watch part of the brewing process through large windows that separate the brewery from the main bar. Six natural ales are brewed – Quayle Ale, Trafalgar Pale Ale, Three Sheets, Victory Bitter, Old Admiral and Nelsons Blood – the latter a rich creamy porter, with bitter coffee and sweet chocolate flavours.

Lord Nelson bar

Fine dining in Nelson's Brasserie

THE LORD NELSON BREWERY HOTEL

ADDRESS
19 Kent St (cnr Argyle St), The Rocks

TELEPHONE
(02) 9251 4044

WEBSITE
www.lordnelsonbrewery.com

RATES
Rooms with shared bathroom $130 double; rooms with ensuite $190 double (extra person $50 per night); rates includes continental breakfast in the brasserie.

HOURS
Mon–Sat 10am–11pm; Sun 12–10pm.

GRUB
The bar menu is available daily 12–3pm. The upstairs brasserie is open daily for breakfast 7.30–9.30am, Wed–Fri for lunch 12–3.30pm, and Tues–Sat for dinner from 6.30pm.

TOP DROP
Choose from the six natural ales produced in the Lord Nelson's boutique in-house brewery, with six other varieties on tap.

NEARBY ATTRACTIONS
The Lord Nelson is within easy walking distance of Sydney's major attractions. It's a 5 min walk to Circular Quay, the Sydney Opera House and the Harbour Bridge, or a 15 min walk to King Street Wharf and the Pitt St Mall. There are also pleasant walks around the foreshore right at the doorstep.

MORE INFO
www.sydney.com
www.visitnsw.com

The '100 per cent natural' tag means the beers are brewed using only malt, hops, yeast and water – no sugars, preservatives or other additives. All are available on tap, and two of the ales – Three Sheets Pale Ale and Old Admiral Dark Ale – are also available in bottles. A number of seasonal ales are also produced throughout the year.

Lord Nelson brewery

If you are hungry, you can have a typical pub meal in the bar, snack on a pork pie or ploughman's lunch, or head upstairs to the elegant Nelson's Brasserie – where the convict-quarried sandstone walls are a feature – for 'innovative Australian cuisine' using the best local and international seasonal produce. It is well named, as 'brasserie' is French for a restaurant serving beer with food, but the restaurant also has an extensive wine list, with a choice of vintages and some magnums.

The nine guest rooms upstairs at the Lord are on two levels above the bar area. Some of the rooms, on the outer side of the building, have beautiful sandstone feature walls. The five rooms on the lower level have shared bathrooms; the four above have ensuites. Two of the ensuite rooms have an additional single bed. All rooms are non-smoking and air-conditioned, with tea- and coffee-making facilities, telephone, fax, fridge, television and iron, and there is high-speed wireless broadband available in all areas of the hotel.

Bar meals at the Lord Nelson

The NEWPORT ARMS

NEWPORT

LOCATION, LOCATION, LOCATION. The Newport Arms has one of the best beer gardens in Australia, perched on a point of land overlooking Pittwater and with views across to Kur-ring-gai Chase National Park. In summer, it is hard to beat as the ideal place to sink a few cold ones. In fact, the leafy west-facing beer garden, which sweeps down to the water and the jetty, is also the perfect spot for sunset drinks all year round while you watch the boats glide by below.

The Newport Arms is perfect for sunset drinks

Long a favourite with surfers, beach-goers and families, the Arms has been owned and operated by the Bayfield family for the past 20 years, but it has been serving drinks since 1880 when it was a hang-out for bushrangers, smugglers and other dodgy characters. Today you're more likely to find families letting the kids loose in one of the three playgrounds while the parents enjoy a sunny afternoon in what is reputedly Australia's – if not the world's – largest waterfront beer garden. The gardens are dotted with a mix of tropical and native trees, dominated by huge canary palms.

... one of the best beer gardens in Australia, perched on a point of land overlooking Pittwater and with views across to Kur-ring-gai Chase National Park.

When businessman Charles Edward Jeannerett teamed up with George Pile to build the hotel, he could see the potential for Newport. Jeannerett owned 20 steamers plying the Parramatta and Hawkesbury rivers, and the wharf he and Pile built adjacent to the hotel resulted in a boom for the area. By the late 1890s, boatloads of daytrippers were coming from Sydney at weekends. The first licensee, William Boulton, bought the hotel from Jeannerett in 1887 and it stayed in the Boulton family until 1919. In 1913 the hotel was rebuilt as a two-storey brick structure with 20 bedrooms, two dining rooms and four parlours. It has survived much, including floods in 1959 and a fire in 1967.

In 1991 the Bayfield family, who had already been running the nearby Dee Why Hotel for 14 years, took over the Arms and began making steady improvements, including facilities such as a children's play area, garden bistro (with a separate area for kids to buy ice-creams, food and soft drinks) and waterside seating, while also rejuvenating the gardens.

Beer garden, the Newport Arms

THE NEWPORT ARMS

ADDRESS
2 Kalinya St, Newport

TELEPHONE
(02) 9997 4900

WEBSITE
www.newportarms.com.au
www.terraceonpittwater.com.au

RATES
$135 single; $175 double or twin; extra person $55 per night. Rates include a light breakfast.

HOURS
Mon–Sat 10–12am; Sun 10am–10pm.

GRUB
Open for brunch weekdays 10.30–11.30am; weekends 9.30–11.30am. Bistro open daily from 11am. Terrace on Pittwater open for lunch daily 12–3pm, and dinner Mon–Sat 6–9pm.

TOP DROP
There are 18 beers on tap (believed to be a world record from a single service point), including a big range of Australian beers.

NEARBY ATTRACTIONS
Newport Beach is just a few minutes' walk, and it is a 15 min drive to Palm Beach (where the television soap *Home and Away* is filmed).

MORE INFO
www.visitnsw.com
www.sydneybeaches.com.au

Today, Newport Beach is only a 45-minute drive from the heart of Sydney, and at weekends the pub is abuzz with activity. There are five bars and three places to eat, including the Garden Bistro in the beer garden and à la carte dining in the Terrace on Pittwater. The bistro's large menu lists pasta, pizzas and main courses including 300 gram grain-fed steaks and a barbecued seafood platter, plus the usual range of pub grub. The up-market award-winning Terrace on Pittwater restaurant has a dedicated kitchen and floor team, and serves contemporary Australian cuisine.

Burger Shack, which opens on Sundays and public holidays for lunch, offers snacks including $17 burgers – a gourmet 200 gram beefburger with salad and chips – as well as chicken satay and chicken schnitzel burgers, fish and chips, a fisherman's basket, nachos and caesar salads.

In the garden, Sydney's largest outdoor pub screen – installed in 2000 in time for the Olympic Games – shows a mix of music videos and sports coverage. In summer, Sunday Chill sees live music in the beer garden from 3pm on Sundays, and there are happy hours from 3–5pm when popular tipples include mojitos and jugs of Pimms or sangria.

Inside there are several areas to relax. Newy's is the public bar where the locals hang out to watch sport on the big screens and have a punt on the action. For a quieter drink, head to the cocktail lounge–style Terrace Bar, which has a sweeping curved bar and walls hung with memorabilia. There's live music here from 7.30pm on Thursdays and Saturdays, and cocktail happy hours Thursdays–Saturdays 8–10pm.

The crowds really turn out for special days at the Arms, such as the annual Pub-to-Pub charity fun run and walk (which raises more than $250 000) in August, the Melbourne Cup 'Fashions Off the Field' beer garden party in November, the East Coast Girl Beach Model Search in October–November, and Fireworks over Pittwater on New Year's Eve and Australia Day Eve. In December, there's always a visit from Santa and his reindeer.

The pub runs a free shuttle bus around Newport and Mona Vale, but if you'd rather stay overnight there is motel-style accommodation, which was added to the hotel in 2002 – eight rooms (seven of which sleep up to three, the other one up to four people) and a family room that sleeps up to six.

A time capsule laid down in 2000 sits in the hotel foyer, in a CUB beer keg. It contains a history of the hotel and the Bayfield family, as well as the Sydney Olympic Games. But if the walls could talk, the tales they'd tell would be of sunshine, laughter, music and the joy of Sydneysiders getting together in one of their favourite pubs.

THE OAKS HOTEL

NEUTRAL BAY

A FALLING ACORN from the magnificent oak tree that dominates the garden bar at the Oaks might startle an unsuspecting patron in autumn – but tradition has it that to be struck by one is very good luck!

The Oaks has been a popular meeting place on Sydney's North Shore – just a 10-minute drive north of the Harbour Bridge – since 1885, and for some it is, quite simply, the best pub in the world. There's no doubt that the weekend throngs drinking, eating, barbecuing and catching up with friends in the large leafy beer garden are having a very good time.

The oak tree has been part of the scenery since August 1938, when it was planted by Kathleen McGill (née Furlong). Members of the Furlong family held the licence for the Oaks from 1918 to 1975. The original 30 centimetre seedling came from the old Anthony Horden's department store in Sydney's George Street, which at that time gave a free oak tree to any patron spending more than £10 in one purchase.

As the tree has grown – now reaching about 20 metres tall and spreading almost as wide – so has the reputation and popularity of the hotel. But it was not the tree that gave the pub its name; rather, it was planted to fit the name. The pub has always been the Oaks, named for the old Oaks Brickworks which was once next door (the site then became used as a tram depot, and is now home to a supermarket).

Everything revolves around the tree – strung with fairy lights that twinkle at night – and the Garden Bar, which are the heart of the Oaks, but there's plenty more to this pub, with several bars and levels, so you can find a quieter place if you choose.

A magnificent oak tree dominates the garden bar

The original seedling came from the old Anthony Horden's department store in Sydney's George Street, which at that time gave a free oak tree to any patron spending more than £10.

At the front of the pub is the 'nineteenthirtysix' bar, named for the year the hotel's former Tramway Bar opened. This area has recently been redesigned, but in keeping with its original Art Deco style. Now, with its leather couches, zinc bar and steel screens, it is where the young crowd hangs out, especially on Friday nights when the resident DJ swings into action. A bar menu – with pizzas, mussels, salads and side dishes – is available here.

THE FACTS

THE OAKS HOTEL

ADDRESS
118 Military Rd, Neutral Bay

TELEPHONE
(02) 9953 5515

WEBSITE
www.oakshotel.com.au

HOURS
Mon–Sat 10–1.30am; Sun 12pm–12am.

GRUB
Weekdays 10am–3pm and 6–10pm; Sat 10am–11pm; Sun 12–10pm.

TOP DROP
There are 14 beers on tap, including a range of local and boutique beers. These include the handcrafted Stone & Wood from Byron Bay, as well as Coopers and James Squire beers.

WHERE TO STAY
There is not much commercial accommodation in Neutral Bay, but the North Shore and city offer many choices. For somewhere not too far away, try Rydges North Sydney, which has hotel rooms and 1- and 2-bedroom suites. www.rydges.com.

NEARBY ATTRACTIONS
Nutcote, the beautiful harbourside home and garden of children's author May Gibbs (*The Complete Adventures of Snugglepot and Cuddlepie*) is now a house museum, at 5 Wallaringa Ave, Neutral Bay; open Wed–Sun, 11am–3pm. www.maygibbs.com.au

MORE INFO
www.sydney.com
www.visitnsw.com

The Oaks' Cue & Cushion rooms have a clubby atmosphere

Other areas include the Steakhouse, the Gourmet Pizza & Beer Cafe and the Cue & Cushion Bar and pool rooms upstairs. The three Cue & Cushion rooms have a clubby atmosphere, with leather chesterfield lounges, blue and red felts on the tables and a jukebox – and one has views overlooking the courtyard and the oak tree.

A feature of the beer garden is the cook-your-own chargrill barbecues. Head inside to the butcher's window and choose your meat, then go back to one of the two large barbies. As ever, mostly men seem to do the outdoor cooking here.

A few steps up from the beer garden and you're in the Garden Palace bar, which has large curved windows looking out to the garden and the oak tree. It's the perfect spot if you want to get out of the sun or the rain.

The Steakhouse serves rump, T-bone, scotch fillet, eye fillet, rib-eye on the bone, New York cuts and lamb rump, as well as sausages and fish steaks. While the Oaks prides itself on its prime steaks, the pub is also famous for its mussel pots – steaming pots of mussels with a side cone of chips.

The Gourmet Pizza cafe has a huge selection of toppings, both gourmet (think Peking duck sausage or marinated pork) and traditional, and a salad bar. For a snack, the menu offers a tasting plate including salt-and-pepper squid and chargrilled chorizo, or you can head to the Oyster Bar for fresh seafood.

Every Sunday there's a family-style roast – slow-cooked rib-eye beef with vegetables – 'just like Mum's' (or better) for $30 per person. And if you're keen to see the latest rugby game or other sporting event, there are big screens in the beer garden and the bar.

The OLD FITZROY *Hotel*

WOOLLOOMOOLOO

THIS HOTEL MAY be a bit hard to find, but for many reasons it's worth the effort to get to the Old Fitzroy in the back streets of Woolloomooloo. It is a pub that retains a lot of its original character, a shabby-chic charm that has been lost at many 'modernised' city pubs, and that's what draws a steady clientele of actors, artists, musicians, writers and media types to its door.

Licensee Gary Pasfield cheerfully describes it as 'a bit grungy', but says that is an essential part of its appeal. 'It's a place to have a drink and a conversation, rather than watching television or the races, and everyone who comes here is through word-of-mouth. People just love it.'

The Old Fitzroy takes its beer very seriously. The pub has two bars and a bistro with seats overlooking leafy Cathedral Street. The main bar downstairs has one of Sydney's largest selections of tap beers, plus a wide range of bottled beers and wines by the glass or bottle. You can sit inside by the fire – there is even a supply of marshmallows for you to roast – or find a table on the footpath outside to watch the world go by. The upstairs bar has six beers on tap, and relaxing lounge rooms with big squashy sofas and armchairs, a pool table, jukebox, and a balcony to sit out on if the weather is balmy.

The Old Fitzroy Hotel in the back streets of Woolloomooloo

The Old Fitzroy is famous for its laksa – more than a dozen different types are on the menu.

Then there's the food. No fancy gastro-pub fare, but something that's unusual for a pub: the Old Fitzroy is famous for its laksa. Steaming bowls of spicy laksa – more than a dozen different types are on the menu – emerge from the kitchen, where the cook, Richard, has been presiding for the past 15 years.

THE OLD FITZROY HOTEL

ADDRESS
129 Dowling St, Woolloomooloo

TELEPHONE
(02) 9356 3848

WEBSITE
www.oldfitzroy.com.au

HOURS
Weekdays 11–12am; Sat 12pm–12am; Sun 3–10pm; public holidays 3pm–12am. Closed Good Friday, Christmas Day, Boxing Day and New Year's Eve.

GRUB
Bistro open weekdays 12–3pm and 6–9.30pm; weekends 5–9.30pm.

TOP DROP
There are 13 beers on tap. Among the most popular are Coopers Green and White Rabbit dark ale.

WHERE TO STAY
There are many accommodation options around Woolloomooloo and Kings Cross, or in the city, to suit all budgets.

NEARBY ATTRACTIONS
It's a short walk to the Domain and the Art Gallery of New South Wales, or any of the city's major attractions. An even shorter stroll will take you to the Finger Wharf at Woolloomooloo.

MORE INFO
http://rocksurfers.org (for the Old Fitzroy Theatre)
www.sydney.com

There are plenty of varieties of this popular Asian treat, and they have the punters coming back for more. The menu lists laksas with barbecued pork and greens; chicken, vegetables and bean curd; mixed seafood; prawns with chicken, vegetables and bean curd in varying combinations; and more ... There are other Asian dishes too, such as beef redang and rice, satays, Singapore noodles, sweet and sour chicken, nasi goreng and curried prawns.

If your tastes run more to traditional pub food, you can order from a range of burgers, all for less than $10, or steak, fish and chips, prawn cutlets and chicken schnitzel for less than $13. Vegetarians won't go hungry either, with dishes including gado gado and three types of meat-free laksa. The bistro also does takeaway.

However, if you're looking for a good night out that involves something besides the pub and its Asian food, the adjoining Old Fitzroy Theatre – an intimate 58-seat venue – can deliver that too. Since 1997, the pub has been home to one of Sydney's first independent theatre companies, the Tamarama Rock Surfers. Over the years, the theatre has staged more than 133 shows, including the premieres of more than 50 new Australian plays, to audiences totalling nearly 90 000.

The Old Fitzroy Theatre puts on up to 12 major productions a year. Each runs for about a month, Tuesdays–Saturdays at 8pm and Sundays at 5pm. Tickets cost $16–$40, the most expensive being for Saturday nights.

Bill posters from the Old Fitzroy Theatre adorn the stairwell

Comfortable and colourful upstairs bar

The upstairs bar has pool tables

In 2010, the pub and the theatre came together for a 'micro-festival' of theatre, music and film over three days. The brainchild of Tamarama Rock Surfers' associate artistic director Phil Spencer and the Old Fitzroy's bar manager Brett Pritchard, it was called Home Brew, and was sold out every night – a success that's been repeated more than once and is likely to continue a couple of times each year. As well as performances and screenings in the theatre, the action moved into the pub itself. While the front bar and restaurant operated as normal, ticket-holders took over the upstairs areas and even the footpath outside.

'I'm not sure exactly how old the pub is,' says Pasfield, who has held the licence since 1999 but has been unable to trace much of its early history. He does know that the original Fitzroy Hotel was renamed the Revolving Battery in the 1980s. A change of ownership saw it revert to the Fitzroy Hotel, but as the locals had always referred to it as the 'old' Fitzroy Hotel, that name was soon made official.

The pub is an easy walk from either the city centre or Kings Cross. It is tucked away on the corner of Dowling and Cathedral streets, about 10 minutes on foot from the historic Woolloomooloo waterfront. During the day, you're likely to find the place full of 'suits' having lunch, but at night there's a mixed crowd of thespians, theatre-goers, backpackers, locals and twenty-somethings on their way to the city nightclubs. At weekends, the Hash House Harriers sometimes use the Old Fitzroy as a start and finish point for their runs, including the annual Red Dress charity fundraiser event. But whenever you make it to the Old Fitzroy, there's bound to be some colour and action. As Pasfield says, it's not like any other pub in Sydney.

LAWSON PARK *Hotel*

MUDGEE

The Lawson Park Hotel is a landmark in Mudgee

FROM THE WIDE balcony of the Lawson Park Hotel – if you are an overnight guest – you can look across the picturesque park from which the pub takes its name, to the Cudgegong River. It's a rare treat in Mudgee, as council regulations forced the removal of many of the historic verandahs that once graced the town's original streetscape. The Lawson Park Hotel escaped the fate of many others, and remains one of the few pubs in town that still has its balconies intact.

If you don't mind climbing the stairs from the back of the garden bar (there's no internal access from the pub) and don't mind sharing a bathroom down the hall, the rooms here are good value. But be warned: the walls are thin. There are seven rooms, with separate bathrooms for men and women. The ceilings are pressed metal and all the rooms have French doors to the wide verandahs that overlook either the street or Lawson Park. There's a spacious lounge – it also has direct access to the verandah – with a television, and a kitchen for overnight guests.

All the rooms have French doors to the wide verandahs that overlook either the street or Lawson Park.

Downstairs, the restaurant and beer garden are popular with local families – there's a children's play area off the beer garden – and visitors. The country-style restaurant and the outdoor area (which is covered) seat about 120 people, and the large main bar has a roaring open fire in winter, around which many a yarn has been told. There's also a sports bar, where the races, football or cricket is usually on the big screens.

The Red Heifer Bar & Grill is renowned for its Angus steaks and deep-dish pies, and you can eat in the bar as well as the dining areas. It's a busy, bustling, friendly place, with a beeper system for meal service, a salad bar and a range of steaks that are all certified Australian Angus beef.

You can cook your own steaks – scotch fillet, rump, New York cut or T-bone – on the chargrill for less than $25, or try the pub's signature deep-dish pies, only $13.95, which come in three versions: lamb, rosemary and tomato; beef, Guinness and green peas; and chickpea, lentils and curry sauce.

A popular spot for lunch

The Lawson Park Hotel is a landmark in Mudgee's colonial streetscape. It was built in the 1860s and was originally known as Tattersalls Hotel. A typical old-style country corner pub, it was lucky to survive that council order to remove wide balconies on Mudgee's old buildings – an order which in recent years has been reversed, and the restoration of old verandahs is now being encouraged.

The park – and the pub – are named for Lieutenant William Lawson, the first European to reach the site of what is now Mudgee, in 1821. A memorial to Lawson, the Centenary Obelisk, stands in the park, erected in 1921 on Market Street and later moved to the park.

In 1813 Lawson had joined Gregory Blaxland and William Charles Wentworth as they made the first successful attempt to find a route across the Blue Mountains. Lawson's knowledge of surveying made him a particularly valuable member of the expedition, and in 1819 he was appointed commandant of the new settlement of Bathurst. While at Bathurst, Lawson undertook three journeys to find a pass through the ranges to the Liverpool Plains. He was unsuccessful but his explorations helped open up the rich pastoral district around Mudgee. James Blackman was the first European settler to cross the Cudgegong River, in 1821, and he was quickly followed by Lawson, who travelled further on to the site of Mudgee, where he later took up 6000 acres (2428 hectares) in the area.

Another famous Lawson also has strong links with the town. The writer and poet Henry Lawson lived in Mudgee for 16 years during his childhood; his mother Louisa was a noted feminist activist of her time.

Nestled in a valley in the central tablelands of New South Wales, about 270 kilometres north-west of Sydney, Mudgee was settled early in 1822 by George and Henry Cox. Today it is home to about 8700 people. The name of the town is derived from the Wiradjuri word 'moothi', meaning 'nest in the hills'.

With its red-earth, clay-based soil, the Mudgee region has proved perfect for grapevines. The first vines were planted in the district about 1856, and today the region produces robust reds, fine chardonnays and other white wines, from 35 boutique wineries. A good time to visit is during the Mudgee Wine Festival, held each September.

The region is also renowned for its lamb, beef, olives and olive oil and honey. A great place to sample and pick up local produce is the Mudgee Farmers Market, held on the third Saturday morning of each month in the grounds of St Mary's Catholic Church (aptly, on the corner of Church and Market streets). There you'll find organic vegetables, olives, honey, nuts, pesto and preserves, goat cheese, jams, jellies and marinades, even fresh yabbies. There's usually live music and you can also get a good coffee.

LAWSON PARK HOTEL

ADDRESS
1 Church St, Mudgee

TELEPHONE
(02) 6372 2183

WEBSITE
www.lawsonparkhotel.com

RATES
Weekdays $50 single and $65 double; weekends $65 single and $80 double.

HOURS
10am–10pm Sun–Thurs; 12pm–12am Fri–Sat.

GRUB
Open for lunch and dinner daily.

TOP DROP
There are 11 beers on tap; the most popular is XXXX Gold. The wine list is exclusively wines from the Mudgee region, as is 90 per cent of the bottleshop stock.

NEARBY ATTRACTIONS
Mudgee Wine Tours runs full- and half-day tours to local wineries, as well as sightseeing tours that take in the nearby town of Gulgong. It also runs a 5-stop progressive lunch tour to local cellar doors. www.mudgeewinetours.com.au Beer lovers might also like to check out the Mudgee Brewery on Church St. www.mudgeebrewery.com.au

MORE INFO
www.visitmudgeeregion.com.au

THE PALACE HOTEL

ADDRESS
227 Argent St, Broken Hill

TELEPHONE
(08) 8088 1699

WEBSITE
www.thepalacehotelbrokenhill.com.au

RATES
Priscilla Suite: $120 double, extra person $25 per night; rooms with ensuite: $70–$120 (most expensive have balcony access); rooms (no ensuite) with balcony access: $45 single, $65 twin, $65 queen; without balcony access: $40 single; $60 double or twin; $40 single for triple room plus $20 per extra person; $60 double for family rooms (sleep 4–6) plus $15–$20 per extra person; $27 per person for dorms (6 share).

HOURS
Daily 5pm–12am.

GRUB
The Side Bar restaurant opens Tues–Fri from 5pm, Sat from 6pm. The cafe opens Mon–Sat 6am–4pm, Sun 8am–3pm.

TOP DROP
There is no beer on tap, but a large range of imported premium labels and boutique Australian beers including Fat Yak, Beez Neez and Big Helga from the Matilda Bay Brewery.

NEARBY ATTRACTIONS
Broken Hill has many attractions. Don't miss the Broken Hill Regional Gallery, as well as galleries of artists Pro Hart and Jack Absalom. Take a drive to the Miners' Memorial at the top of the hill overlooking the town.

MORE INFO
www.visitbrokenhill.com.au

THE PALACE HOTEL

BROKEN HILL

The Palace Hotel, Broken Hill

SOMETIME IN THE 1970s – nobody seems quite sure exactly when – Mario Celotto set about painting an expansive and extravagant tribute to Botticelli's *The Birth of Venus* on the ceiling of his Broken Hill pub. Mario's Palace Hotel became famous for the magnificent folly. Celotto, a migrant who had arrived in Australia from Italy in 1949 and (rumour has it) offered to buy the pub while drinking at the bar one day in 1973, put out a challenge for anyone who could do better on the blank wall next to it. He offered £1000 but no-one took him up on it. To this day, the space remains blank.

But the other walls do not, being a riot of colour, waterfalls, naked women, lush meadows and Aboriginal hunters, created at Mario's request by Aboriginal artist Gordon Waye, from Augusta. He was given free rein to paint whatever he wanted, the only stipulation being that it had to include a water feature so that the pub would feel like 'an oasis in the outback'. The murals almost upstaged the glitz and glamour of actors Terence Stamp, Hugo Weaving and Guy Pearce in the hugely successful 1994 Australian movie *Priscilla, Queen of the Desert*, and turned the pub into a national star in its own right after it was used as a location for the film.

Mario's Palace began life as a coffee palace. Commissioned by the temperance movement and built in 1889, it was one of the first three-storey buildings in Australia, an elegant establishment for the well heeled, a sedate and sober alternative to the many rowdy pubs of the outback mining town of Broken Hill. One of its most stunning features – from the outside – is the verandah, believed to be one of the longest of its style in the Southern Hemisphere. The hotel was ultimately unprofitable as a coffee house – understandably, the locals preferred a cold drink – and in 1892 a liquor licence was granted.

In its heyday the Palace Hotel was a grand place to stay. It contained a fine dining restaurant, the Pavilion, offering silver service with starched white tablecloths and capable of competing with anything that city hotels could offer. Upstairs there was a Ladies Parlour, family dining rooms, smoking rooms, correspondence rooms and a mix of 'bridal suites' with ensuites and rooms with shared bathrooms.

What is now the Side Bar was initially made up of shops that opened on to Sulphide Street. Under the staircase, a timber stairwell leads to the cellar, a bar and pool hall. As the coolest part of the building, the cellar was the place where hotel patrons would retreat from the harsh and blistering heat of Broken Hill summers.

In 1919 the hotel was sold to a group of mine managers and was used as a returned soldiers' hostel run by the RSL, offering indoor bowls, a gym and a place for veterans to restart their lives after their service in World War I. Later it reverted to being a pub.

Then came Mario, who owned the hotel from 1974 and changed its name to Mario's Palace Hotel in 1988. After his death in 2001, the hotel continued to trade for some time but closed in 2007. The building stood empty for two years, until in 2009 it was sold to a consortium of Broken Hill locals who began an ongoing process of renovation while still retaining the retro look the pub is famous for.

'We opened the accommodation first, and then started opening the bar a few nights a week,' says manager Esther La Rovere, one of the new owners. 'Now we are opening for dinner as well, and hope to extend that to lunch in the near future.'

The amazing murals are Mario's legacy

There's live music in the main bar every Saturday night and cocktail specials in the ground-floor Side Bar, or you can head up the sweeping staircase to the Balcony Restaurant, a popular spot for tapas and cocktails on hot summer nights.

There are now 48 guest rooms, including newly renovated balcony and ensuite rooms, family, singles and doubles, and the renowned Priscilla Suite. All the rooms are unique, some with hand-stencilled wallpaper (by Mario) and others with florid red and orange 1960s and '70s carpets. Some have been renovated with all mod cons, including wi-fi internet access, while others are still in their near-original state. However, all rooms are air-conditioned and have a television, iron, and tea- and coffee-making facilities.

In the 1970s Mario Celotto set about painting an expansive and extravagant tribute to Botticelli's *The Birth of Venus* on the ceiling of his Broken Hill pub.

Nine deluxe rooms have ensuites, with bath tubs, and open onto the wonderful balcony. Other rooms are 'classic older-style pub rooms' with the ladies and gents bathrooms in the hallway, and there's a mix of singles, twins, doubles, triples, family rooms and six-share budget dorms. The Priscilla Suite, with its lavish murals, is unchanged since scenes from the movie were shot in it. It has two rooms, one with a queen-sized bed and two singles, the other with twin beds; there's an ensuite and balcony access.

'We are passionate about the Palace and we recognise the potential of the building and its historical significance,' says La Rovere. 'We really want to restore it to its former glory.'

PEEL INN

NUNDLE

The Peel Inn's corner location in Nundle

HAPPY CROWDS SPILL out onto the verandah and mingle under the trailing grapevines in the beer garden at the Peel Inn on a busy weekend. It's a mixed crowd – middle-aged motorcycling couples, families with kids from teens to babies, touring cyclists and couples on weekend getaways. Publican Robert Schofield and his family take it all in their stride – after all, they've been in the business for generations now.

Few of those around the bar or eating in the country-style bistro are likely to give a thought to how the Schofields came to be here, but if you pause in the hallway the extraordinary story of this family pub is spelt out in the pictures hanging on the walls. The pretty village of Nundle, 60 kilometres south-east of Tamworth, with its lovely old stone buildings, seems an unlikely setting for a gripping tale of fortunes won and lost. But that's what happened. Robert Schofield's grandfather won the pub on the turn of a card in a tense poker game nearly 150 years ago and his descendents have run it almost ever since.

Robert Schofield's grandfather won the pub on the turn of a card in a tense poker game nearly 150 years ago and his descendents have run it almost ever since.

In 1860, the same year that William McIlveen built the Peel Inn, John Schofield and his brother Thomas arrived in Australia from Manchester aboard the ship *Dorrigo*. McIlveen's inn was a single-storey brick building with a shingle roof and a verandah on two sides. Popular with the gold diggers who flocked to the region to seek their fortune, it was, according to newspaper reports of the time, the biggest rum hotel north of Newcastle.

John Schofield, a carpenter, was one who came to try his luck in the goldfields. Two years later, as he faced McIlveen across a card table, McIlveen wagered everything he owned – his precious pub – and lost. For the next 60 years, the Schofield family ran the hotel, with John's 11 children all being born there. His youngest son Victor added the balcony in 1914, creating the look of today's hotel.

In 1922, after John Schofield's death, the hotel was sold to Annie Prisk, but it was not to stay out of the Schofield family for long. In 1950, a third generation, grandsons Jeff and

Guy Schofield, bought the hotel from Doug Stortenbecker, and it has remained in the family from then on. Since 1967, the licensee has been Robert Schofield, who now runs the pub with the help of son Nathan and his family. In another strange twist of fate, Robert's cousin Kerry married Di, the great-great-granddaughter of William McIlveen, uniting the two families.

Meals, rooms, coffee and more

There are plenty of reasons to visit Nundle, with a calendar of special events year-round in the region. One of the major local attractions is the annual Nundle Go for Gold Chinese Festival, which runs for two days over Easter, featuring Chinese dragon parades, colourful dancing, martial arts and, of course, Chinese food. The festival is run in honour of early settlers who worked in the goldfields, and the town – including the pub – is strung with Chinese lanterns.

If you're a dog owner, the best time to visit is the first Sunday in May when the Great Nundle Dog Race is run on the Nundle Recreation Ground. With its origins in an argument between two local farmers over who had the fastest dog, the race began in 1979 and is now the most important fundraiser of the Nundle Public School Parents & Citizens Association and attracts families and their dogs from all over the area. The main event, the Great Nundle Dog Race, is only open to working dogs, but the day also has 20 other races for all types of dogs and is one of Nundle's major tourist draws.

The Peel Inn is a great base to stay in the region, no matter what your reason for visiting Nundle. Ten rooms open out onto the huge 6-metre-deep verandah that wraps itself around the second storey of the hotel. Simply furnished, some with antique washstands, bentwood chairs from the hotel's original dining room, timber shutters and pressed-tin walls, the rooms are unfussy and unspoiled. Most rooms share a bathroom down the hallway.

Breakfast is available for overnight guests, as well as for drop-ins. There's no menu; everyone gets the same thing – cereal, orange juice, bacon and eggs, toast, and tea or coffee. After breakfast you can plan your day as you sit in the bar, or if the weather's fine on the wide front verandah or in the large garden bar, overhung by grapevines.

Later in the day, the Peel Inn's 'famous homemade' pie, with peas, mash and gravy, goes down a treat with diners, who also have the choice of such pub staples as chicken schnitzel, steaks, burgers and fish and chips, and more unusual offerings including locally smoked trout. The second Wednesday night of each month has a food theme, offering something different such as Italian, Indian, pizza or roasts.

PEEL INN

ADDRESS
Jenkins St, Nundle

TELEPHONE
(02) 6769 3377

WEBSITE
www.peelinn.com.au

RATES
$45–$60 single; $65 twin or double; $80 double with ensuite.

HOURS
Daily 11–12am.

GRUB
Open for dinner 6pm daily, except Friday 6.30pm.

TOP DROP
A full range of popular beers is available.

NEARBY ATTRACTIONS
The Nundle Woollen Mill, about 2 min walk from the pub, runs 45 min guided tours that show the mill in action (and there's a shop to buy great woollen items). The Nundle Courthouse Museum and the Odgers & McClelland Exchange Store are also worth a visit.

MORE INFO
www.nundle.info

The PRINCE *of* WALES *Hotel*

GULGONG

On the footpath outside the Prince of Wales Hotel, one of Gulgong's oldest buildings, is a cryptic symbol marked on a ceramic tile. To the initiated, the travellers who walked the roads looking for work, food or somewhere to sleep, it would be read as 'dangerous drinking water'.

The Prince of Wales Hotel

ON THE FOOTPATH outside the Prince of Wales Hotel, one of Gulgong's oldest buildings, is a cryptic symbol marked on a ceramic tile. To the initiated, the travellers who walked the roads during the gold rush of the 1870s and the depression of the 1930s looking for work, food or somewhere to sleep, it would be read as 'dangerous drinking water'.

Pub grub at the bar

The tile is one of 70 on the Gulgong Symbol Trail, designed by local potter Chester Nealie and placed along Mayne Street and through Coronation Park, a reminder of the secret language used to mark the 'lie of the land'. Other symbols leave the messages 'dangerous people', 'money usually given here' and 'angry dogs'.

Licensee Rowena Ellis, born and bred in Gulgong, laughs when it is mentioned; it's all part of the rich history of her home town, 294 kilometres (or about four hours' drive) north-west of Sydney, between Dubbo and Newcastle.

Gulgong was once famous as the 'Town on the Ten Dollar Note' – at least until the old paper money was replaced by polymer notes in 1993 and Gulgong and its famous son, the writer Henry Lawson, were replaced by Dame Mary Gilmour. Lawson's links with the town are an integral part of its appeal. Each year, the Gulgong Henry Lawson Heritage Festival is staged over the Queen's Birthday long weekend in June, and his presence is everywhere, including in the bar at the Prince of Wales, where a full-size model of the poet is on the wall.

The Prince of Wales has been offering country hospitality since the late 1800s. Rowena's parents Meg and John bought it in 1976 'when women weren't even allowed in the bar' and their daughter has been running it (this time around) since 2005. After a five-year stint as manager and licensee from 1995 to 2000, Rowena pursued a different career path for a few years but came back to the hotel when the former licensees moved out without warning, leaving the pub an empty shell. She took on the challenge of getting it back up and running.

'There was literally nothing in it,' she recalls. 'No chairs, no tables, no beer.' Her first task was to refurnish and re-establish the pub before moving on to bigger renovations, including providing more accommodation.

'When I came into the hotel I had a lot of dreams and ideas of different things I wanted to do with the business,' says Rowena. 'My parents trusted me to do these things and the ideas have worked, with the help of great reliable staff.'

Plants and corrugated iron add atmosphere

The pub's original five guest rooms have been supplemented by seven modern motel units immediately behind it. During the week, the accommodation is usually used by contract workers at the local coalmine, but at weekends Rowena's marketing efforts have seen it become a popular spot for girls' weekends away (packages include meals, winery tours and massages). All the motel rooms have air conditioning, electric blankets, a bar fridge, microwave, wi-fi access and flat-screen televisions with DVD players. The rooms in the pub have shared bathrooms, the motel rooms have ensuites.

With its terracotta-tiled floor, lots of pot plants, wall murals, and use of corrugated iron, the pub is warm and welcoming and gives no hint of its former empty state. There are two pool tables, and live bands play on Friday nights.

THE PRINCE OF WALES HOTEL

ADDRESS
97 Mayne St, Gulgong

TELEPHONE
(02) 6374 1166

WEBSITE
www.princeofwalesgulgong.com.au

RATES
Hotel rooms: $45 double or twin; $55 family room. Motel rooms: $106 double or twin; family room $106 double plus $20 per extra person.

HOURS
Mon–Sat 9–12am, Sun 9am–10pm.

GRUB
Continental breakfast available daily, and a full breakfast menu at weekends 8am–12pm. Open daily for lunch 12–2pm, and dinner 6–8pm.

TOP DROP
There are eight beers on tap: VB, Carlton Draught, Carlton Dry, XXXX Gold, Bundy Draught, Cascade Light, Tooheys New and Tooheys Old. The wine list features only wines from the Mudgee region.

NEARBY ATTRACTIONS
Next door to the pub is the Prince of Wales Opera House, the oldest continually operating opera house in Australia. Don't leave town without visiting the Henry Lawson Centre (www.henrylawsongulgong.org.au). The Gulgong Town Trail is a self-guided walk (get a brochure from the visitor centre) through the town's history.

MORE INFO
www.gulgong.net

Prince of Wales back bar

From the kitchen, still run by Meg Ellis, two full-time chefs create an extensive menu including homemade pizzas, Asian-inspired specials (think red beef curry or garlic prawns), and two sizes of steaks – 400 grams and 600 grams – all for under $25. There are also light meals, and a 'coffee and cake' menu.

Next door is the Prince of Wales Opera House. Built in 1871 as a large timber and bark music hall, the opera house was used to entertain the townspeople and goldminers during Gulgong's heyday when the town was home to 20 000 people. When the gold rush ended a decade later, the townspeople continued to make good use of the theatre. In the 1880s the Gulgong Amateur Dramatic Club used it regularly, and Henry Lawson saw his first theatrical production (*The Pirates of Penzance*) there. Dame Nellie Melba once sang on its stage, and Les Darcy slugged it out in a boxing ring here.

The theatre closed in the 1960s but by the mid-1970s it had been saved by the revived Gulgong Amateur Dramatic Society and is still going strong. Today it is the venue for performers in the annual Henry Lawson Heritage Festival and the Gulgong Eisteddfod, is used by the Gulgong Musical and Dramatic Society and hosts world-famous visiting performers such as pianist Roger Woodward and jazz musician James Morrison.

About 130 buildings in the town are listed by the National Trust. The narrow streets – which follow the grid marked out by the goldminers' canvas town – are lined with clapboard and iron buildings, decorated with iron lacework and wide verandahs. A statue of Henry Lawson stands in the park between Medley and Herbert streets.

Prince of Wales garden bar

THE PUB WITH NO BEER

TAYLORS ARM

SING JUST THE first couple of lines of 'The Pub With No Beer', with its familiar country tune, and it's almost certain that every Australian around you will be able to chime in with the rest of the lyrics! Country singer Slim Dusty's mega-hit of the 1950s still resounds, and pilgrims still make the trek to rural New South Wales to have a beer at the bar of the Pub With No Beer.

The road to Taylors Arm (population 50) and its famous country pub is a beautiful drive, along a winding route that runs for about 30 minutes from the Pacific Highway at Macksville, about halfway between Sydney and Brisbane. There's no fear of getting lost – signposts herald your destination all the way!

The Pub With No Beer

The Pub With No Beer began life as the Cosmopolitan Hotel. Built over five years and first licensed in 1903, the pub looked very similar then to how it does today. The Cosmopolitan's fortunes fluctuated through the hard times of the Depression and war years, rising during the boom period after World War II when timber mills were busy and the then new banana industry was yielding good profits for farmers.

Parsons was working as a timber cutter when he wrote the song about the characters who frequented the old pub at Taylors Arm.

In those days, pubs were given a certain quota of beer from the brewery. However, being the only pub on the route through the valley, no traveller could pass it without stopping for a drink and the story goes that one day, when the pub was full of thirsty patrons ... it ran out of beer! There are other versions of the tale, but this seems the most plausible.

This story inspired songwriter Gordon Parsons to immortalise the pub in what became one of Australia's most famous songs. Parsons was working as a timber cutter when he wrote the song about the characters who frequented the old pub at Taylors Arm. He tried it out at parties around the area, and refined it during a tour with Slim Dusty and Chad Morgan.

THE PUB WITH NO BEER

ADDRESS
4 Main Rd, Taylors Arm

TELEPHONE
(02) 6564 2100

WEBSITE
www.thepubwithnobeertaylorsarm.com.au

RATES
$50 for queen room; $55 for room with queen bed plus single bed; $60 for queen bed and 2 single beds; bunk rooms $15 per person.

HOURS
Mon–Sat 10–12am;
Sun 10am–10pm.

GRUB
The Cow Hide Bistro opens daily for lunch, and Fri–Sat nights for dinner.

TOP DROP
Handcrafted boutique beers from Murrays Craft Brewing Co., as well as most well-known beers.

NEARBY ATTRACTIONS
At the back of the pub, you'll find the historic Talarm Church, built in 1928 and relocated to Taylors Arm in 2003. It is now full of interesting memorabilia, including a large collection of beer cans.

MORE INFO
www.visitnsw.com

Bar at the Pub With No Beer

Slim was looking for a B-side for his recording of 'Saddle Boy', and asked Parsons if he could use 'A Pub With No Beer'. It was 1957, and the song was played on Radio 2UE in Sydney by disc jockey Bob Rogers. The rest is history. The song went to Number 1 on the 2UE chart, on all Sydney charts and then nationally. It remained in the Australian charts for six months. In England huge sales saw it earn a silver record while in Ireland it went to the top of the charts and stayed there for 10 weeks. Eventually, it was released in 11 countries.

The song put the tiny township of Taylors Arm and its bush pub on the map for thousands of visitors – from all over Australia and overseas. The influx of patrons has seen changes at the pub over the years, the original small bar being expanded, a bistro added and accommodation moved to a separate building.

'A Pub With No Beer' sold more copies than any other Australian recording at that time. Slim Dusty received the first gold record awarded in Australia and the first and only gold 78 rpm record ever awarded. Gordon Parsons' contribution to Australian country music was recognised in 1982 with his induction into the Australasian Music Roll of Renown at the Tamworth Country Music Festival.

Memorabilia relating to the song, the singers and the pub cover the walls, including framed copies of early records, historic photos and newspaper clippings, and on Sunday afternoons there's live music on the pub's wide verandah. In the summer the action is on the outdoor stage in front of the grassy picnic area and beer garden.

'True blue' tastes – steaks, seafood and specialties such as dark ale pie and curried sausages – are offered by the kitchen of the Cow Hide Bistro, which is bright and cheerful, with red-and-white-checked tablecloths.

Having come all this way, some folk get the urge to stay, and if you do, there's homestead-style accommodation available just across the lawn in front of the pub. There are double rooms with queen-sized beds, as well as family rooms with bunks for children. Another option is the free camping ground on the oval opposite the pub.

Today, there's plenty of beer on hand but be warned: no fuel is available in Taylors Arm, so fill up before you head there.

THE ROYAL HOTEL

HILL END

THE CLOCKS AT either end of the dining room in the Royal Hotel have stopped. One says 12.40, the other shows 10.20. They're not the only sign that this is a town that is – to some extent at least – frozen in time.

More than any other town in Australia, Hill End is a living snapshot of what life was like during the 1870s gold rush. According to the NSW National Parks and Wildlife Service, which has administered the town since 1967, Hill End's collection of historic working-class cottages and village buildings is 'without parallel' in Australia. It is also probably one of the prettiest towns you can visit.

Hill End is 72 kilometres from Mudgee, with 2 kilometres of unsealed road at the end, or 85 kilometres from Bathurst via Sofala, with the final 7.5 kilometres being unsealed. Care should be taken on the road, especially in wet weather when the dirt sections can be very slippery.

The Royal Hotel, Hill End

Hill End is a living snapshot of what life was like during the 1870s gold rush. It is also probably one of the prettiest towns you can visit.

The road from Bathurst brings you into an avenue of European trees planted by pioneering goldminer Louis Beyers in the 1870s, and in autumn it is a blaze of red and gold. Where Beyers Avenue meets the village centre, one of the first buildings you come to is the Royal Hotel.

The Hill End Historic Site encompasses and protects the village's buildings, among them the Royal, one of 27 hotels built in the town to cater for the population boom during the gold rush. Opened in 1872, today it is the only pub in Hill End.

At the time of the gold rush about 8000 people lived in and around Hill End. The town not only had all those pubs, but three banks, two newspapers, a brewery and a mile-long stretch of shops. Life went on to the sound of huge stamp batteries that crushed the ore, working around the clock in the continual search for gold. It was said that the noise of the stampers was so constant that when they broke down, the townspeople had trouble sleeping because of the silence.

Now the town is quiet all the time; about 100 residents remain here and the only people who pass through are tourists wanting a look at how life once was.

It's hardly surprising to learn that Hill End has been a popular haunt for artists, starting with Russell Drysdale and Donald Friend in the late 1940s. They were followed by others including Jeffrey Smart, Margaret Olley, John Olsen and Brett Whiteley. Today, a new generation of artists is also finding inspiration in the historic landscape, and an artist-in-residence program is run in partnership by the NSW National Parks and Wildlife Service and the Bathurst Regional Art Gallery, using Murray's Cottage, once the home of Donald Friend, and Haefliger's Cottage, once owned by Paul Haefliger and Jean Bellette. The Jean Bellette Gallery, in the national park information centre, exhibits work by artists based in the Hill End area, as well as those who have been artists in residence.

The Royal Hotel sign

The village's existing buildings – and some empty plots of land – are all marked with signs created using 80 historic photographs taken in the 1870s by pioneer photographer Beaufoy Merlin, depicting scenes from the era. Among the buildings are the original Hill End post office, courthouse, school, general store, cottages and a couple of churches. It is easy to picture what life would have been like during the gold rush, and you can also take a 2-kilometre walk to the Bald Hills mining area, which will take you past the old cemetery.

The Royal Hotel offers comfortable accommodation for up to 22 people, in single, twin or double rooms, with shared male and female bathrooms down the hall. There is also a family room that sleeps four. All rooms have a balcony, either with a town view or overlooking the shady beer garden at the back of the hotel. The guest rooms were refurbished with new colonial-style furniture in 2007, giving it a feel in keeping with the gold-rush era.

The period feel extends to the dining room, which takes orders at a hole-in-the-wall beside the beer garden but delivers to your table. The menu offers both traditional Australian pub choices and a Chinese menu. There are lace curtains and tablecloths, with a mixture of bentwood and plastic chairs; don't expect to have to dress up to dine here.

In the bar, the pub provides everything they think the clientele of mainly tourists will want – a pool table, video jukebox with more than 2000 songs to suit all tastes, a poker-machine room, and an arcade-style games machine with 39 'old school' games (think Pacman, Donkey Kong and Space Invaders). For a quieter time, you might prefer the garden bar, where in the late afternoon it's possible to spot grazing kangaroos and other wildlife.

Give yourself a couple of days in Hill End; after one, you'll just be starting to wind down.

THE ROYAL HOTEL

ADDRESS
Beyers Ave, Hill End

TELEPHONE
(02) 6337 8261

WEBSITE
www.hillendnsw.com.au

RATES
$40 single; $65 double; $70 twin; $100 family room (sleeps 4). Rates include a self-serve continental breakfast until 10am.

HOURS
Mon–Sat 11–12am;
Sun 10am–10pm.

GRUB
The bistro is open daily for lunch 12–2pm, and dinner 6.30–8pm.

TOP DROP
There are 5 beers on tap: Tooheys New, XXXX Gold, VB, Carlton Draught and Cascade Premium Light.

NEARBY ATTRACTIONS
Head to the NSWNPWS office and museum in Hospital La (walk, because the badly rutted road is 4WD only!) and pick up a brochure for a self-guided historical walk around the village. There is no signage to the museum/information centre but anyone can direct you there. Other attractions are the La Paloma Pottery, Craigmoor (the grandest house in Hill End, usually open on long weekends) and tours of the Bald Hill Gold Mine.

MORE INFO
www.environment.nsw.gov.au and (02) 6337 8206 for the information centre.

The ROYAL HOTEL

SOFALA

SANDRA TOMKINSON PULLS up a chair in front of the fire in the lounge and happily tells the story of the country pub that has been in her family for more than five decades.

Sofala's Royal Hotel, built in 1862

The Sofala Royal Hotel as it stands today was built in 1862 but there was a single-storey hotel on the site as early as 1851. The original owners were Moritz Mendel and his wife Annie. He was a Prussian, she was English, a member of the family who owned Abbey Shoes. They met on the boat to Australia and married during the voyage.

Despite the romantic beginnings, the Mendels didn't prosper. After his wife and one of their children died within a short space of time, Moritz committed suicide and was buried in the cemetery in Sofala. Their descendents still come to Sofala to stay in the pub.

The Royal was built at the height of Sofala's goldmining boom. Today, the laid-back village is little more than a couple of streets but it lays claim to the title of the oldest surviving gold town in Australia – 'and you can still find gold here', says Sandy. Commercial goldmining in the district had finished by the late 1940s, but for those who want to try their luck in the river behind the pub, gold dust can still be found (you can buy or hire equipment from the souvenir shop).

Commercial goldmining in the district had finished by the late 1940s, but for those who want to try their luck in the river behind the pub, gold dust can still be found.

Sofala is 245 kilometres north-west of Sydney and 45 kilometres north of Bathurst in the Turon River valley. It sprang up after the discovery of gold at Summerhill Creek in early 1851 and within months a huge tent city had formed and the hotel and general store had been built. But the gold boom was something of a flash in the pan, the population swelling to 10 000 and then rapidly declining. The Turon Hills was Australia's second biggest goldfield, but by the middle of 1854 the diggers were moving on from Sofala to new fields and the town was shrinking. Still, there was a booking office for Cobb & Co, where coaches bound for Bathurst, Orange and Forbes stopped, and a couple of banks.

Of the original 40 hotels (and countless sly grog shops), the Royal is the only one that remains. Sandy's parents, Frank and Eileen Farrell, took over the pub in 1955 and Sandy took it on in the 1990s. Her mother's name is still above the door.

On the other side of Denison Street is the old weatherboard general store, which with its ornate lacework is one of the village's grandest buildings. Many other significant buildings have also survived, including the police station and gaol (1890s), the post office (1879) and the former Sofala hospital, originally built in 1874 as a courthouse. Other historic buildings are now private homes.

Public bar, Royal Hotel, Sofala

If Sofala's quiet charm takes hold and you find enough of interest to keep you overnight, the pub has six guest rooms, all furnished in period style with iron bedsteads. Two are double rooms, the others have a double bed and a single. All have doors to the verandah, front or back.

The walls of the front bar are covered with photographs, history and memorabilia relating to the pub and the town. Behind the bar, an array of shiny sporting trophies dating back to the 1930s charts the success of the village cricket, football and tennis teams. Apart from the locals, you're likely to be chatting at the bar with campers and bushwalkers, the occasional bus tour group or families who visit during the school holidays.

The picturesque streetscapes also make Sofala a favourite spot for photographers, artists and film-makers. In 1947, Russell Drysdale captured the main street and its timber buildings in his famous work *Sofala*. It was also the setting for some of the scenes from the movies *The Cars that Ate Paris* (1974) and *Sirens* (1994).

The pub no longer serves meals, but there's a licensed restaurant, Cafe Sofala, at the end of Denison Street, the Gaol Cafe is on the hill above the main street and the Lolly Shop in the post office serves lunch. And nothing is more than about two minutes' walk from everything else in this village. In the summer, the river is a great place to cool off and the garden bar out the back of the hotel has a barbecue for those who want to use it. There's a pool table in the lounge.

A good time to visit Sofala is for the annual Sofala and District Agricultural and Horticultural Show, held in late February at the Sofala Showgrounds. Events include woodchopping, iron man and women events, sheepdog trials and the best of the best relay, as well as displays of antique machinery, art and craft, poultry and pigeons, snakes and photography.

THE ROYAL HOTEL

ADDRESS
Denison St, Sofala

TELEPHONE
(02) 6337 7008

RATES
$35 per person.

HOURS
Open from 12pm Sun–Fri and 11am Sat.

TOP DROP
Beers on tap include VB, Tooheys New, Tooheys Old and Hahn.

NEARBY ATTRACTIONS
A walking guide to the historical points of interest in the village is available from the Sofala Souvenir Shop in Denison St. About 12 km from Sofala is the Turon Technology Museum, showcasing 1850s–1950s power technologies – steam turbines, hot-bulb engines, internal combustion engines, diesel engines and more; open mainly on weekends and public holidays.

MORE INFO
www.sofalagold.com
www.bathurst-nsw.com

The SILVERTON Hotel

SILVERTON

THE TOURISTS ARE circling outside the Silverton Hotel. Most of them are men, of course, walking around and taking a good long look at the car parked outside the pub's front door.

Mel Gibson may have long departed these parts, but the spirit of *Mad Max* lives on in the outback town of Silverton. His V8 Interceptor, which once held the prime parking spot in town, has moved next door to the souvenir shop, and there's a new vehicle in its place.

Nothing ever stays the same. No-one knows that more than the people of Silverton, who have learned to adapt to changing circumstances over the years. The town that once was the centre of a mining area now hosts film crews on a regular basis and has been catering for the growing tourist market over the years.

The Silverton Hotel

The distinctive red-dust landscape around Silverton has made it one of Australia's most popular filming locations, with dozens of feature films and countless television commercials being shot here over the past 40 years. Many locals had roles as extras in *Mad Max II*, which was filmed around Silverton in 1981 and is arguably the most memorable movie set here. If you've seen the television mini-series *A Town Like Alice*, or the movies *The Slim Dusty Story*, *Razorback*, *Adventures of Priscilla, Queen of the Desert*, *Mission Impossible II* or *Dirty Deeds*, you've caught a glimpse of the Silverton Hotel.

The distinctive red-dust landscape around Silverton has made it one of Australia's most popular filming locations, with dozens of feature films being shot here over the past 40 years or so.

Once considered a 'ghost town', Silverton has undergone a tourism-led revival in recent years, with its unique setting in the middle of the Mundi Mundi Plain, about 25 kilometres north-west of the mining city of Broken Hill, only partly responsible. For such a tiny place, there's plenty to see and it's easy to spend a day here.

The pub is the focal point of the town, its walls crammed with movie-making memorabilia (as well as plenty of souvenirs). Publicans Peter and Patsy Price, who took over the Silverton Hotel in 2010, have made considerable improvements to the old place.

THE SILVERTON HOTEL

ADDRESS
Layard St, Silverton

TELEPHONE
(08) 8088 5313

WEBSITE
www.silverton.org.au/hotel.htm

HOURS
Mon–Sat 9am–late;
Sun 10am–10pm.

GRUB
Food is available when the hotel is open.

TOP DROP
There are four beers on tap: XXXX Gold, Hahn Super Dry, Hahn Light and Tooheys New.

WHERE TO STAY
Silverton is short on accommodation unless you want something very basic. Penrose Park Recreational Reserve has cabins, bunkhouses, campsites and caravanning facilities, with toilet and shower blocks. Camping: $7 for adults, $15 for a family of 4, $5 each additional child. Bunkhouses: $40–$85, sleeping up to 8 people.

NEARBY ATTRACTIONS
The Mad Max Museum, the passion of collector Adrian Bennett, opened in late 2010 and is home to a large collection of *Mad Max* memorabilia including photographs, costumes, and original and replica vehicles including two Interceptors. Open daily 9am–5pm in winter, 10am–4pm in summer. Tel: (08) 8088 6128.

MORE INFO
www.silverton.org.au

Silverton's old church

The most noticeable change, on arrival (especially to return visitors) might be the new car out the front. 'I call it the love child of the Interceptor,' says Price of his creation, forged from the shell of an old VW Beetle. It's not the only Beetle in town, of course: further up the hill the much-photographed pair painted by Peter Browne have been displayed for years, resplendent with their distinctive emu faces.

The original Silverton Hotel opened in 1884 to cater for the town's growing population of miners. When the town was founded in 1883, it had a population of 250 but within months that had doubled. A larger, two-storey building replaced the first hotel only a year later to cope with demand. In its heyday, the town had about 3000 residents and boasted a newspaper, masonic lodge, gaol, hospital, jockey club, football team and Methodist church. The pub burnt down in 1918 and its licence was transferred to the former post office, the building that still welcomes thirsty travellers today.

The Australian trade union movement, later so successful in Broken Hill, began in Silverton in 1884 as the Barrier Ranges Miners' Association. Its main role was to help injured miners and their families. In 1886 the association formed a branch of the Amalgamated Miners' Association of Australasia, which pushed for workers' rights under the banner 'United we stand, divided we fall', and unionism was born in the region.

The Broken Hill Proprietary Company Limited (now BHP Billiton) was formed in the former Silverton Hotel in 1885. Ironically, the region's rich ores that Silverton were built upon were the cause of its eventual decline, as larger mines opened in nearby Broken Hill. The Silverton Municipal Council was taken off the New South Wales state register in 1899, leaving the state government in control of the town; many of its buildings were transported to Broken Hill by teams of donkeys, camels or bullocks.

Although fewer than 60 people live in Silverton today, the town has a vibrant cultural life, boosted by tourism and the film industry. The landscape that was once home to miners is now inspiring a new generation of artists, and the Silverton galleries attract people from all over the world.

And some things don't change. One of those is the famous Silverton Hotel hot dogs – twice the size of any you'll be able to order at most pubs, and available with a range of different sauces. There are other, lighter, snacks as well, and Peter and Patsy Price have created a new dining area in the old pub, along with a new bar outside and they've put a cover over the beer garden. They're planning to build accommodation out the back, and to create a permanent stage area for live music acts.

THE STAR HOTEL

MACKSVILLE

The Star Hotel overlooks the Nambucca River

THE NAMBUCCA RIVER flows right past the door of the Star Hotel, and it's not uncommon to see boats pulled up at the hotel jetty, just off the main highway through Macksville.

The impressive facade of the elegant riverside pub is the first thing you see when coming into Macksville on the Pacific Highway from the north. Then you cross the Macksville Bridge, turn left and you are at the door.

The Star Hotel was built in 1885 by pioneers Hugh McNally and Angus Mackay, after whom the town is named. The original inhabitants of the region were the Kumbaingeri or Ngamba Aboriginal people, but European timber cutters began felling cedar in the area in the 1830s and 1840s, and were followed by dairy farmers.

Now owned by the Partridge family, the pub has undergone extensive renovations and refurbishment in recent years to bring it to its present glory. John and Jenny Partridge and their business partner Steve McEvoy bought the Star in late 2001, after already being involved in the successful rejuvenation of the Federal Hotel in Bellingen, in which they still have an interest, the Coast Hotel in Coffs Harbour, and other hotels in Kempsey, Nambucca Heads, Armidale and Ballina. After two years, they sold the lease but in 2009 they bought it back and now own the Star in partnership with their sons Ben and Adam.

'We really aim at the family market,' says Adam, who manages the hotel, and chose the upstairs verandah, with its fabulous river views, as the setting for his wedding to Kendall on Valentine's Day 2009.

The 'new look' pub is open and relaxed, with the bar flowing into the bistro area, and the beer garden at the side ensuring river views from almost every spot. There's

The pub is a popular drawcard for fishermen, who can easily pull up at the jetty, just as passing motorists find a spot to park their cars.

THE STAR HOTEL

ADDRESS
16 River St, Macksville

TELEPHONE
(02) 6568 1008

WEBSITE
www.starhotelmacksville.com.au

RATES
$80 queen room; $70 twin share; $50 single; $45 triple-share bunk room.

HOURS
Mon–Sat 10–12am;
Sun 10am–10pm.

GRUB
Daily 12–2.30pm and 6–9pm.

TOP DROP
There are 11 beers on tap, the most popular being Coopers Pale Ale and Tooheys Old.

NEARBY ATTRACTIONS
Visit Mary Boulton's Pioneer Cottage and Museum, a replica of a settler's home that brings the pioneering history of the district to life. The cottage is a bit further along River St from the Star Hotel, and is open Wed and Sat afternoons.

MORE INFO
www.visitnsw.com

banquette seating in the bistro and a picture window looks out onto a leafy courtyard. A new sweeping staircase leads to the upstairs verandah, which seats 60 and is stylishly casual, with cane furniture, hanging baskets and lantern lights. Off the verandah is an intimate alcove with an elegant sofa, just the spot for a cocktail or two.

A colourful alcove at the Star Hotel

The beer garden seats 50 people under a pavilion-style roof that ensures year-round use, and has a Tiny Tots play area in the corner, making it the spot that families gravitate to.

The Nambucca River is one of Macksville's main attractions and the pub is a popular drawcard for fishermen, who can easily pull up at the jetty, just as passing motorists find a spot to park their cars. 'There's a houseboat company further down the river, and sometimes people who are houseboating for the weekend will anchor off from the pub and bring the dinghy in for a beer or lunch,' says Adam.

With its location on the Pacific Highway about 500 kilometres north of Sydney – about halfway to Brisbane – the pub is a good place to break the road trip for lunch, a snack or an overnight stop. It's also a popular destination and stopover for motorcyclists and it's not uncommon to see a row of shining bikes parked outside.

The menu features all the classic pub grub, as well as daily specials and a kids' menu. Among the popular dishes are oysters from the Nambucca River, served three different ways (natural, kilpatrick or with fresh limes and wasabi oil) or a mixed dozen for $26. Another classic offering is the surf & turf, a 300 gram scotch fillet topped with fresh seafood in a garlic cream sauce ($30). The steaks are all 120-day grain-fed beef from the New England region of New South Wales, aged for six to eight weeks.

For those who want to stay overnight, there are ten rooms upstairs, sharing three bathrooms. All the rooms have flat-screen televisions, and there's a mix of double or twin rooms, plus some with a double and single bed. One room has a set of bunks and a single bed. Rooms at the front of the pub are slightly more expensive. There's a small communal kitchen off the hallway, ideal for making a simple breakfast or a cup of tea.

Unless you are keen on fishing, there's not a lot to do in Macksville, a town of about 3000 people that is mainly a service centre for the surrounding tropical fruit, vegetable and dairy farms. But it's a pleasant place to stop for a while, and if you want a taste of country life the time to visit might be the weekend after Easter, when the annual Macksville Show is held.

The WALCHA ROAD Hotel

WALCHA ROAD

The Walcha Road Hotel

WHEN FIRE RAGED through the historic Walcha Road Hotel in the early hours of a November morning in 2004, the locals were worried that they might have lost their pub. Over four hours, the blaze was beaten back by firefighters using 11 tankers from eight brigades in the district. Water was pumped from Surveyors Creek, which runs behind the pub, to help quell the flames. However, by the end all that was left standing of the beloved Walcha Road watering hole was a few rooms downstairs and one end of the bar.

But licensee Suesann Long – who was in Queensland on holiday when the pub burnt down – and her partner Gary wouldn't see their customers without a 'local' for long, and an old railway dining car was soon installed on a set of disused tracks next to the hotel ruins. The carriage was converted to a makeshift bar, which continued to trade for several years until the hotel was rebuilt. It re-opened on the third anniversary of the fire, 10 November 2007.

When the pub burnt down an old railway dining car was soon installed on a set of disused tracks next to the hotel ruins. The carriage was converted to a makeshift bar, which continued to trade until the hotel was rebuilt.

Today, there's not much at Walcha Road, which is 19 kilometres west of Walcha (pronounced Wal-ka), off the Oxley Highway, and about 70 kilometres from Tamworth, in the northern tablelands of New South Wales: just a few houses, a one-man police station and the pub. The original hotel was built in 1860, and the railway line north from Sydney, which passes through Walcha Road, came through in 1882.

Walcha Road, between the larger centres of Tamworth and Armidale, served as the train stop for the agricultural Walcha district and as such carried a large volume of goods including wool and livestock. In 1911 alone, about 8750 bales of wool were transported from Walcha Road to Sydney. Livestock and goods are no longer carried by train, and the necessary yards and sheds have been removed.

The new pub building brought locals and visitors better facilities – inside and out. The bar is larger, the dining room seats 60, verandahs were added at the back and a function room was created upstairs, replacing accommodation and lounge rooms.

Instead of rooms inside the pub, the hotel now has three purpose-built self-contained rooms in a timber building adjacent to the hotel, but tucked below the road level. Each has a double bed, kitchen sink, fridge, ensuite (with a bath as well as a shower), wardrobe,

THE WALCHA ROAD HOTEL

ADDRESS
1539 Wollun Rd, Walcha Road

TELEPHONE
(02) 6777 5829

WEBSITE
www.walcharoadhotel.com

RATES
$120 double in the hotel rooms; $60 double in the railway carriage.

HOURS
Daily 11am–late.

GRUB
Open daily for breakfast, from 7am for guests, lunch 12–3pm, and dinner 6pm–late.

TOP DROP
Beers on tap are XXXX Gold, Tooheys New, Hahn Extra Dry and Hahn Light. There's also all the standard beers and a good wine list.

NEARBY ATTRACTIONS
The historic village of Walcha is worth a wander around, and about 19 km east of Walcha on the Oxley Hwy you'll find the lovely Apsley Falls. The shire is home to the magnificent Macleay Gorges and boasts some 205 000 ha of national parks, wilderness and state forest. Parts of Werrikimbe National Park are World Heritage–listed.

MORE INFO
www.walchansw.com.au

The Walcha Road Railway Bar is now accommodation

The Walcha Road Hotel entrance

chair, fan, heating and – most importantly – electric blankets for those cool New England nights. The railway carriage has also been converted to accommodation, with a double and two single beds – and the old bar is still in place.

Take some time to read the framed handwritten lyrics on the bar wall, a song composed by local singer Tony Kennedy, 'The Ballad of the Walcha Road Fire'.

Suesann Long is proud of the food that comes out of the state-of-the-art kitchen, which has been well reviewed by Sydney critics. Among the specials you can expect to tempt you from the menu are confit leg of duck with a green peppercorn brandy sauce, duck à l'orange, tournedos rossini, veal marsala and fillet mignon.

Despite the lack of anything else at Walcha Road, the pub still attracts a good following for its food and its cosy atmosphere. Here's a place where you truly are away from it all. And in the winter, there are log fires burning in the grate.

KING O'MALLEY'S
IRISH PUB

CANBERRA

King O'Malley's Irish Pub, Canberra

Look up and you'll see many collected treasures ... a penny-farthing bicycle hangs from the ceiling, and high above are spinning wheels, old brass keys, sea trunks and other curiosities.

THERE'S A FINE irony about a pub named after a passionate teetotaller, a man who used his power and influence to introduce prohibition to the Australian capital. That's what hotel owner Peter Barclay thinks – and his customers tend to get the joke when they discover the answer to the question 'Who was King O'Malley?'.

O'Malley was an American who came to Australia in 1893. He so wanted the power that a seat in Australia's first Federal Parliament would bring that he even claimed to be Canadian (a prerequisite was that candidates must be Commonwealth citizens). O'Malley eventually achieved his goal, becoming a member of the South Australian Parliament and later Federal Minister for Home Affairs. He founded the Commonwealth Bank, championed votes for women and was involved in the development of Australia's trans-continental railway.

He also picked the location of Australia's capital, so it seemed a fitting tribute when his great admirer Peter Barclay opened a pub in Canberra and named it after him. However, Barclay thinks it unlikely O'Malley would have welcomed the gesture, as he fiercely opposed alcohol, which he referred to as 'stagger juice'.

O'Malley introduced the law that prohibited the sale of alcoholic beverages in Canberra from 1911 until it was overturned in 1928 by a public referendum. But Peter Barclay

Dining at King O'Malley's Irish Pub

believes that O'Malley was 'a man of his times' and if alive today might have views closer to what is now considered responsible service of alcohol. O'Malley, he says, was a 'true practical politician' who was known to buy drinks for potential voters while he chatted to them in hotels.

King O'Malley's opened in 2000 on Canberra's City Walk, and has since grown organically, as an old pub would have, explains Barclay. Established in a building that had been a YWCA since the 1940s, it has expanded into surrounding shop areas. The slate-floored entry leads to eight distinct areas, including a cosy snug lined with copies of Hansard.

King O'Malley's presence is everywhere, and his Irish heritage is celebrated. An impressive bust of O'Malley sits to one side of the main bar, and there are old photos of him in the Snug. Look up and you'll see many collected treasures related to his life and times. A penny-farthing bicycle hangs from the ceiling, and high above are spinning wheels, old brass keys, sea trunks and other curiosities. There are Celtic touches throughout the pub, including a Blarney Stone (kissing not required) – but this is no formula Irish bar. It has a genuine feel, without kitsch.

Drink here and you're likely to be rubbing shoulders with lobbyists and political players of all persuasions – and hearty debate is sure to be in full swing. O'Malley's is warm, inviting and full of nooks and crannies to sup in. In winter, a fire burns in the bluestone fireplace and mulled wine is on offer.

Australian fare with an Irish touch is served at King O'Malley's. As well as typical pub fare, you'll find dishes with Irish monikers like beef and Guinness pie, Limerick lamb, the Cork classic (eye fillet steak), the shamrock (a pasta dish) and the King's special (eye fillet steak with bacon and 'the King's own' brandy and tomato sauce). For dessert, go all out with the Donegal date pudding with ice-cream and a drizzle of caramel sauce. There's a kids' menu: the usual chicken nuggets and chips, ham and cheese pizza, and pasta with bolognaise sauce. Families are welcome – high chairs are available and there are even change tables in the toilets.

Peter Barclay was awarded an OAM in 2007 for his charitable work, so it's not surprising that he sees community involvement as a key part of traditional pub life. Barclay and his staff support the World's Greatest Shave for the Leukaemia Foundation and 'Movember' to raise funds for and awareness of men's health issues.

Apart from these, all sorts of events are held at King O'Malley's, from salsa dancing to chess matches, trivia nights and live entertainment. A small stage hosts comedians and musicians; the pub is renowned for its music. On Mondays, there's jazz, local rock bands play on Thursdays, Fridays and Saturdays, and on Sunday nights musicians gather around an old bluegum table to play traditional Irish folk music.

KING O'MALLEY'S IRISH PUB

ADDRESS
131 City Walk, Canberra

TELEPHONE
(02) 6257 0111

WEBSITE
www.kingomalleys.com.au

HOURS
Mon–Sat 11am–late,
Sun 12pm–late.

GRUB
Open for lunch and dinner,
11am–10pm.

TOP DROP
There are 10 beers on tap, including Guinness, Kilkenny, Coopers and Fat Yak, and Bulmer's cider. Or of course there's always an Irish coffee, served with a hit of Jamesons Whiskey.

WHERE TO STAY
Historic Olims All Seasons Hotel has been welcoming guests since 1927 – the same year Old Parliament House was opened – and is now classified by the National Trust. The 127-room hotel is within walking distance of major attractions. Rates start from $433 for a double Heritage Room.
Tel: (02) 6243 0000.
www.olimshotel.com.au

NEARBY ATTRACTIONS
It's a short walk to many of Canberra's attractions, including the Legislative Assembly, the Canberra Museum Gallery and the National Film and Sound Archive.

MORE INFO
www.visitcanberra.com.au

WIG & PEN

CANBERRA

Wig & Pen, Canberra

Perched on the side of the bar, the glass and stainless steel structure is filled with fresh hop flowers, herbs and spices, and truffles. The ale flows through it before reaching the beer glass with an extra hit of flavour.

GOOD THINGS COME in small packages. That's the philosophy behind the Wig & Pen, Canberra's only brewpub.

The brainchild of microbiologist and enthusiastic 'beer aficionado' Lachie McOmish, the Wig & Pen has been part of the Canberra social scene for nearly two decades. In 1991 McOmish began thinking seriously about establishing a micro-brewery in Canberra. The dream came to fruition as the Wig & Pen a few years later, after he had successfully sourced the essentials: premises, a brewer and the brewing equipment.

A charming and cosy little shopfront in the heart of the national capital was found for the home of the new venture and a brewer was found in Richard Pass, a talented home brewer with a keen palate. The necessary equipment was sourced from the extract-only Craig Brewery in Sydney's Darling Harbour, which closed in 1992, and was adapted to be able to create the Wig & Pen's full mash brewhouse.

After several years, and with a number of awards to his credit including Champion Small Brewery at the 1998 Australian International Beer Awards, brewer Richard Pass moved on. Current head brewer Richard Watkins, who has been at the Wig & Pen for the past

'Modus Hoperandus' with truffles

15 years, has seen it go from strength to strength, consistently winning awards for its beer in Australia and New Zealand, becoming one of the most awarded breweries in Australia. The pub has also taken out numerous Best in Class and Champion Trophy awards at the Australian International Beer Awards.

In 2009 the Wig & Pen took its Kembery Regional Ale to the production line and bottled the award-winning brew. Due to space constraints at the Wig & Pen, Watkins brewed and bottled this beer at a larger facility, De Bortoli Wines in Bathurst.

The pub now offers 16 beers, including four hand-pumped real ales and several barrel-aged Belgium styles aged in the Wig & Pen's own barrel facility. There are six regular brews and another six seasonal brews, including a wheat beer and a Bavarian-style Doppel Bock, as well as two hand-pressed ciders. From the balanced fruitiness of the Kembery Ale to the Velvet Cream Stout, described as 'a robust chocolate and coffee extravaganza', and numerous one-off batches, there's always something tasty, interesting and unique to drink at the Wig. And this is also one of the few places in Australia serving hand-pumped real ale.

Fancy a Bob's Armpit? Or perhaps a glass of Venom, or a Firey Aztec? The creativity behind the beers extends to the names they've been given! Bob's Armpit, in case you were wondering, is a 'funky wild Belgium-inspired' beer, a Firey Aztec is a chocolate chilli stout, and Venom is a double American pale ale.

One of the most interesting features of the bar – for those who are into the brewing side of things – is a cylindrical feature they call the 'Modus Hoperandus', created by

Wig & Pen barrels

Wig & Pen bar

Watkins. 'It's pretty unique,' he says. 'There are a few others in pubs around Australia, but I made them all.' Perched on the side of the bar, the glass and stainless steel structure is filled with fresh hop flowers, herbs and spices, and truffles. The ale flows through it before reaching the beer glass with an extra hit of flavour.

To complement its large range of beers, the Wig & Pen provides traditional pub food in generous servings. Nothing is priced over $13 and the choice ranges from a ploughman's lunch to curries (beef vindaloo or a butter chicken), fish and chips, or bangers and mash with the Wig's own Velvet Cream Stout gravy. The gravy is also recommended on a roast beef or chicken roll (with chips).

From the garlands of hop flowers around the bar to the interest generated by being able to watch the brewing process through the glass, and the warm wood panelling and furniture, the bar is intimate and inviting. Designed in the style of English pubs, it adopted a name in keeping with its proximity to Canberra's law courts and press gallery.

On Sunday afternoons you can take part in (or just come and listen to) the Wig & Pen musos' jam session. Depending on the timing, you might be propping up the bar alongside university students, politicians, public servants, judges or journalists.

WIG & PEN

ADDRESS
Canberra House Arcade, Alinga St, Canberra

TELEPHONE
(02) 6248 0171

WEBSITE
www.wigandpen.com.au

HOURS
Weekdays 12pm–12am, weekends 2–10pm.

GRUB
Open for lunch weekdays 12–2pm, and dinner weekdays 5–9pm, Sat 4–9pm.

TOP DROP
Among the 16 different beers brewed on the premises, the regulars are Amber Hefeweizen, Kiandra Gold Pilsner, Ballyragget Irish Red Ale, Kamberra Kolsch and Wig & Pen Pale Ale.

WHERE TO STAY
Medina Executive James Court is a short walk away, on Northbourne Ave. It has 150 self-contained apartments with rates from $170 for a 1-bedroom apartment or around $250 for a 2-bedroom apartment. The complex has a restaurant, swimming pool and health club. www.medinaapartments.com.au

NEARBY ATTRACTIONS
All of Canberra's attractions are within easy reach, including the Australian War Memorial, Canberra Museum and Gallery, National Museum of Australia and more.

MORE INFO
www.visitcanberra.com.au

Victoria

Opposite (clockwise from top): Middle Park Hotel; Beelzebub's Jewels, Holgate Brewhouse, Woodend; Grand Pacific Hotel, Lorne; Craig's Royal Hotel, Ballarat.

The ESPLANADE *Hotel*

ST KILDA

The 'Espy', St Kilda

Grungy rather than glamorous, 'The Espy' is the place to come for the best in live bands, from rock to hip-hop.

IT'S GRUNGY RATHER than glamorous, but the Esplanade Hotel is a true icon of the bayside suburb of St Kilda. If entertainment is what you look for in a pub, then you can't go past it.

Since 1878 'The Espy' has held a special place in the hearts of pub-goers looking for music. In the early days, the entertainment was provided by string quartets but today this is the place to come for the best in live bands, from rock to hip-hop. With its unbeatable location overlooking the St Kilda foreshore and Port Phillip, the front bar and small outdoor area at the front of the pub are always packed on a summer afternoon, but the action moves inside when the music starts.

All the big names have performed here – everyone from John Farnham and Paul Kelly to The Kills and Hot Hot Heat, as well as international heavy-metal acts Ed Guy and Deeds of Flesh, hip-hop artists DJ Cash Money, Steinski and Peanut Butter Wolf, and dance music's leading DJs from the USA and UK. And the Espy's the place to find up and coming talent too, not just in the music world. Comedians like Dave Hughes and Rove McManus started out with gigs at the Espy, and the hotel is also the venue for the SBS television production 'Rockwiz'.

Art Deco–inspired public bar in the basement

There are six bars in the pub, which have roaring open fires in winter, and three stages: the Front Bar/Lounge, the Gershwin Room and the Public Bar. The Gershwin Room is the stunning former grand dining room of the Esplanade Hotel, restored to its original splendour, with gold-leaf walls, an elaborate ceiling and lots of period detail including hand-rendered motifs, as well as an open fireplace.

The Public Bar was renovated and re-opened in July 2005. Originally home to Melbourne's first female-only club, the Primitive Room, the space had been bricked up and untouched for more than 35 years until renovations began in 2004. Now the historic underground bar has Art Deco–inspired imagery, original pressed-tin mouldings, a pit area with comfy black couches, Russian tattoo artwork from the early 1940s and the original floor tiling. Seating in the main area of the bar is a collection of tall wooden church pews.

Originally known as the Nimrod Room, the Espy's Front Bar is almost legendary among performers. With its fabulous bay views, it has bands on the bill every day of the week, with the pub averaging 50 bands over all three stages each week. And the best news is that a lot of the entertainment – especially early in the night – is free. No wonder the pub packs them in. From around 5.30–6pm on Fridays, Saturdays and Sundays you can catch Espy regulars in the Front Bar; the music starts a bit later on Tuesday and Wednesday nights – around 8.30pm.

Crowds come for the best live bands

THE ESPLANADE HOTEL

ADDRESS

11 The Esplanade, St Kilda

TELEPHONE

(03) 9534 0211

WEBSITE

www.espy.com.au

HOURS

Mon–Wed 12pm–1am, Thurs–Fri 12pm–3am, Sat 8–3am, Sun 12pm–1am (long weekends till 3am).

GRUB

The Espy Kitchen is open Mon–Wed 12–11pm, Thurs–Fri 12pm–2.30am, Sat 8–2.30am, Sun 8–1am (long weekends till 3am).

TOP DROP

Beers on tap include Carlton Draught, VB, Fat Yak, Pure Blonde and Stella Artois.

WHERE TO STAY

The Novotel St Kilda is a couple of doors down from the Espy towards Luna Park. It has 209 rooms and suites from around $145. www.novotelstkilda.com.au

NEARBY ATTRACTIONS

The Espy is in the heart of St Kilda, just around the corner from the action in Fitzroy St, the shops, restaurants and cake shops of Acland St, and the fun of Luna Park. Straight ahead, over the walkway, is St Kilda beach and the historic pier. On Sundays, the Upper Esplanade becomes a colourful craft market under the towering palm trees that line the Esplanade.

MORE INFO

www.thatsmelbourne.com.au
www.visitvictoria.com

The Gershwin Room

For a quick bite to eat before seeing a band, or just a place to relax and enjoy the fantastic views over St Kilda beach, the Espy Kitchen has two levels, a mezzanine area seating 70 people and a downstairs area for another 50. The place to be is upstairs, with its balcony and full-length windows looking out over the Esplanade, providing a stunning view of the bay: head here at sunset. The mezzanine also has a large window overlooking the Front Bar stage, which is opened for major events, effectively joining the two spaces.

The Espy Kitchen's menu has a mix of traditional pub favourites: steaks, fish, soup of the day, salads, pastas and Asian rice dishes. Breakfast is served at the weekends and you'll be catered for whether you need a full 'recovery' feed or just a coffee and a newspaper to read.

Don't worry too much about what to wear for your big night out at the Espy. There's no dress code, unless you plan to wear track pants or steel-capped boots. Anything else is considered just fine, because it's not about what you wear. It's all about the music.

The sunny outdoor area

CARLTON

HOTEL LINCOLN, ONE of Melbourne's popular gastro-pubs and one of its oldest licensed establishments, has taken on a contemporary image in recent years. A striking decor for the dining room, changing exhibitions of contemporary artists' works, an appealing lack of pretension and its city-fringe location in Carlton has made it a favourite with academics, trade unionists, artists, students, office workers and night owls.

Hotel Lincoln was first registered as a pub in 1854. It was given a facelift in 1939 and when it re-opened the profile of Abraham Lincoln was frosted on the window of the bar to attract US servicemen in Melbourne during the war. The Art Deco–styled front bar was 'too good to change', says owner Jon Burford, who has retained much of the feel of the traditional bar, even down to the cracked terrazzo floor. There's a fireplace too, but it's more for atmosphere than warmth.

'We're famous for not making parmas. We're trying to push the envelope a bit, with dishes like steak and kidney pudding, pigs' trotters and black pudding.'

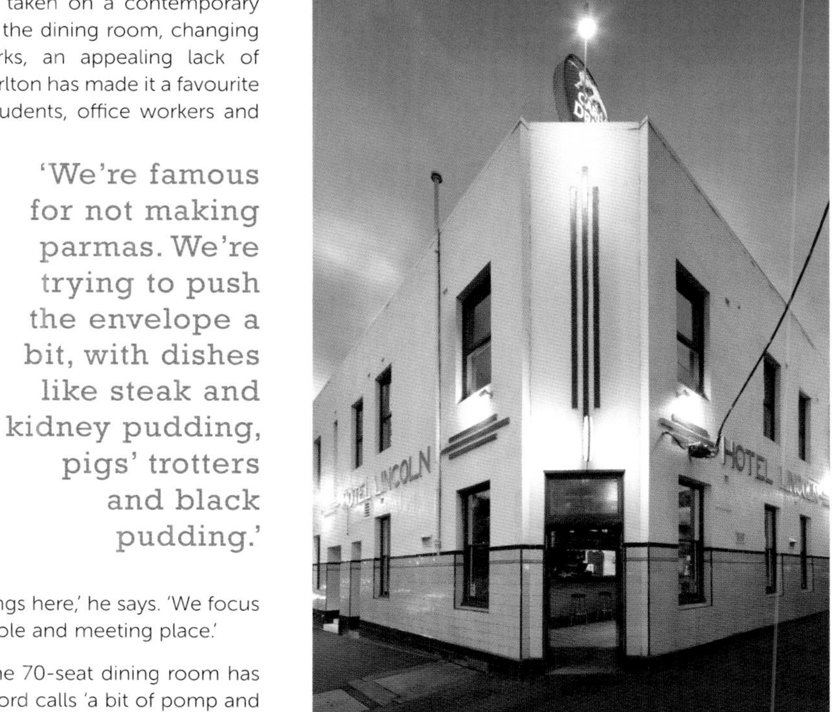

Hotel Lincoln, Carlton

'Because we are near to Trades Hall, this was very much a workers pub and there have been lots of political meetings here,' he says. 'We focus on the front bar as a traditional watering hole and meeting place.'

The bar may have stayed the same, but the 70-seat dining room has been given a modern edge with what Burford calls 'a bit of pomp and ceremony'. It is strikingly stark, with white lacquered panels and white leather chairs in a room with dark grey walls, charcoal mirrors and a black carpet.

Head chef Ross Beeley brings his traditional training (French and Middle Eastern) to the menu's scope, while still maintaining a seasonal focus, with as much as possible sourced from local producers. Just about everything is produced in-house, from salting and curing meats to baking bread twice daily. There is also a focus on offal, in traditional English fashion.

'We're famous for not making parmas,' says Burford. 'We're trying to push the envelope a bit, with dishes like steak and kidney pudding, pigs' trotters and black pudding.'

HOTEL LINCOLN

ADDRESS
91 Cardigan St, Carlton

TELEPHONE
(03) 9347 4666

WEBSITE
www.hotellincoln.com.au

HOURS
Sun–Thurs 12–11pm, Fri–Sat 12pm–12am.

GRUB
Open for lunch 12–2.30pm and dinner 6–9pm Sun—Thurs, and 12–3pm and 6–9.30pm Fri–Sat.

TOP DROP
Boutique beers are the focus, with Hargreaves Hill ESB the most popular beer sold. Carlton Draught is on tap (even though there's deliberately no label on the tap). There are around 300 labels on the wine list.

WHERE TO STAY
Downtowner on Lygon has 5 styles of contemporary, 4-star rooms and apartments, including king, executive, spa, apartment and family rooms, from around $165 per night; it is a block away on Lygon St. www.downtowner.com.au

NEARBY ATTRACTIONS
Close to Carlton's legendary Lygon St, and only a short distance from major attractions including the Old Melbourne Gaol, Melbourne Museum and IMAX theatre, and Carlton Gardens.

MORE INFO
www.thatsmelbourne.com.au
www.visitvictoria.com

Art @ The Lincoln

The hotel has a classic bar menu in addition to its dining-room menu. No bookings are required for the bar, it's just a matter of popping in and grabbing a table or propping yourself up at the bar for a counter meal. What you might find on the blackboard menu are six or seven items to share (samosas, oyster plates, a bowl of fried whitebait with aioli, fried chicken wings) and six bar meals, perhaps including a soup of the day, beer-battered fish'n'chips, pork and fennel sausages (but with braised pearl barley rather than mash), corned beef with mash and green beans, a vegetable curry, or the Hotel Lincoln's beef burger. All bar-menu mains are $15.

Look for the dedicated charcuterie menu as well as a lunchtime special 'the classic ploughman's lunch', featuring slow-cooked and then charred house-aged Victorian beef, freshly baked sourdough bread, beetroot pickle, cloth-wrapped cheddar, duck rillette, tomato and apple chutney, cornichons and horseradish cream.

The contemporary focus is not confined to the decor and the menu. One section of the bar is devoted to Art @ The Lincoln, a changing two-wall work of contemporary exhibitions staged in partnership with the nearby Ian Potter Museum of Art at the University of Melbourne. The exhibitions are designed to showcase contemporary artists' responses to the pub.

'It changes every three months, and is another element of trying to engage with our customers because it's a great conversation piece,' says Burford. 'Our aim is to encourage creative reflections on pub culture: the good, the bad and the ugly.'

And in case you are wondering, there are no pokies in this pub.

The front bar

MIDDLE PARK HOTEL

MIDDLE PARK

THE FLAG OF the 2010 Melbourne Cup winner, Americain, hangs proudly above the doors to the bar at the Middle Park Hotel. It's a sure sign that this is a pub where the sports-mad will feel right at home – but that doesn't mean just giant screens and cheering patrons.

Memorabilia is everywhere, covering all types of sport, but it doesn't overwhelm or detract from the comfortable feel of this bayside pub, which has been licensed since 1889. With a location just opposite Gate 1 of the Australian Formula One Grand Prix track at Albert Park, it seems somehow fitting that sport is the theme here. On the other side of the pub is Middle Park village and just beyond is Port Phillip in one direction and the city centre in the other.

The hotel entrance is marked with a red canopy on Armstrong Street, and the small lobby has a reception desk and intimate guest lounge with leather chairs and a fireplace. The restaurant and bar areas form a horseshoe around the central Victorian staircase that leads to the 25 guest rooms.

The public bar is cavernous, at 70 metres, believed to be the longest in the country. Counter meals, at $12 each, are served here. There are five choices, which change about every three months, but you might find things like Irish stew, soup and a sandwich, coq au vin, pork cordon bleu (a rump schnitzel) or smoked haddock florentine among them. At the back of the bar are five booths, each with its own plasma screen television. On Sundays, head here for cool jazz sounds from 6–9pm.

For the dining room, with its massive antler 'chandelier', consulting chef Paul Wilson has created a menu that uses primarily

Middle Park Hotel

There are fun touches … the door tags taken directly from 1970s Sandman van slogans that read: 'Don't laugh, your daughter could be inside' or 'If this room's rockin' don't come a-knockin'.'

The public bar

Victorian and organic produce, with a focus on rare breed meats from small specialist suppliers. The weekend roast could be Warialda Belted Galloway or Red Angus beef, Wessex saddleback pork or Blackface Suffolk lamb, for example, while other meats from 'boutique' breeds feature throughout the year's seasonally changing menu. Signature dishes channel hotel classics such as prawn cocktail, scotch eggs and chicken kiev, or eggs royale in the morning. The wine list is exclusively Victorian labels.

Hotel suites have claw-foot baths

The monogrammed carpet up the stairs leads to traditional pub rooms – but with ensuites and modern style. The rooms are large and light, with high ceilings, original architraves and white plantation-style shutters. The decor is black and white with fire engine–red splashes from the pure wool blankets, scatter cushions and

Monogrammed carpet on the stairs

fun touches here and there.

Most rooms also have built-in window seats, with about half the rooms overlooking the street (but windows are double-glazed to cut out noise). There are LCD televisions, and the walls are hung with a collection of Rennie Ellis photographs depicting life in Melbourne over five decades – a mix of great Victorian sporting moments, social life and rock'n'roll (the King suite features Mick Jagger). The hotel's two suites have gas fireplaces and claw-foot bathtubs in the ensuite (as well as the double-headed showers found in all). Every room has an iPod dock.

There is a minibar with a difference: a basket containing Victorian wines (Craiglee, Shadowfax, Yering Station and TarraWarra) and other locally made treats such as Grand Ridge and Three Troupers beers, and Cocoa Farm dark and buttermilk chocolate.

There are fun touches too. The brightly coloured coat hooks, and the door tags taken directly from 1970s Sandman panel van slogans that read: 'Don't laugh, your daughter could be inside' or 'If this room's rockin' don't come a-knockin'.' Another surprise – possibly unique to this hotel – is a locked bedside drawer marked with a red 'X'. What's inside? You have to ask for a key to find out, but a hint is that it is an 'adults-only' minibar specially designed for the bedroom.

Surprises are all part of the experience at the Middle Park – and that's the way they like it.

Rooms are large and bright

MIDDLE PARK HOTEL

ADDRESS

102 Canterbury Rd, Middle Park

TELEPHONE

(03) 9690 1958

WEBSITE

www.middleparkhotel.com.au

RATES

From $250 for a double room to $800 for King suite, or $1000 for King apartment premier suite. Prices vary depending on the season and length of stay.

HOURS

Daily 11–1am.

GRUB

Bar meals available daily 12–11pm; restaurant open for lunch 12–3pm and dinner 6–10pm.

TOP DROP

Seventeen different beers come out of 45 taps in the bar, ensuring that almost every taste is covered.

NEARBY ATTRACTIONS

The Middle Park Hotel is on the opposite side of Canterbury Rd to Albert Park, with its enormous lake and 225 ha of gardens. There are walking and cycling tracks, kayak and sailboat hire, a public golf course, and the park is also home to the Melbourne Sports and Aquatic Centre. The Australian Formula One Grand Prix is held at Albert Park every March. In the other direction, it is a few blocks' walk to the South Melbourne and Middle Park beaches.

MORE INFO

www.visitmelbourne.com
www.thatsmelbourne.com.au

MITRE TAVERN

MELBOURNE

Melbourne's oldest pub, the Mitre Tavern

THERE'S NO QUESTION that Melbourne's oldest pub, the Mitre Tavern, is a pretty blokey place. In fact, on a Friday night when the after-work crowd packs into the beer garden there are about five men to every woman among the hundreds of revellers, says publican Ben Addison.

They've been pouring drinks at the Mitre since 1867, in a lane that was doubtless a rough and rowdy spot in those days. In modern Melbourne, it's not quite as trendy as some other laneways, but coming across the pub while wandering in the city is like discovering a little piece of olde England.

The feeling persists inside, where low ceilings (and doorways!), lots of timber, open fires in winter, hunting prints and the odd deer's head on the wall give the Mitre a very old-fashioned feel. It's a huge hit with British expats too, says Addison, but hastens to add – unnecessarily – that this is definitely not 'a theme pub' nor in any way twee.

> Low ceilings (and doorways!), lots of timber, open fires in winter, hunting prints and the odd deer's head on the wall give the Mitre a very old-fashioned feel but this is definitely not 'a theme pub'.

Pull up a bar stool and you might find yourself chatting to a 'suit' from the insurance, banking, recruitment or financial sectors. This is very much the business end of Melbourne ... but that doesn't mean it's not an eclectic crowd. Mohawk hairstyles don't even raise an eyebrow if they walk in.

The two-storey Gothic-style building was first a private home, and has been documented by the Melbourne City Council as the oldest building in Melbourne. In 1868 Mr Henry Thompson became the first of many publicans at the Mitre Tavern. Hunting, racing and sporting men made it their favoured meeting place, with members of the first Victorian Polo Club and the Melbourne Dog Club holding their meetings here. And with its proximity to the law courts, and to Temple Court and Chancery Lane, it was also a place where some distinguished patrons quenched their thirst.

Across the road from the Mitre is the Savage Club, built by Australia's first baronet, Sir William Clarke. The mistress of his son, Sir Rupert Clarke, a woman called Connie

The public bar

Waugh, is said to have hanged herself in the Mitre and her ghost is believed to haunt the tavern. In 1930 the hotel was bought by the Royal Insurance Company, which planned to demolish it to make room for additions to its Collins Street building, but the Mitre stubbornly hung on until 1937 when the company had a change of heart.

Downstairs, the bistro offers hearty pub food, with free pizza on Thursday night and a free sausage sizzle in the garden bar on Friday night. There's trivia on Monday at lunchtime and on Tuesday and Wednesday nights. The dining area seats up to 100 and is furnished in a rustic-looking way. The walls are adorned with murals and hand-carved boards, some dating back to early last century. The menu has traditional favourites including burgers, pastas, parmas, a beef and Guinness pie, steaks and more.

Head upstairs to the Mitre Steakhouse and Grill – where a premium steak will cost you $30–$40 – and it's a much more formal affair, with big leather dining chairs, a fireplace, leadlight windows and a 'clubby' feel. There's a small bar off the side of this dining room.

The extensive beer garden runs the length of the tavern off Bank Place and is an unexpected find, tucked between city office towers. There are a few small trees planted down one side, and the space has heaters in winter and a retractable awning to cover it in case of rain or extreme heat. It claims to be the largest beer garden in Melbourne's CBD, with seating for 200 and standing room for many more. For many patrons it's a welcome contrast to the smart cocktail bars that are popular today, and a small reminder of a simpler way of getting together with friends.

Wall decorations

MITRE TAVERN

ADDRESS
5 Bank Pl, Melbourne

TELEPHONE
(03) 9670 5644

WEBSITE
www.mitretavern.com.au

HOURS
Mon–Sat 11am–late; closed Sun.

GRUB
Mon–Sat 12–3pm and 5pm–late.

TOP DROP
There are 14 beers on tap, including Pure Blonde, Carlton Draught, Stella Artois, Coopers Pale Ale, Guinness, Moo Brew, Peroni, Fat Yak Pale Ale and Asahi.

WHERE TO STAY
Metro Apartments on Bank Pl is almost directly opposite the Mitre Tavern, and has 4-star studio and 1-bedroom apartments priced from around $115–$130. www.metroapartmentsmelbourne.com

NEARBY ATTRACTIONS
Bank Pl runs between Collins St and Little Collins St, in the heart of the city, and is an easy walk to all major attractions. You can also walk 2 blocks to Flinders St and jump on the free City Circle tram which runs to most attractions.

MORE INFO
www.visitmelbourne.com
www.thatsmelbourne.com.au

MORNING STAR *Hotel*

WILLIAMSTOWN

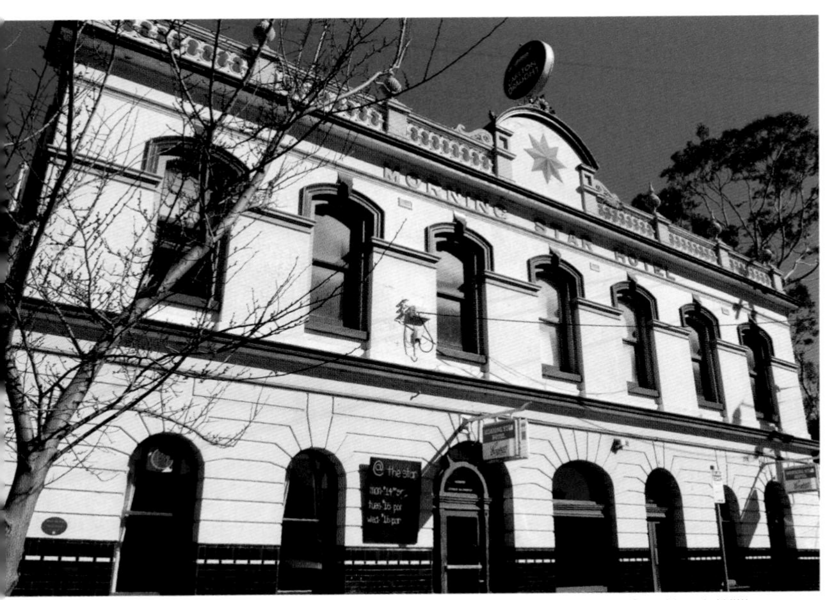

Morning Star Hotel, Williamstown

A STROLL BY the bay is one of the highlights of Williamstown, a south-western suburb of Melbourne that prides itself on its nautical heritage. Williamstown has been home to naval shipbuilding since 1860 and retains much of its maritime village charm, the historic buildings of Nelson Place along the waterfront now housing cafes, restaurants and shops.

But it's well worthwhile getting beyond the first couple of blocks from the water to delve a little deeper into what makes Williamstown tick, and one place to do that is at the Morning Star Hotel. This is very much a local pub, a little off the beaten tourist path, and somewhere you'll find surprisingly good food, people willing to have a bit of a chat at the bar and a large sunny beer garden away from the crowds.

There has been a pub on this site since 1869, and the present hotel has been here largely unchanged (on the outside at least) since 1889. The large dining room offers modern gastro-pub cuisine in a setting that's comfortable for everyone, from tradies in their fluoro safety jackets to couples at tables for two by the window or groups of ladies at lunch. Historic photos of Williamstown hang on the walls, there are ornate ceiling roses overhead as well as a large stone fireplace, and the whole room is decorated in heritage colours. Side windows overlook the large paved garden bar, with bright azaleas in pots.

At the front of the pub is an old horse trough. It may have been there since the pub was built, at a time when there were 45 hotels in Williamstown and everyone got around in a horse and buggy.

Early in the week, cheap eats are on the menu; so Monday–Wednesday you'll see specials such as steak and chips or the Star parma for less than $16. The à la carte menu in the dining room offers seriously good food, including roast duck, fish of the day (grilled barramundi, perhaps), fish and chips, bangers and mash, and steaks from the grill, and an extensive wine list. There's a kids' menu too.

In the bar, the menu includes a trio of dips, bruschetta, salt-and-pepper calamari, and a mini yum cha for $15. The day's specials – usually three of them – are available both in the bar and the dining room, and there's usually a vegetarian option among them.

A central hallway – the bar is on one side, dining room on the other – leads to a smaller lounge at the back of the pub, which has a big-screen television (and there is one in the bar too) and some big comfy lounges for those who want a quieter spot.

At the front of the pub is an old horse trough. It may have been there since the pub was built, at a time when there were 45 hotels in Williamstown and everyone got around in a horse and buggy. The Morning Star's first licensee, Amelia Sarah Kingston, was killed when her buggy overturned as she travelled the short distance from the hotel to the waterfront to pick up her husband.

Today, the Morning Star is a short walk from the Williamstown train station; however, a much more interesting way of reaching it is to board the ferry at Melbourne's Southgate and travel down the Yarra River and across the bay. It takes nearly an hour, but gives you a new perspective on the city and Port Phillip. When you alight, look back for views of the city skyline through the masts of the boats bobbing on the water.

The old horse trough outside

Gem Pier is dominated by the World War II minesweeper HMAS *Castlemaine*, a product of the Williamstown dockyards and now a maritime museum, and the waterfront park, Commonwealth Reserve, which has a band rotunda and the anchor from HMAS *Nelson* to look at. Running almost the length of the waterfront, Nelson Place is lined with interesting historic buildings – most dating back to 1870 – including former hotels, newspaper offices, banks and a 19th-century barber shop, as well as the Modern Buildings, built in 1909. Many of these buildings now house restaurants and cafes.

If you have lunched at the Morning Star and feel like a walk, head a couple of blocks over to the Williamstown Botanical Gardens (the barman will point you in the right direction). Ornate iron gates open into these restful gardens, where the four lawns – Golden Elm, Liquidamber, Sunset and Four Corners – are well used, especially when the sun's shining. Established in 1860, the gardens originally belonged to a small group of 'scientific and pleasure' gardens that tested how well European species would grow in the new colony of Australia. A stroll through the palm-lined pathways will bring you out to the seafront.

MORNING STAR HOTEL

ADDRESS
3 Electra St, Williamstown

TELEPHONE
(03) 9397 6082

HOURS
12–11pm Sun–Wed, 12pm–1am Thurs–Fri, 12pm–12am Sat.

GRUB
Open for lunch 12–2pm and dinner 6–9pm daily.

TOP DROP
Coopers Draught, Premium Light, Pale Ale and Premium Lager are all on tap, along with Guinness and Bulmer's cider.

WHERE TO STAY
Punthill Williamstown is a modern apartment hotel offering contemporary studios and 1- and 2-bedroom apartments, all with private balconies. Rates start at around $165. www.punthill.com.au

NEARBY ATTRACTIONS
Step aboard the WW II minesweeper HMAS *Castlemaine* at Gem Pier and get a feel for how life was for the seamen of yesteryear (www.hmascastlemaine.com). Along the street from the Morning Star is the Williamstown Historical Society Museum, in one of Hobsons Bay's oldest structures, the Mechanics Institute, a National Trust building dating from 1860; open Sun afternoons. The bluestone Timeball Tower on the point at the eastern end of Nelson Pl was built by convict labour in the late 1840s; originally a lighthouse, it operated as a timeball for passing ships until 1926 and is now part of Point Gellibrand Coastal Heritage Park.

MORE INFO
www.visitvictoria.com

YOUNG & JACKSON

MELBOURNE

Young & Jackson, Melbourne

CHLOE. LIKE SO many truly famous people, she only needs one name. Tell any Melburnian (or indeed, perhaps any Australian) that you are going to have a beer with Chloe and they know instantly who – and where – you mean. 'Having a beer with Chloe' at Young & Jackson has been a rite of passage for generations of young Melburnians, embodying two of the city's icons.

'Having a beer with Chloe' at Young & Jackson has been a rite of passage for generations of young Melburnians.

Young & Jackson is one of Melbourne's oldest remaining pubs and still one of its liveliest. Home to Australia's most famous nude, a painting of a young Parisian by Jules Lefebvre, it stands on Melbourne's busiest corner, ensuring there is always something happening.

To make the most of that view – looking out to the impressive Victorian edifice of Flinders Street Station, the modern lines of Federation Square and the towering presence of St Paul's Cathedral – take a table in the cafe or head upstairs to Chloe's Bar. But to immerse yourself in the action, go straight through the main doors and into the Long Bar, where sports fans gather, or the Main Bar.

Y&J has plenty of options, depending on the occasion or your mood. Everyone from 18 to 80 comes to Y&J, whether they are sporting fans (of any kind), the pre-theatre crowd heading to the Arts Centre, or just meeting up with friends before a night out. The Long Bar and the Main Bar, with their pressed-metal ceilings and wonderful leadlights, are usually crowded and noisy, but upstairs are several areas where you can have a quiet drink or a meal in the restaurant. Smokers and cider-lovers can head out into the fresh air of the tiny rooftop garden, with its artificial grass and apple-green theme. This is Australia's only dedicated cider bar, with eight ciders on tap (including Scrumpy Jack from French oak barrels) as well as an extensive range of Australian and imported bottled ciders.

Young & Jackson Hotel (formerly Prince's Bridge Hotel) has been the place 'where Melbourne meets' since 1861. Arguably Australia's most famous pub, it was opened by John P. Toohey, who later went on to found the Standard Brewery in Sydney, which

Chloe's Bar, with the famous painting

produced Tooheys beer. In 1875 Irish goldminers Henry Figsby Young and Thomas Joshua Jackson became licensees of the pub, and renamed it Young & Jackson Hotel. The partnership ended in 1890 but Young carried on the licence with his sons Harry and Reginald.

Who was Chloe? Her real name was Marie and her career as a model began in Paris. Throughout her life, Chloe has kept company with artists, poets, wharfies, prime ministers and drunks, soldiers and sailors, celebrities, bushies, labourers and art connoisseurs. Marie was immortalised by French art teacher Jules Joseph Lefebvre, but little is known about her, except she was about 19 years old and that about two years after the painting was done, she threw a party for her friends and then killed herself by drinking poison. The reason for her suicide is thought to be unrequited love.

Chloe was first exhibited in the Paris Salon in 1875, a showcase exhibition of the work of the leading French Academy masters – and she caused a sensation, winning both the gold medal and acclamation from Salon judges, critics and the public. But when she was first displayed in Young & Jackson, there was a scandal. Then owned by Dr Thomas Fitzgerald, after three weeks of backlash about the exposure of such nudity she was removed; Dr Fitzgerald then hung *Chloe* in a front room of his home (but

The bell rings for 'last drinks'

YOUNG & JACKSON

ADDRESS
Cnr Swanston and Flinders sts, Melbourne

TELEPHONE
(03) 9650 3884

WEBSITE
www.youngandjacksons.com.au

HOURS
Mon–Thurs 10–12am, Fri 10–3am, Sat 9–3am, Sun 9–12am. Cider Bar open 12pm–12am Sun–Thurs and 12pm–3am Fri–Sat.

GRUB
Restaurant open daily 12–2.30pm for lunch, and for dinner Sun–Thurs 5.30–9pm and Fri–Sat 5.30–9.30pm. Bar food available during normal trading hours.

TOP DROP
There are 30 beers and 9 ciders on tap.

WHERE TO STAY
Just a block away on Flinders St, the Rendezvous Hotel Melbourne is a grand and historic hotel. Built in 1913 as the Commercial Travellers Club, it has been beautifully restored. It has 340 rooms, priced from around $190 double. www.rendezvoushotels.com

NEARBY ATTRACTIONS
Y&J is within shouting distance of all Melbourne's inner-city attractions, including Federation Sq, the two art galleries – NGV International and NGV Australia – Royal Botanic Gardens, Southbank and more. The Melbourne visitor centre is directly opposite the pub, in Federation Sq.

MORE INFO
www.visitmelbourne.com
www.visitvictoria.com

Quieter bars are upstairs

visible to the passing public) and this was also deemed unacceptable to some, so she was moved to a back room.

Henry Figsby Young was an art collector, with a private collection of more than 200 works on display throughout the hotel. He purchased *Chloe* at Dr Fitzgerald's estate auction in 1909, and brought her back to Y&J, where she held pride of place in the Main Bar for nearly 80 years. He could not have dreamed of the legend he was creating.

Chloe became known as the 'Queen of the Bar Room Wall' and for many young men was the only naked woman they ever saw before going to war. Today, ANZAC Day is the biggest of the year for the hotel, which holds Melbourne's only licence to serve liquor from 6am that day. The dawn service crowd heads straight up St Kilda Road from the Shrine of Remembrance to Y&J when the formalities are over.

In 1987, when the Bond Corporation owned the hotel, *Chloe* was moved from the Front Bar. Some believed her relocation to a quiet bar upstairs (then renamed Chloe's Bar) was to take her out of the public eye, so she could eventually be removed or sold. There was a public outcry and the National Trust stepped in to make her part of the hotel's heritage listing. Now *Chloe* cannot leave the hotel at any time, except for restoration work. About 50 people a day come in simply to have a look at her.

But there are plenty of other reasons to drop in to this pub. Bands play in the Main Bar on Friday and Saturday nights, and the Sunday Session (3–6pm) has blues and rock. There's also live entertainment every public holiday eve from 9pm, with bands and a DJ.

The cafe looks out to Flinders Street

BLUE DUCK INN

ANGLERS REST

IN 1912, A successful miner called Billy O'Connell bought a slab hut operating as a butcher shop, got himself a hotel licence and prepared to open a pub at the confluence of three great alpine rivers – the Cobungra, the Bundarra and the Mitta Mitta – in the Victorian High Country. He knew it would be a good business, because the planned main road was to run right past the door.

When the government refused to approve the survey plans for the new road, O'Connell took a tin panning dish and wrote 'Blue Duck' on it. He nailed it up outside his pub and the name was born. A 'blue duck', in miner's terms, is the same as a white elephant, a mining lease that fails to produce gold. And that's what Billy O'Connell thought his pub – still doing a flourishing trade today – would be.

The Blue Duck Inn, Anglers Rest

A 'blue duck', in miner's terms, is the same as a white elephant, a mining lease that fails to produce gold. And that's what Billy O'Connell thought his pub would be.

The original slab building, cut from local timber and built in 1900, had been selling fresh meat to miners on the walking track from Omeo to the goldfields around Mt Wills. In the early 1920s, O'Connell carted two houses from Omeo – room by room – through the bush on horse drays to replace the old building. One is the existing building of today's Blue Duck Inn, and the other – on the site of today's accommodation – became the home where he and his wife Lillian raised their nine children.

Another of Billy O'Connell's legacies is the small log building behind the pub. Known as State School number 4286, O'Connell built it in 1926 when five of his children were of school age. The Education Department provided a teacher to be shared with

Self-contained cabin accommodation

the school at Glen Wills; he rode his horse between the two schools, dividing his week between them.

In spite of the pessimistic name he gave his hotel, O'Connell's pub was discovered by keen anglers from Melbourne who valued its location near the best trout fishing around. Among the regular visitors was Sir Harold Clapp, head of the Victorian Railways. In the 1930s, Clapp arranged for apprentices at the Newport rail yards to cast the Art Deco bronze duck – now painted a bright blue – that still stands at the gate.

After the O'Connell family left in 1946, the Blue Duck's fortunes were mixed and the licence was relinquished in 1967 when the local gold ran out. The building was used for various purposes until 1998, when the Blue Duck regained its licence and resumed trading as a country pub.

Today, the same High Country hospitality is to be found, with hearty meals and simple accommodation. The Blue Duck's isolation, surrounded by 400 000 hectares of Alpine National Park, is no deterrent to those who know the beauty of its location. You might arrive and find there's a horse tied up outside, or perhaps a line up of touring motorcycles ... everyone's welcome. The à la carte menu is complemented with a good range of Victorian wines; the signature dish is a 400 gram scotch steak. On chilly days, there's an open fire to relax beside, and in summer the best place is on the verandah overlooking the Cobungra River and an historic old bridge. Artists and photographers delight in it, and part of the charm for many is that this is a place where

The pub is surrounded by the Alpine National Park

The Art Deco bronze duck

television and mobile phone reception is almost non-existent. You can relax with a drink by the river, splash around in a swimming hole if it's warm enough, read a book on the lawns or go birdwatching – the 'blue duck' at the gate has real feathered friends including robins, parrots, rosellas, wrens and magnificent wedge-tailed eagles.

The Duck has six two-bedroom self-contained cabins. Each has a gas stove, fridge, cutlery and crockery, and tea- and coffee-making needs. The ingredients for a cooked or continental breakfast can be purchased to prepare in your cabin or on the guest barbecue. The cabins consist of a main room with the kitchenette, wood fire and a double or queen bed, a sofa and a dining-room table, while the second room has a double bed and a set of bunks or a single bed, and there is an adjacent bathroom.

Getting to Anglers Rest is part of the fun. From Melbourne, you can take the Princes Highway to Bairnsdale and Omeo and then travel 30 kilometres on a winding bitumen road which will bring you right to the Duck's front door. Or you can come through Mount Beauty and Falls Creek, across the beautiful Bogong High Plains to the Omeo Highway and from there it is just 11 kilometres to the Blue Duck. Other routes will take you through the pretty village of Bright and the ski village of Mount Hotham before hitting the Omeo Highway. The drive from Melbourne will take about five hours, but some of it is along the 270-kilometre Great Alpine Road, a truly spectacular part of Australia, and worth exploring. Travellers from the north come through Albury to Tallangatta and Glen Wills, along the Mitta Mitta valley, on a partly unsealed road.

The Blue Duck Inn closes for the winter, after the snow season starts, from the Queen's Birthday weekend in June until 1 September.

Entrance to the Blue Duck

BLUE DUCK INN

ADDRESS
Omeo Hwy, Anglers Rest

TELEPHONE
(03) 5159 7220

WEBSITE
www.blueduckinn.com.au

RATES
Cabins from $130–$150 double, or $60–$70 per person if there are three or more guests.

HOURS
Daily 11am–11pm (but change according to the season; often closed Mon Sept–late Dec).

GRUB
Meals available Wed–Sun and public holidays for lunch 12–2pm and dinner 6–8pm; daily during Victorian school holidays.

TOP DROP
Carlton Draught is on tap, with a range of other Australian and imported beers available in cans and stubbies.

NEARBY ATTRACTIONS
Whitewater rafting on the Mitta Mitta River is a great way to see the beauty of this region. Rafting Australia runs trips for beginners and advanced paddlers June–Nov. Entry points into the Mitta Mitta are within a few km of the pub. www.raftingaustralia.com.au. There are also guided horseriding treks and fly-fishing tours run in the area.

MORE INFO
www.visitvictoria.com

CRAIG'S ROYAL *Hotel*

BALLARAT

Craig's Royal Hotel, Ballarat

THIS LANDMARK HOTEL is aptly named. Since it opened in 1853, it has played host to a long line of regal visitors, including dukes and duchesses, as well as knights and dames and other famous names.

While still a pub at heart, an ambitious restoration project completed in 2010 has given it some of Ballarat's finest accommodation, in keeping with its long reputation for tradition and elegance. Ballarat's first officially licensed pub, it played an important part in goldfields history. Opened by Thomas Bath in 1853, two years later it was the venue for the Royal Commission of Enquiry into the Eureka Stockade uprising. Walter Craig bought Bath's Hotel (as it was then called) in 1857.

Walter Craig had a dream that his horse Nimblefoot would win the Melbourne Cup, and of his own death. Both premonitions came true that year, 1870.

In 1867, the royal patronage began: Queen Victoria's second son, Prince Alfred, Duke of Edinburgh, visited Ballarat and was hosted in Craig's Prince's Room, specially prepared for him. Over the years, others followed – Prince Albert Victor and Prince George, the Duke and Duchess of York (later to become King George V and Queen Mary), the Duke of Clarence, the Duke of Windsor and the Duke and Duchess of Gloucester.

There were other famous visitors too. In 1867 poet and horseman Adam Lindsay Gordon ran the stables at Craig's, Mark Twain stayed during an Australian tour in 1895 and Dame Nellie Melba famously sang from the balcony of the Reading Room in 1908 on one of her many visits to Ballarat. Lord Kitchener stayed at the hotel, as did Sir Robert Menzies and Sir Donald Bradman.

Over a drink in Craig's Bar you may hear the amazing tale of how Walter Craig had a dream that his horse Nimblefoot would win the Melbourne Cup, and of his own death. Both premonitions came true that year, 1870.

Current owners John and Mary Finning, who bought the hotel in 1999, took six years to fully restore the entire hotel to stunning effect. The plush lobby is a taste of what is

Elegant surroundings for a quiet drink

to come, but the bars, gaming room and the light-filled courtyard atrium bistro ensure it hasn't lost its country pub feel.

Handmade brickwork, elegant archways and marble fireplaces are featured throughout. Each of the 41 guest rooms is different in size, shape and look, furnished with antiques personally sourced by Mary Finning. 'Classic' and 'superior' rooms are beautifully furnished in period style and some have spa baths, but the hotel's 'deluxe' rooms and 'royal suites' are jaw-droppingly gorgeous. Among the most extravagant are one of the two chinoiserie-styled rooms, which has an intricately carved 600-year-old Chinese wedding bed, and the lavish Melba Suite, with an antique mahogany bed; other rooms have brass beds or four-posters. The best views are from the Tower Suite. Modern 'necessities' such as plasma televisions (hidden inside cabinets), air conditioning, hairdryers and internet access have been cleverly integrated without detracting from the overall effect.

Fine food in the Gallery Bistro

CRAIG'S ROYAL HOTEL

ADDRESS
10 Lydiard St Sth, Ballarat

TELEPHONE
(03) 5331 1377

WEBSITE
www.craigsroyal.com.au

RATES
$230–$460 double, including continental breakfast.

HOURS
Main bar open daily 10am–10pm.

GRUB
Craig's Coffeeshop open weekdays 8am–6pm and weekends 9am–6pm. The Gallery Bistro open daily for breakfast 7–10am, lunch 12–2.30pm and dinner 6–9pm.

TOP DROP
Beers on tap include Carlton Draught, Classic Blonde, Amber Ale, Heineken and Hahn Light.

NEARBY ATTRACTIONS
Craig's Royal Hotel is within walking distance of many of Ballarat's attractions, including the Art Gallery of Ballarat (home of the original Eureka flag). A little further out of town, the city's major tourist attraction is Sovereign Hill, a re-created gold-rush era village that is one of Australia's best outdoor museums. www.sovereignhill.com.au

MORE INFO
www.visitballarat.com.au
www.visitvictoria.com

The Foyer Lounge

There are two restaurants and two bars. The plush Foyer Lounge has velvet and studded leather sofas, potted palms and antiques, and is popular with the pre-theatre crowd heading to historic Her Majesty's Theatre across the road. For a more casual drink, the main bar has big-screen television for the sports fans, and for jazz head to Craig's Bluestone Cellar bar. On Friday and Saturday nights there's piano music in Craig's Bar, where the cocktail names are linked to the hotel's history (try a Nimblefoot).

The large glass-roofed conservatory that now encompasses the historic courtyard offers informal dining from breakfast through to dinner. In the coffee shop, take a seat at the big communal table for brunch or coffee (and they do takeaway too).

In keeping with its regal aspect, high tea is served every Sunday at Craig's at 3pm. Bookings are essential, and the cost includes a short tour of the hotel, explanation of the history of Craig's and a look at the suites and banquet rooms.

Old gas lamp

A Chinese wedding bed adorns one guest bedroom

The FARMERS ARMS

DAYLESFORD

The Farmers Arms, Daylesford

Beer is still pumped straight from the keg, you'll find local news and historical photos on the walls, a wood fire in the corner, and the bar has retained its period charm.

SQUIZZY, TUBBY AND Wally know there'll always be a spot for them at the bar at the Farmers Arms. Three small brass plaques, engraved with their names and marked 'Reserved', claim their places at the end of the bar in recognition of their long patronage of this popular Daylesford pub. It is known for great food that attracts visitors from miles around, but the Farmers Arms is still very much a 'local' where everyone's happy to meet new faces and have a chat.

Over the past decade, the hotel has developed a well-deserved reputation for fine dining. That hasn't changed, but the style and atmosphere is now more relaxed without sacrificing any of the quality. Susanne Devine and Claire Levine have owned the Farmers Arms since 2009 and have introduced a more informal style of dining, with communal tables as well as an option to eat at the bar or at smaller tables around the main dining room. Your fellow diners at a communal table may be local farmers or business folk, daytrippers or weekend visitors from Melbourne – only an hour and a half or 180 kilometres down the freeway – or overseas travellers looking for an authentic Australian country pub.

THE FARMERS ARMS

ADDRESS
1 East St, Daylesford

TELEPHONE
(03) 5348 2091

WEBSITE
www.farmersarmsdaylesford.com.au

HOURS
Daily 11.30am–late.

GRUB
Daily for lunch 12–3pm and dinner 6pm–late.

TOP DROP
On tap you'll find Carlton Draught, Alpha Pale Ale, Dogbolter Dark Lager, Fat Yak Pale Ale, Stella Artois, Asahi, Cascade Premium Light and Bulmer's cider.

WHERE TO STAY
Balconies B&B in the heart of Daylesford has 9 stylish double rooms with ensuites, from $175. For luxury and indulgence, the Lake House on the edge of Lake Daylesford has 33 rooms and suites from around $275. www.lakehouse.com.au

NEARBY ATTRACTIONS
Behind Daylesford's main street is the Convent, a 3-level historic 19th-century mansion that now houses a gallery, small museum, a chapel, cafe and shops (www.theconvent.com.au). At nearby Hepburn Springs, indulge in spa treatments and hot pools at the Hepburn Bathhouse & Spa, one of about a dozen day spas in the district (www.hepburnbathhouse.com).

MORE INFO
www.visitdaylesford.com
www.visitvictoria.com

'Some locals eat here several times a week, and we probably have a mix of about 50/50 locals and visitors,' says Susanne. 'We decided that we wanted to move away from having a restaurant to bring it back to much more of a true pub feel. Everyone has really embraced it, and we're finding that people are lingering that bit longer, maybe because it is more relaxed.'

The front bar

The dining room is a large open space with an 18-seat communal table in the centre, and smaller tables for two or four around the room. Fresh flowers, eclectic artworks and collectibles keep things interesting and there's a friendly buzz about the room when the tables start filling up. The former pool room, off the front bar, is now another dining space, with pressed-metal ceilings, rich red walls and lampshades that add warmth, especially at night. There's another 14-seat communal table in here, or high tables with stools to perch on.

The menu changes often but may include dishes like pheasant or duck, or perhaps a rabbit and tarragon pie with thick kipfler potato chips, an aged porterhouse steak with rocket and jus, or slow-roasted pork belly with mash, broccolini and a smoky chilli relish. It's deceptively, deliciously simple, and you'll also find tasty new takes on pub staples like fish and chips and curries.

The original timber hotel that stood on the corner of East and Knox streets went the way of so many old pubs, and burnt down. The current distinctive red-brick corner hotel has been standing since 1857. Beer is still pumped straight from the keg, you'll find local news and historical photos on the walls, a wood fire in the corner, and the bar has retained its period charm. Some wag has planted a set of antlers on the goat's head mounted above the bar, which is strung with medals from a local sporting team.

On Friday night there are raffles in the front bar, with several prizes on offer to benefit local charities. Winners may go home with a bottle or two, some local free-range eggs, or the big prize of the night, a meat tray. The charity of choice benefits each week until $2000 has been raised, then another charity gets a turn.

If you needed any other excuse to visit Daylesford, one of Victoria's prettiest towns, there are plenty. Part of 'spa country', it is full of small galleries, homeware shops and foodie outlets, and there are about a dozen day spas to choose from in the region if you fancy a bit of pampering.

GRAND PACIFIC HOTEL

LORNE

THE GRAND PACIFIC Hotel was the first hotel on the Great Ocean Road. By the time the road was built – between 1919 and 1932 – the hotel was already more than half a century old and was well loved by visitors to the beautiful seaside town of Lorne, a reputation that holds fast today.

Memories of earlier visits to the Grand Pacific are still uppermost in many guests' minds, whether they are just stopping off for a drink or spending the weekend or longer. This is a pub that holds a nostalgic place in the hearts of many Australians, particularly Melburnians.

'Most of the locals have grown up here,' says general manager Bryce Newcombe. 'It's their pub and they love nothing more than sitting in the bar talking about the old days.' The locals' bar is the old 'fishos bar', now called F2, which has a pool table with the best pier view, tiled floors for sandy feet straight from the beach across the road and live music on Sunday afternoons. The wrap-around glass doors open up in summer and the atmosphere is laid back.

Grand Pacific Hotel, Lorne

Stroll on the pier when you're here; at the right time of year (June–September) you might see the migrating humpback whales pass by.

When the pub was first built, in 1875, guests would arrive from Melbourne or Geelong by boat. The Lorne Pier, in front of the hotel, was built for their convenience and it became a focal point for the town. When Henry Gwynne opened the existing impressive three-storey hotel in January 1880, he delivered one of the best views in town. Later, the pier was used to bring in supplies for the road building and as a base for workers toiling on it. By 1922 the Great Ocean Road – built after World War I by returned servicemen in honour of their fallen comrades – had reached Lorne, making the town much more accessible. The world's biggest war memorial, the road took 16 years to build by hand, using picks, shovels and dynamite. Victoria's Lieutenant-Governor declared it officially open at a ceremony near the Grand Pacific Hotel, the site where the project's first survey peg had also been hammered into the ground.

For today's visitors, many memories are linked to the 1970s when the Grand Pacific was renowned for its live entertainment and as a rock hotel – until its refurbishment in the mid 1990s, the ballroom had a false ceiling installed for better acoustics. Acts which performed there included AC/DC, the Screaming Jets, Australian Crawl, Skyhooks and Kylie Minogue.

GRAND PACIFIC HOTEL

ADDRESS
268 Mountjoy Pde, Lorne

TELEPHONE
(03) 5289 1609

WEBSITE
www.grandpacific.com.au

RATES
$65 double room; $75 queen room; $99–$120 king room; $95 Pacific Pier queen room; $125 Grand Pacific spa king room; $160 1-bedroom apartment or 2-bedroom town house; $175 2-bedroom apartment; $210 3-bedroom apartment.

HOURS
Open from 8am (if you want a coffee); bar open 11am–late.

GRUB
Open for breakfast weekends 9am–12pm; daily for lunch from 12pm, and dinner from 6pm. From Boxing Day to Australia Day, cafe open daily from 5pm.

TOP DROP
Try local beer from the Otway Brewery, the most popular being the pilsner-style Prickly Moses Summer Ale and the darker Red Ale over winter. Others on tap include James Squire Golden, Boag's Draught, Heineken and Kirin.

NEARBY ATTRACTIONS
Continue along the Great Ocean Rd to the great sandstone pillars in the sea called the Twelve Apostles (although now there are only 8 left). The drive meanders for 106 km from Torquay through Lorne and on to Warrnambool.

MORE INFO
www.gor.org.au
www.lovelorne.com.au

Today the ornate plaster ceiling has been revealed again and the room – with beautiful stained-glass windows and a view of the pier – is once again a ballroom, but one that converts into a family-friendly cafe for casual dining and entertainment in summer evenings (from Boxing Day to Australia Day).

The facade, the ornate balconies, the sandstone interior walls and the ocean views may have changed little from the building's earliest days, but the 19 hotel rooms, from the doubles to the spa suites, have had stylish makeovers. All rooms have queen- or king-sized beds, televisions and video. Guests have exclusive access to the verandah; the ten front rooms that face the sea have floor-length sash windows that you can step through. Some rooms have spas and the two queen rooms have a view of the pier. There is also a modern extension at the back of the pub with 15 one- to three-bedroom apartments.

On the last Sunday morning of each month the ballroom is the venue for a local craft and produce market, just one of many events that make the pub an integral part of Lorne life. There's also the annual Harvest Dinner, featuring only local produce, and New Year's Eve is huge, with live entertainment in the ballroom and fireworks off the pier.

But the biggest event of all is the Lorne Pier to Pub, which has been held for more than 30 years and is officially the largest open-water swim in the world (it made the *Guinness Book of Records* in 1998). Organised and run by volunteers from the Lorne Surf Life Saving Club, the course is 1.2 kilometres from the Lorne Pier to the foreshore in front of the LSLS clubhouse (and the Lorne Hotel, the other pub). Each year 4000 people swim across Louttit Bay and the event has now grown to a three-day sporting festival that also includes the Mountain to Surf Fun Run and the Surf Boat Race Classic.

The Grand Pacific's bars and restaurant areas all have large floor-to-ceiling windows to take in the stunning views. The menu changes often, but includes everything you would expect, including a curry of the day, beef and Guinness pie, steak sandwiches, steaks, seafood and pizza. Monday night is lamb shank night, Tuesday is gourmet pie night, on Wednesday the special is a curry, and on Thursday indulge in a chicken parma. Nightly specials are $25 including a glass of house wine or a pot of beer.

Outside, you'll find another piece of nostalgia is parked at the front of the pub, a Kombi courtesy van (named Joy, after a former barmaid) that will run patrons the short distance into town. Take a stroll on the pier when you're here; at the right time of year (June–September) you might see the migrating humpback whales pass by.

The Grand Pacific bar; the pub's courtesy Kombi van, Joy

HEALESVILLE HOTEL

HEALESVILLE

WHEN MICHAEL KENNEDY and Kylie Balharrie decided on a day out at Healesville Sanctuary in April 2000 and stopped at the Healesville Hotel for lunch, little did they expect that the historic pub would soon be their own.

'We knew the hotel was for sale and over a bottle of rosé and some lunch in the hotel garden with friends on a lovely sunny day, we thought that we could run a place like this. By that July we had moved to Healesville with our two-year-old daughter!' says Kylie.

The couple put their hearts and souls into their new business, and the Healesville Hotel has constantly evolved since then. Within a couple of months, they had reopened the hotel restaurant, with new timber floors, lots of fresh flowers, wine displays, and furniture and paintings that embraced the character of the building.

'We are both passionate about good food and wine, and we appreciate this area and the bounty of what it produces, the beauty of the hills and the fantastic local community,' says Kylie.

The century-old hotel looks out on the main street of Healesville. The front bar is made up of a series of rooms with high pressed-metal ceilings, polished floors and Persian rugs. In winter the bar is warmed by open fires while in warmer months the garden bar with its shady umbrellas is a popular spot to while away a sunny afternoon.

The bar and bistro menus offer seasonal and regional cooking including pub classics – with a twist. The fish'n'chips are made with beer batter, the steaks are dry-aged, the shepherd's pie – a regular weeknight special, teamed with a glass of wine for $25 – uses local slow-cooked lamb. On

Healesville Hotel

The dining room has old-world ambience, with a pressed-metal ceiling, and wicker chairs plus an old industrial milliner's table that seats 14 as the centrepiece.

HEALESVILLE HOTEL

ADDRESS
256 Maroondah Hwy, Healesville

TELEPHONE
(03) 5962 4002

WEBSITE
www.yarravalleyharvest.com.au

RATES
Mon–Thurs $100 per room, Fri and Sun $130 per room; Sat room and 3-course à la carte dinner for 2 $315; Sat room, dinner and breakfast for 2 $365.

HOURS
Daily 12–11pm.

GRUB
Cafe daily 8am–4pm; bar and bistro daily 12–11pm; à la carte dining room Wed–Sun lunch 12–4pm and dinner 6–11pm.

TOP DROP
There is a large selection of cold beers and local cider on tap including Coopers, the local brew Hargreaves Hill, James Squire, Guinness and Napoleon & Co. cider.

NEARBY ATTRACTIONS
Healesville Sanctuary, Badger Creek Rd, is a great place to see native animals including kangaroos, dingos, koalas, wombats, wedge-tailed eagles, lyrebirds, reptiles and more. The sanctuary opened in 1921 to preserve endangered species and educate the public. Visit its Wildlife Health Centre hospital to see veterinarians caring for injured or orphaned wildlife. The cafe here is operated by the Healesville Hotel. www.zoo.org.au

MORE INFO
www.visitvictoria.com

Old-world ambience in the dining room

Thursday night, have a curry (perhaps coconut pork and snake bean) and a beer, and on Fridays a roast for two is only $20 each. Even the bangers and mash stands out from more ordinary fare – these are pork and fennel sausages from the hotel's own butcher shop, served with roasted pumpkin and sage, baby spinach and jus. Order at the bar; bookings are not usually taken, but there are plenty of tables and the wait is usually not longer than the time it will take you to have a relaxed drink.

The dining room has old-world ambience, again with a pressed-metal ceiling, and wicker chairs plus an old industrial milliner's table that seats 14 as the centrepiece. The menu is more formal than the bar's. At night, the room is candlelit, in winter there is an open fire, and in summer the tables spill out into the courtyard when things get busy.

'Our approach to food has been to embrace the region and the season and this is reflected in the dining-room menu and the classic dishes in the bar,' says Kylie.

Produce is sourced locally, either from the couple's own nearby farm or from the kitchen garden, which between them provide salad greens, herbs, lemons, artichokes, garlic and asparagus. The weekly menu also features produce grown by Yarra Valley farmers, including eggs, figs, berries and citrus.

The huge wine list – more than 300 labels – also has a great selection by the glass. Whether you fancy French bubbles, a pinot gris or one of the local wines from Yeringberg or Mount Mary, the list includes delicious offerings from the Yarra Valley and beyond.

If you feel inclined to stay and explore the Yarra Valley a little longer, the Healesville Hotel has seven spacious, stylish and brightly painted and restored guest rooms (again, with those wonderful pressed-metal ceilings). Each room is different but all have queen-sized beds, television and tea- and coffee-making facilities. There are three bathrooms at the end of the hallway (take the handmade local soap you'll find in your room).

Across the side lane leading to the beer garden, the old bottleshop has been converted into the bustling Healesville Harvest cafe, where breakfast is served. The cafe is also a popular option for lunch, with a selection of appealing seasonal salads, soups, pies, frittatas and the like. You can also stock up on local produce – jams, sauces, nuts, fudge and more – to take home with you.

MILDURA GRAND HOTEL

MILDURA

THE ART DECO edifice of the Mildura Grand Hotel has always been a traffic-stopper, but its growth in recent years has added to its stature. No longer just a hotel – if it ever was 'just' – the Mildura Grand is now a complex that encompasses three acclaimed restaurants, a modern brewery pub and a pizza cafe.

The main hotel building on Seventh St, overlooking the Murray River, is flanked by two drinking holes. On the Deakin Avenue side is the Grand Sports Bar, occupying the space that for many years was home to the original Spanish Grill restaurant. This was a prominent part of the hotel and did a roaring trade with the locals, but closed in 1989. A new Spanish Grill has been created inside the hotel; there is nothing Spanish about it but the name has been kept for old times' sake.

On the other side of the hotel, on Langtree Avenue, is the Mildura Brewery Pub, which opened in the former Astor Theatre in 2004. The magnificent Art Deco cinema building has been restored to its former glory with a modern twist that enables patrons to watch the operation of the new state-of-the-art brewery inside it.

The magnificent Art Deco cinema building has been restored to its former glory with a modern twist that enables patrons to watch the operation of the new state-of-the-art brewery inside it.

Entrance to the Mildura Grand Hotel

The disused theatre, which dates back to 1924 (and was remodelled in 1937), came with the Mildura Grand Hotel when the hotel was bought by Don Carrazza and his family in 1989. The brewery development has retained many of its design features – even the cinema's screen is situated among the brewing vats and remains in occasional use.

Courtyard gardens at the hotel

The brewery produces six beers: Desert Premium Lager, Honey Wheat Pale Ale, Stefano's Pilsner, Mallee Bull Heavy Ale, Storm Cloudy Ale and Sun Light, the latter named for the region's warm and sunny climate, which boasts 77 days on average each year when the temperature exceeds 30 degrees Celsius. The brewery also makes seasonal beers from time to time. Brewery tours are available (bookings essential), and you can also sample the beers with a tasting tray.

A traditional Sunday roast is on the menu every week for lunch and dinner, and for those with a hearty appetite – and who like a challenge – the pub runs a 'Pub Parmi Army Challenge'. Tell the staff you'd like to try it, and you'll be served a parmigiana that's four times the size of a normal one, with wedges and salad. Patrons who can eat the whole meal within 20 minutes receive a Parmi Army certificate and are inducted into the Parmi Army Hall of Fame. This culinary challenge is open to all any day at lunch and dinner times.

The hotel complex extends down Langtree Avenue

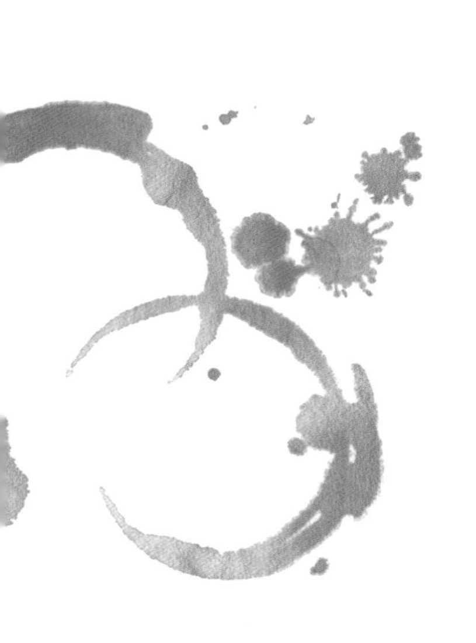

The Art Deco facade of the Mildura Grand

The Mildura Grand began life in 1891 as the Mildura Coffee Palace. After the Carrazza family's association with the hotel began, it gradually developed a national reputation for great food and hospitality. In 2006 it was sold to the hotel company Day Group.

With five restaurants and four bars, the Grand has became famous in more recent years largely for its association with celebrity chef Stefano de Pieri (Don Carrazza's son-in-law), whose multi-award-winning Stefano's is among the restaurants at the hotel.

There are 102 guest rooms, ranging from comfortable standard doubles to larger suites, some with balconies and garden views, and plush State suites with king-sized beds. The Presidential Suite (the most expensive) is Art Deco–inspired, with a large marble bathroom and a spa bath. The hotel also has a heated outdoor swimming pool, sauna, gymnasium and free wi-fi for guests.

In a central position between Sydney, Melbourne and Adelaide, Mildura sits on the banks of the Murray River in north-western Victoria. Mildura was established in 1887 by the Chaffey brothers as an irrigation colony and is now the centre of a major agricultural region. The main road into the town, Deakin Avenue, was named after Alfred Deakin, the Victorian Minister for Water Supply who later became Prime Minister.

The brewery produces six beers

MILDURA GRAND HOTEL

ADDRESS
Seventh St, Mildura

TELEPHONE
(03) 5023 0511 or 1800 034 228

WEBSITE
www.qualityhotelmilduragrand.com.au
www.mildurabrewery.com.au
www.stefano.com.au

RATES
$115–$210 double; $240–$420 suite. Rates include breakfast. Extra person $30. Children 11 and under stay free in parents' room.

HOURS
Mon–Thurs 12pm–late;
Fri–Sun 11am–late.

GRUB
Mildura Brewery: weekdays for lunch 12–3pm and dinner 6–9pm, weekends an all-day menu; Stefano's restaurant: Tues–Sun from 7pm (bookings essential); Stefano's Cafe Bakery: Mon–Sat 7.30am–3pm, Sun 8.30am–3pm; New Spanish Bar & Grill: Tues–Sun 6pm–late (wine bar from 5pm); Seasons: Mon–Sat 6pm–late.

TOP DROP
Mildura Brewery produces a range of 6 beers along with seasonal beers.

NEARBY ATTRACTIONS
W. B. Chaffey's home, Rio Vista House, can be visited at 199 Cureton Ave. It is now the home of the Mildura Arts Centre and includes the regional Art Gallery and Sculpture Park as well as the performing Arts Theatre.

MORE INFO
www.visitmildura.com.au

ROYAL HOTEL

QUEENSCLIFF

Royal Hotel, Queenscliff

The Royal Hotel is a rabbit warren of cosy bars and dining areas furnished with an eclectic mixture of furniture, artwork and collectibles against rich colours and the patina of the past.

THE GRAND ITALIANATE edifice of the Royal Hotel greets visitors to the seaside town of Queenscliff even before the main street is reached. It would be easy to drive past and then get caught up in admiring the many heritage buildings in the town – including several other impressive-looking pubs – so that you don't go back. And that would be a shame, for the Royal is not only Queenscliff's oldest hotel, it is also the most charming.

Built in about 1854, the Royal Hotel is a rabbit warren of cosy bars and dining areas furnished with an eclectic mixture of furniture, artwork and collectibles against rich colours and the patina of the past. A central staircase inside the main entrance hall leads to the guest rooms, while corridors off it in several directions lead to bars and eating areas. A tiled verandah under the front archways is a great place for a coffee.

The front lounge bar has a two-way fireplace, small mosaic-topped coffee tables, a banquette topped with leopard-print cushions and a view of the street. You can eat here or in the more formal dining room on the other side of the main entrance, or take the corridor to the back, where a larger and less formal restaurant – with an area of big squashy leather couches – leads out to the bluestone courtyard. There's a barbecue out there, as well as a kids' play area with a sandpit and trampoline. The tiny public bar has a television – as does the lounge – and yet another room off the bar has a pool table in it (free to play). On Friday nights there's live music in the front bar from 8pm.

The menu has the usual range of pub grub, from parmas and steaks to salt-and-pepper calamari and curries, and there's also a blackboard menu of specials daily, with lunch from as little as $10 and dinner from $12.

Stephen Wilson, who has had the pub for 20 years, is the latest in a line of owners that includes Cliffy Splatt, who ran it for a decade from 1883 and put his name in leadlight above the front door.

The paint may be peeling in a few places, and a little TLC may be needed here and there, but the ten period-style guest rooms have charm too. Five of them have access to the verandah, with views of the sea, and four of these have romantic queen-sized four-poster beds. Only one room has an ensuite; the others share bathrooms but all rooms have a wash basin in them.

The hotel is within easy walking distance of Queenscliff's main thoroughfare, Hesse Street, and all major attractions. With its elegant Victorian-era streetscapes, churches and fishermen's cottages, Queenscliff is a popular tourist haunt 106 kilometres from Melbourne, just inside the entrance to Port Phillip on the Bellarine Peninsula.

Originally a fishing village, Queenscliff was settled in the 1850s and soon became a strategic defence post and an important cargo port, servicing steamships trading in Port Phillip. Its two lighthouses were built in 1862–63. Fort Queenscliff was built between 1879 and 1889, and was the most heavily armed defence post in the Southern Hemisphere, operating as the command centre for all the forts around the port.

Rich interior colours

By the 1880s, Queenscliff was a popular seaside destination for Melburnians, who arrived by paddlesteamer. The opening of a railway line to Geelong in 1879 brought increasing numbers of visitors and the Royal Hotel soon had competition. Numerous hotels – then called coffee palaces – were built, including the Palace Hotel (now the Esplanade Hotel), the Vue Grande Hotel and the Queenscliff Hotel.

Dining areas

Today's visitors explore the town's art and antique galleries, soak up the history, or picnic under the towering pine trees along the foreshore. Some arrive by ferry from Sorrento on the Mornington Peninsula. Charter boats depart from Queenscliff with divers and fishermen, and you can also swim with seals and dolphins. Others prefer to just cast a line off the Queenscliff pier.

One of the most popular times to visit is for the annual Queenscliff Music Festival, held on the last weekend of November, which attracts both local and international acts. The Queenscliff Seafood Feast, focusing on the bounty brought in by local fishermen, is held annually on Good Friday to raise funds for the Royal Children's Hospital.

THE FACTS

ROYAL HOTEL

ADDRESS
34 King St, Queenscliff

TELEPHONE
(03) 5258 1669

WEBSITE
www.queenscliff.com.au

RATES
$90–$130 double; extra person rate $30.

HOURS
Daily 11.30am–late.

GRUB
Daily for lunch 12–2.30pm and dinner 5.30–9pm.

TOP DROP
Carlton Draught and Heineken are on tap.

NEARBY ATTRACTIONS
Queenscliff has 3 museums: the Queenscliffe Historical Museum, the Fort Queenscliff Museum and the Queenscliffe Maritime Museum, which has displays depicting the maritime history of Queenscliff and southern Port Phillip, wrecks, lifeboats, rescues, early diving equipment, artefacts from shipwrecks, a lighthouse display, and historic charts and maps of Port Phillip and the coastline of Victoria. Sat nights in Aug–May the Bellarine Railway runs the Blues Train, a progressive party featuring Australia's best blues musicians rocking to the sway of a vintage steam train. www.bluestrain.com.au

MORE INFO
www.queenscliff.org
www.visitvictoria.com

ROYAL MAIL HOTEL

DUNKELD

The Royal Mail Hotel, Dunkeld, with Mt Sturgeon behind it

WITH A MULTI-AWARD-WINNING fine-dining restaurant, a host of up-market accommodation options and a backdrop of stunning mountains, the Royal Mail at Dunkeld is no ordinary pub.

Most people make the 260-kilometre drive from Melbourne on the strength of the Royal Mail's reputation for sensational food and wine. But this lovely hotel, built in 1855 and more recently updated, still retains its public bar where you can play a game of pool, meet the locals and get a simple but delicious bar meal for as little as $18.

> Most people make the drive west from Melbourne to the hotel on the strength of the Royal Mail's reputation for sensational food and wine.

Dunkeld – and the Royal Mail – is set against the most southerly mountains of the Grampians' Serra Range, Mt Sturgeon (or Wuragarri, in the language of the local Chap Wurrung people), followed by the Piccaninny (Bainggug) and Mt Abrupt (Murdadjoog).

Historically, Dunkeld was a vital link to the Western District for the Cobb & Co Royal Mail Service, which gave the hotel its name. The township was originally called Mount Sturgeon but in 1854 was renamed Dunkeld by settlers who were reminded of their Scottish home by the local scenery.

The Royal Mail was established in 1855 and is the only one of five hotels built in the town to have survived. In 1997 the owners, Dunkeld Pastoral Company Pty Ltd, embarked on a project to modernise the building while retaining its historical significance. Using local sandstone and retaining part of the original structure in the front wall of the building and the bar–dining room, the hotel took on the shape that it has today.

Under executive chef Dan Hunter the Royal Mail has developed a reputation for excellent food and wine, in a unique style that uses the bounty of the hotel's kitchen gardens, fruit orchards, egg-laying hens and a greenhouse for growing herbs.

The restaurant, which seats 40, offers seasonally changing tasting menus for omnivores and vegetarians for $160 and $130 respectively, with accompanying wines for $115. This is an experience in which to indulge, and needs at least three or four hours of your time. The 60-seat bistro has an à la carte menu with main courses priced at $25–$40. In the bar, where you don't need to book, there is a traditional bar menu with an emphasis on quality. Dishes may include rainbow trout with potato, broccoli and almonds, steaks – Sher wagyu rump or Hopkins River sirloin with potato fondant, carrot, and a shallot and white wine sauce – or a Glenloth free-range chicken parma with chips.

The Royal Mail houses one of the most comprehensive and varied wine cellars in Australia, including one of the country's leading collections of Bordeaux and Burgundy. A selection of 2300 local and imported wines is offered from an inventory of 26 000 bottles. Cellar tours and wine tastings are held every Saturday at 4pm at a cost of $15.

As a popular weekend destination, the Royal Mail has a wide range of accommodation options, all of which give guests access to the hotel facilities including the heated outdoor swimming pool. The accommodation is divided between the hotel itself and the nearby Mount Sturgeon property.

In Dunkeld, the rooms are in and around the landscaped gardens of the hotel. There are double or twin garden-view rooms, double or twin mountain-view rooms and deluxe mountain-view rooms, which have king-sized beds and luxury bathrooms (with heated floors). All have a bar fridge, tea- and coffee-making facilities and a flat-screen television; the mountain-view rooms have a phone.

Guest room

There is also a one-bedroom luxury king apartment and two two-bedroom apartments, which have a queen-sized bed in one room and twin beds in the other. These have kitchenettes and entertainment units, and the two-bedroom apartments have balconies with views of Mt Sturgeon. An option for larger groups is the four-bedroom Mulberry House, directly across from the Royal Mail Hotel on Parker Street, which sleeps 11.

The original Mount Sturgeon Homestead is also open to guests, along with eight one- and two-bedroom bluestone cottages on the property, about 5 kilometres from the hotel. Built by Chinese workers in the 1870s as shearers' quarters, these are a peaceful retreat, with huge, comfortably worn brown leather armchairs, an open fireplace, a CD player and patchwork quilts on the beds. The water tank against the back wall cunningly conceals your bathroom. There's a kitchen with a microwave and a barbecue outside, but there's no television, no phone and no mobile phone reception.

ROYAL MAIL HOTEL

ADDRESS
98 Parker St, Dunkeld

TELEPHONE
(03) 5577 2241

WEBSITE
www.royalmail.com.au

RATES
$165–$380 double room with breakfast; $325–$365 double 1-bedroom apartment with breakfast; $305–$335 2-bedroom apartment (sleeps 4) with breakfast; $210–$295 for 1-bedroom or $305–$335 for 2-bedroom cottages. Extra person $45.

HOURS
The public bar open 12pm daily.

GRUB
Restaurant open for dinner Wed–Sun from 6.30pm. Bistro open daily for lunch 12–2.30pm and dinner 6–9pm. Bar meals served 12–2.30pm Tues–Sat and 12–3pm Sun, and 6–9pm Tues–Sat.

TOP DROP
There are more than 60 local and imported beers. The Royal Mail's cellar houses one of the largest wine collections in Australia.

NEARBY ATTRACTIONS
Dunkeld has 3 art galleries, a second-hand bookshop, museum, golf course and arboretum. There are 8 walking trails within a 5 min drive of the hotel. Dunkeld Open Gardens and Galleries, 1st weekend of each month, has tours, demonstrations and Q and A sessions with local horticulturalists, botanists and artists.

MORE INFO
www.discoverdunkeld.com.au
www.visitvictoria.com

TANSWELL'S COMMERCIAL *Hotel*

BEECHWORTH

Tanswell's Commercial Hotel, Beechworth

WITH A NEW chef, newly renovated rooms and a brewery out the back, Beechworth's oldest surviving hotel, dating from 1853, is looking to a bright future. Tanswell's Commercial Hotel has seen a lot during its time – including, it's said, the sight of the infamous bushranger Ned Kelly drinking in the bar.

The original pub, a single-storey shingle-roofed building known simply as the Commercial Hotel, was built in Beechworth's main street in 1853 but later burnt down and was replaced by the town's first two-storey structure. In 1871 it was sold to Thomas Tanswell, who added his name to it and had greater plans for the business. In 1873 he opened the brick Tanswell's Commercial Hotel, with leadlighting around the bar bearing his name and a grand cast-iron lace and timber verandah.

Beechworth is a gold-rush town that later became the administrative and legal centre for north-east Victoria and an important coaching and trade stop on the route connecting Melbourne and Sydney. Liquor licences were first granted in Beechworth in 1853 and by the end of that year the town already had five pubs, including the Commercial. By 1874, there were more than 60 licensed premises but the new Tanswell's was the grandest of them all. Local legend even has it that Ned Kelly was a patron. True or not, the hotel certainly hosted some important guests, including the Governor of Victoria, who stayed here during a visit to the region in 1906.

Crawford and Co, a large local coaching firm, occupied premises behind the hotel.

Tanswell's Commercial Hotel has seen a lot during its time – including, it's said, the sight of the infamous bushranger Ned Kelly drinking in the bar.

They specialised in coach building and stabling, and delivered mail and passengers around Victoria's north-east. The current stables date from 1892, and since 2004 have been home to the Bridge Road Brewery, which is accessed through a laneway entrance which leads to its beer garden and children's play area.

Thomas Tanswell left his name

The Tanswell family sold the hotel in 1967 after almost a century in their ownership, but the name remained. In 2011 chef James Cleeve, who ran Beechworth's Green Shed Bistro for nearly ten years, became the licensee and set about establishing a reputation for good-quality traditional pub grub alongside some more sophisticated fare. You'll still find bangers (Irish pork sausages) and mash, and fish and chips on the menu, but there's also a confit of duck leg with apple, pear and walnut salad, or cuttlefish and chilli risotto, onion and goat's cheese tart, steamed mussels and freshly shucked oysters. And, of course, there's also a kids' menu.

Upstairs there are 12 guest rooms and a self-contained one-bedroom apartment. The rooms, refurbished in 2011, offer queen, double, twin and single beds and share four bathrooms. The spa apartment has a separate bedroom and a living area with spa, bathroom and kitchen, and access to the verandah overlooking the main street. It has period features including pressed tin and ceiling roses. All rooms have wi-fi connections.

Beechworth is a popular destination for road cyclists and mountain bikers, and the hotel is bike friendly, with a lockable bicycle shed for guests. One of Australia's best rail trails – old railway lines converted to bicycle tracks – the 98-kilometre Murray to Mountains Rail Trail, goes right through the middle of Beechworth.

The hotel is part of Beechworth's interesting streetscape

TANSWELL'S COMMERCIAL HOTEL

ADDRESS
40–44 Ford St, Beechworth

TELEPHONE
(03) 5728 1480

EMAIL
tanscom@bigpond.net.au

RATES
Single $55, queen $75, spa apartment $150. Rates include continental breakfast.

HOURS
Daily 11am–late.

GRUB
Daily for lunch 12–3pm and dinner 6–9pm.

TOP DROP
There are 12 beers on tap, including Carlton Draught, Cascade Light, Coopers Sparkling Ale, Leffe and 4 from Bridge Road Brewers (Robust Porter, Beechworth Pale Ale, Australian Ale and a German-style wheat beer Hans Klopek's Hefe Weizen).

NEARBY ATTRACTIONS
Beechworth has 30 National Trust–listed buildings; the most interesting is the courthouse where bushranger Ned Kelly was committed for trial in 1880. In Aug Beechworth stages a weekend re-enactment of the hearing and trial. Take a guided tour of the courthouse, including the dock in which Ned sat, the judge's chambers, clerk's room, sheriff's office, jury room and remand cells. Kelly also spent time in Beechworth Gaol, which is open for tours, and the Burke Museum also has much Kelly memorabilia.

MORE INFO
www.beechworthonline.com.au

WALHALLA'S STAR HOTEL

WALHALLA

Walhalla's Star Hotel

TUCKED IN A lush valley in the Victorian Alps, the village of Walhalla was once one of the world's richest goldmining towns and home to 2500 people. The gold ran out in 1914 and Walhalla was quite simply abandoned. Today it is home to only 11 people (when everyone's at home).

In the late 1800s, Walhalla had ten hotels, three breweries and seven churches; the Star Hotel was Walhalla's most famous gold-rush hotel. It was the terminus for the Cobb & Co coach that serviced Walhalla until 1910, when the railway finally came to town. However, the advent of the railway arrived too late for Walhalla because by 1915 all the mines had closed and the trains provided an easy way to carry away nearly all of the town's buildings and machinery. It was soon a ghost town.

The original Star Hotel was destroyed by fire in December 1951. But over the past two decades the hotel – and the village – has risen from the ashes and abandonment. Buildings are being restored and new ones – such as Walhalla's Star Hotel – are being erected to replace those lost. Walhalla's Star Hotel was rebuilt on the same site as the original, opposite the historic band rotunda, and opened in early 1999. The facade is a replica of the original but the interior is designed for modern needs.

The advent of the railway arrived too late for Walhalla because by 1915 all the mines had closed and the trains provided an easy way to carry away nearly all of the town's buildings.

When Walhalla's Star Hotel owner Michael Leaney began his ambitious project to breathe new life into the town, the first stage was finally getting electricity connected to Walhalla. And the town hasn't looked back, attracting more than 100 000 visitors a year keen to spend time wandering the picturesque leafy street lined with cute timber cottages. Most are daytrippers and weekenders from Melbourne – it is only 180 kilometres or two-and-a-half hours' drive from the city – or travellers looking for a good stopover point on the Sydney–Melbourne coastal drive.

For somewhere so small, there are a surprising number of things to do in Walhalla, and Leaney is happy to point you in the right direction, whether it be to tour a goldmine or

The unusual bar

explore the cemetery. His hotel is truly once again the heart of the village.

Walhalla's Star Hotel is small, comfortable and stylish. It has 12 air-conditioned guest rooms, all of a good size, some with verandahs overlooking the street. A cosy guest lounge has a small library of books and CDs, a guest computer and tea- and coffee-making facilities. There's a guest bar, with an old-fashioned honesty system, but no television, either in the rooms or the public areas of the hotel. 'It's all about leaving your day-to-day life behind and relaxing,' says Leaney.

The guest rooms are all doubles; children under 12 are not catered for. All have king-sized or twin beds, and three rooms are triples. All rooms are of the same standard – but may be a different colour! They all open either onto the first-floor verandah or to the cottage garden. Each room has a CD player and radio, writing desk, wi-fi (with a $5 connection fee), armchair and sofa. There are ceiling fans, heating and electric blankets. All rooms also have ensuites with showers, but no baths as all the water is tank water. One of the four ground-floor guest rooms is designed for people with limited mobility and access to the hotel is via a ramp with increased door widths for easy use by wheelchairs.

Guest room

Dinner is served in Parker's Restaurant, which has an à la carte menu. The curved bar is made of corrugated-iron sheets with a timber top and manages to be modern rather than rustic looking, and there's a wood fire for chilly mountain nights. The GreyHorse Cafe next door is open daily for lunch and snacks.

Getting out and exploring is part of Walhalla's attraction. One of the best places to start in understanding the Walhalla story is at the Long Tunnel Extended Gold Mine where you can take a tour to see what it was all about. Gold was discovered in the area in 1863 and one of the first mines to be successful was the Walhalla, named by its Scandinavian manager after the home of the god Odin in Norse mythology. The success of the Walhalla Mine attracted even more people to the area to search for gold and before long the town's name had been changed from Stringers Creek (after the first man to find gold here) to Walhalla. But the richest mine turned out to be the Long Tunnel in the centre of town; it yielded more than 50 tonnes of gold.

WALHALLA'S STAR HOTEL

ADDRESS
Main Rd, Walhalla

TELEPHONE
(03) 5165 6262

WEBSITE
www.starhotel.com.au

RATES
$219 double or twin room, $249 triple (either 1 king bed and 1 single, or 3 single beds). Rates include continental buffet breakfast.

HOURS
The hotel does not have a public bar but hotel guests have 24-hour bar access.

GRUB
Parker's Restaurant is available to guests for dinner most nights mid-week and Sat; bookings essential.

TOP DROP
A wide selection of local Gippsland wines is available.

NEARBY ATTRACTIONS
Take a guided tour of the Long Tunnel Extended Gold Mine, ride a narrow-gauge train through lovely bushland with the Walhalla Goldfields Railway, explore the historic cemetery, take a ghost tour and potter in the small shops and museums. Walhalla is at the end of the Australian Alps Walking Track (which runs 650 km from Canberra), but the best option for visitors is the 2-day guided 40 km walk developed by the Star Hotel and nearby Mt Baw Baw Alpine Resort (www.greatwalhallaalpinetrail.com).

MORE INFO
www.visitwalhalla.com
www.visitvictoria.com

South Australia

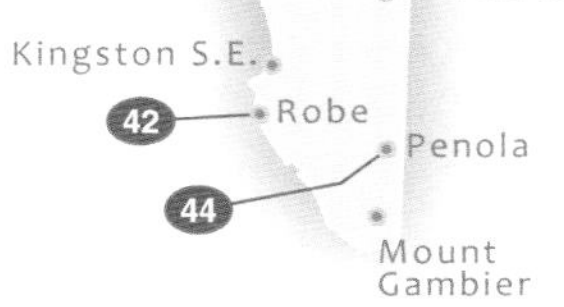

Opposite (clockwise from top): Prairie Hotel, Parachilna; Largs Pier Hotel, Largs Bay; The Edinburgh Hotel, Mitcham; Kimba Community Hotel Motel.

METROPOLITAN

REGIONAL

PRAIRIE HOTEL
LICENSED SINCE 1876

The
SHED &
FRONT BAR

The EDINBURGH *Hotel*

MITCHAM

The Edinburgh Hotel, Mitcham

'DULL MOMENTS ARE craved at times, but it doesn't happen much – thank heavens!' says Alison James, the licensee at the Edinburgh Hotel in the Adelaide suburb of Mitcham. After spending 16 years of her hotel career at this popular pub, Alison says there's never a dull day.

Patrons at the Ed are a mixed bunch, from local 'tradies' and social club members in the Front Bar, where there are still meat raffles on Friday nights and Saturday mornings – something that Alison says is quite rare in a pub these days. The raffles 'bring a lot of local colour, and they are a great bunch of people,' enthuses Alison, who sees everything from weddings to hundredth birthdays, twenty-firsts, school dinners and wakes in the course of a typical week.

'Tuesday night is our "uni" night and has been for 20 years or so. We have live music on Friday and Sunday nights and a DJ on Tuesday nights. Businessmen and -women come mainly for lunches, particularly on Fridays, and we also look after a lot of group meetings through the week. We are reasonably close to Centennial Park' – the cemetery and crematorium – 'and so we average three or four wakes a week because we have the outside garden and a selection of function rooms.'

The pub is as popular with twenty-somethings as it is with senior citizens or Rotarians, although they might choose different bars to drink in. 'We are really a beer, wine, scotch and vodka pub but our Sunday $5 bloody marys, which are amazing, are also very much appreciated this side of town,' says Alison. 'We are known for being the only hotel in South Australia to house-pour Johnnie Walker Black, Tanqueray gin and other top lines in spirits. People love it!'

In the Front Bar there are still meat raffles on Friday nights and Saturday mornings – something quite rare in a pub these days.

The Edinburgh Hotel is in the heart of Mitcham Village, one of South Australia's original outlying settlements, now only ten minutes from Adelaide's CBD. Built in 1869, it was at that time one of six licensed premises in the area. The original stone building looked a bit like a cottage and is now the central part of the hotel; the impressive parapet and pediment above it, along with the southern wing, were added some time in the 1870s, while the northern wing was added in 1914.

Saved from the threat of demolition in 1974, the hotel has since been extensively renovated and enlarged and is now classified by the National Trust of South Australia. It is within the Historic (Conservation) Zone – Mitcham Village and is also on the State Heritage Register.

Dining in the cafe atrium

Robert Nesbit held the licence until 1874 when the hotel became the first of a chain of hotels owned by Charles Edward Mallen, a brewer. The hotel stayed in the Mallen family until 1978 when it was bought by current owners, Chris Codling and Danny Djurasevich. At that time, Alison James became the licensee.

'I started working here in 1989, but I left after about eight years and had done other things for about four years when the owners asked me to come back to the Ed to help build the business,' she says. 'I've been here again for more than eight years and love it because it is such a varied hotel that offers so much choice to people. The owners meet me every week for a catch up; we work well as a team and they are very mindful of the historic surroundings and the importance of spending money on the hotel to keep it looking great.'

Whether it's the Front Bar, the Village Bar or live music in the beer garden on Sunday afternoons, there's always something happening at the Edinburgh. Wine tastings are frequent, with the biggest the annual Shiraz Day on the last Sunday in June, when more than 250 shiraz labels are available to taste. The event has been running for around 20 years, and it attracts about 700 people – many of whom come from interstate especially for it. In recent years, cider tastings have also proved popular.

The Front Bar does a $12 'pint and parma' deal, and there's family dining in the cafe atrium at the back of the hotel. The cafe menu is extensive, while a more limited version is available in the bar including oysters (natural or beer-battered), dips, crumbed prawns and platters.

Many come to the Ed for the award-winning bottleshop, which has a huge and diverse wine selection including a whole cellar of burgundies. Alison says there has recently been a surge of interest in unusual beers, with buyers keen to take home mixed six-packs of interesting brews from smaller producers.

THE EDINBURGH HOTEL

ADDRESS
1–7 High St, Mitcham

TELEPHONE
(08) 8373 2700

WEBSITE
www.edinburgh.com.au

HOURS
The Front Bar is open Mon–Sat 10–12am (closed Sun); Village Bar is open Mon–Sat 11–12am and Sun 11am–10pm.

GRUB
Mon–Sat from 10am for cake and coffee; lunch daily 12–3pm and dinner 6–9pm (Sun 6–8pm).

TOP DROP
About 25 different beers are on tap, including boutique beers such as Vale Ale, Budvar from the Czech Republic, James Squire Amber, Monteiths Black, Mad Brewers Noir Stout and Coopers Vintage.

WHERE TO STAY
Tiffins on the Park, on Greenhill Rd, Parkside, about 5 km from Mitcham, has 54 suites and guest rooms, priced from $99 per night. www.tiffinsonthepark.com.au

NEARBY ATTRACTIONS
The Edinburgh Hotel is the start of a 2 km self-guided Mitcham Village Walk through Mitcham Village Historic (Conservation) Zone and surrounding areas. Two other walks take in St Michael's Church and Upper Mitcham, and the 3 Mitcham cemeteries. Brochure and maps for the walks are downloadable from www.mitchamcouncil.sa.gov.au

MORE INFO
www.southaustralia.com

LARGS PIER HOTEL

LARGS BAY

With its three-storey arcaded facade, the Largs Pier looks more like a European palace than an Australian hotel.

Largs Pier Hotel, Largs Bay

FOR THE BEST view of the majestic Largs Pier Hotel, you should be on the water. It's easy, then, to imagine how those arriving by ship would have seen it at the end of a long sea voyage ... like something from a dream, a magnificent mirage shimmering on the waterfront to greet them.

Some still see it that way, as passengers on cruise ships coming into Port Adelaide are frequently among those dining at this wonderfully restored seaside pub. With its three-storey arcaded facade, the Largs Pier looks more like a European palace than an Australian hotel.

Elegant it may be (some liken it to Raffles in Singapore), but the Largs Pier is renowned in South Australia as one of the great rock pubs. The Largs has been a starting point for some of Australia's top bands in the early stages of their careers, and it is still fostering new

talent. Every Friday night there are acoustic performers in the Largs Bar from 5–8pm to kick off the weekend.

Stylish modern guest rooms in the heritage section of the hotel

With a pedigree of performers that includes Bon Scott (who met his wife at the Largs Pier Hotel after a gig in 1971) and AC/DC, Diesel, Cold Chisel, Little River Band and the Angels – to name just a few – the Largs Pier has been *the* place to go for great pub music since the 1970s. Jimmy Barnes immortalised it in his song 'Largs Pier Hotel' which he launched in the hotel bar in 2010 in front of an enthusiastic standing-room-only crowd.

Built by the Largs Bay Land and Investment Company in 1882, the hotel opened on the same day as the Largs Bay Pier and Railway, and the area immediately became a major destination for mail steamers and an important seaside resort for South Australia. For two decades, the Largs Pier Hotel was the first port of call – and first temporary residence – for arriving European immigrants. The hotel has always been ahead of its time; in 1953 it opened Australia's first drive-through bottleshop and it also served Adelaide's first counter meals.

Largs Bay is about 16 kilometres from the Adelaide CBD, on the Lefevre Peninsula, just beyond the heart of Port Adelaide. Although you are still in suburbia when you visit the Largs Pier, it's easy to forget how close the city is when you look out to sea from the verandah of the hotel.

The Largs Bar has a 'Raffles' feel

The hotel's interior lives up to the exterior's promise. At the top of the sweeping grand staircase (there is no lift), the 15 high-ceilinged 'heritage' bedrooms are luxurious without being fussy, and have a modern style, ensuites with spa baths, room service and windows that open to the sea air. Nine of the rooms have doors that open on to the balcony. When choosing your bedroom, remember that Room 11 is reputedly haunted!

On the ground floor, the Largs Bar looks like it belongs in the tropics. With swinging 'punkah' ceiling fans, potted palms, wooden shutters and a lovely wooden bar, it leads out to a sheltered terrace with tables overlooking St Vincent Gulf, and is just the place for a beer, a cocktail or a glass of wine. If the weather's chilly,

LARGS PIER HOTEL

ADDRESS
198 Esplanade, Largs Bay

TELEPHONE
(08) 8449 5666

WEBSITE
www.largspierhotel.com.au

RATES
Heritage rooms: $159 standard; $184 deluxe; $205 deluxe spa or corner room; $245 executive spa suite. $10 surcharge Sat. Motel rooms: $154 single or double; $174 family room. Extra person $20 adult, $10 child under 12. Cots $10.

HOURS
Bars open from 9am daily until 10pm weekdays and 12am weekends.

GRUB
Open for breakfast 6.30–11am daily; lunch 12–3pm and dinner 6–9pm Mon–Thurs; all-day dining 12–9pm Fri–Sun.

TOP DROP
The range of beers on tap includes Carlton Draught, Cascade Light, Carlsberg, Coopers Pale, Coopers Clear, Pure Blonde, Carlton Dry and Vale Ale, plus Bulmer's cider.

NEARBY ATTRACTIONS
Historic Port Adelaide has many attractions including the South Australian Maritime Museum, where you can board a full-scale replica of a sailing ketch. The Bond Stores in Lipson St are the museum's main gallery. Climb the lighthouse, built in 1869, and take in the views of the port. www.history.sa.gov.au

MORE INFO
www.southaustralia.com

Largs Pier

you will find a cosy spot at the end of the bar, where there's a log fire, leather couches and low tables. And if you don't fancy the noisier restaurant area, the bar menu offers only a slightly more limited choice. Wood-fired pizzas are available daily for dinner and Friday–Sunday for lunch.

The Pier Restaurant, in an extension on the other side of the hotel, has been designed in a similar way to the bar but has a more contemporary feel and is popular with families and music lovers. A small stage in the corner hosts the music and tables extend out to a large deck.

On the other side of the original hotel, an old dance hall has been linked to the building and converted to 19 motel rooms (including one fully self-contained unit), all of which have individual direct street access to the Esplanade.

Largs Pier Hotel verandah

WALKERS ARMS

WALKERVILLE

WHEN THE OLD Walkers Arms burnt down in 2007 – the result of an electrical fault – the owners, the Dean Group of Hotels, saw a huge opportunity to create a new hotel from the ground up that would set unparalleled standards in sustainability. The hotel had been trading in the Adelaide suburb of Walkerville, 3 kilometres from the CBD, since 1848 and it had been rebuilt twice before – in 1880 and 1970 – but they were determined that this new incarnation would be like no other hotel.

Walkers Arms, Walkerville

The new Walkers Arms has embraced the idea of eco-sustainability with gusto. Everything here has been thought through, down to the smallest detail, taking the pub from 'old school' to 'very, very cool', in both its decor and its use of technology.

> In the restaurant you'll find something you don't see every day: a large doughnut machine which churns out 1440 sweet circles every hour.

Walk into the lobby of the hotel and the first thing that you'll see are a number of giant-sized white wing chairs, like something out of *Alice in Wonderland*. More of them are dotted throughout the hotel, and they are favourite places for guests to take photographs.

Reds and greens – the colours of life – are predominant in the decor. The most striking feature is the distinctive artwork of Adelaide artist Emma Hack, who was commissioned to create work about 'life'. Her strong visual designs, with intense colours and using circular motifs, symbolise the rebirth of the hotel. The designs have been created using magnified DNA sequences of butterflies and insects, and the theme has been carried through into the soft furnishings and even the carpets. It's all crisp, minimalist and very hip.

The public areas of the hotel are a large modern bar area, a massive garden courtyard and two dining areas. The main 120-seat restaurant is a buffet offering a carvery, with Asian and other international options, all provided by a team of 30 chefs and 20 kitchen staff serving around 6000 meals a week. Everything is made on the premises (as much as possible) including pastries, jams, sauces – all part of watching the hotel's carbon

WALKERS ARMS

ADDRESS
36 North East Rd, Walkerville

TELEPHONE
(08) 8344 8022

WEBSITE
www.walkersarms.com.au

RATES
Standard room $150 double; deluxe spa room $200 double.

HOURS
11–12am Sun–Thurs and 11–2am Fri–Sat.

GRUB
Buffet restaurant operates 2 lunch sittings daily, 12.30–1.30pm and 1.30–3pm, and 2 dinner sittings, 5.30–7.30pm and 7.30–9.30pm. À la carte restaurant open Mon–Thurs lunch 12–2.30pm and dinner 6–9pm, Fri–Sun all-day dining 12–9pm. Late-night pizza available Fri–Sat 9–11pm.

TOP DROP
Among the popular beers on tap are Vale Ale, McLaren Vale boutique beers, as well as Bulmer's cider.

NEARBY ATTRACTIONS
Walkers Arms is 3 km from the CBD. If you are interested in sustainability, take a 'green' city tour to learn about the 'green' sites and initiatives of Adelaide with a professional guide. Walking tours might include the South Australian Museum's Bio-Diversity Gallery, Botanic Gardens, Adelaide Central Markets, Adelaide Zoo and more. For information, contact South Australian Tourist Guides Association, 0419 861 320.

MORE INFO
www.southaustralia.com

footprint, which extends to the choice of beer and wines, with local labels preferred. In the restaurant you'll also find something you don't see every day in your local pub: a large doughnut machine which churns out 1440 sweet circles every hour. On the other side of the huge marble fireplace that flanks the buffet seating, the à la carte restaurant has booths and tables for another 80 diners, alongside a stunning 14-metre-long marble-topped bar.

Beer garden with super LED screen

In the garden, changing lights against the wall of the hotel can be used to 'colour' the white building for special events, such as pink for breast cancer awareness, yellow for Daffodil Day, and so on. Another 120 or so seats are provided in the garden bar, which has two super-sized video screens – one side a full screen, the other a montage of nine smaller LCD screens (so you can have sport on one side and a chick flick showing on the other). Booths around the outside of the garden bar have individual television screens, with iPod docks for screening your own movie or slide show. And just so you are never without entertainment, there are also LED promotion screens on the bar taps and in the bar toilets (really worth checking out).

The green theme is everywhere

When the Arms reopened in mid-2010, it had recycled about 90 per cent of the demolition material and construction waste, was able to generate all its own electricity and had implemented systems to ensure it was as eco-friendly as possible. This involved design features to enable the use of renewable energy sources, natural gas and water recycling, as well as natural ventilation, lighting and temperature control wherever practicable. Even the carpet is specially designed, made of compressed sugarcane to reduce noise and retain heat. Double-glazed windows keep out the traffic noise as well as assisting in temperature control.

Solar panels installed on the hotel roof generate 5 kilowatts of energy each day, running the entire hotel without drawing electricity from the main grid.

A 91 000-litre water tank under the hotel carpark is used for watering the drought-resistant plants chosen for the landscaping, and rainwater is used for all toilets. Taps in the bar and restaurant toilets are on timers to conserve water.

The 14-metre-long marble-topped bar

The 20 guest rooms (double the number of the former hotel building) are equally eco-sensitive. There are 12 standard rooms and eight spa rooms. Electronic key cards activate (and switch off) the power – all except that most important item, the alarm clock, which remains on even when the card is removed (they've thought of everything).

Large plasma-screen televisions in all the bedrooms – on a swivel for ease of viewing from all corners of the room – also have the ability to act as laptop monitors. And there's wireless internet access throughout the hotel.

Indoor dining flows out to the garden bar

THE AUSTRAL HOTEL

QUORN

The Austral Hotel bar

WHEN PUBLICAN NADINE Garrad stands at the bar of the Austral Hotel, she can look out onto the main street of Quorn. When she does, she often imagines what it was like in days gone by ... particularly in the 1940s when the street would have been filled with soldiers heading off to war. The train station from which they departed is across the way and the pub was often the last place they visited before boarding the troop trains. Quorn was constantly busy back then, with about 50 trains a day passing through the town during and immediately after the war.

'In those days the pub served the railway and the troops, with the CWA [Country Women's Association] feeding them. Now we cater to the local farmers, commuters to Port Augusta and the tourists passing through,' says Nadine.

Built in 1878, the Austral was the first pub in town to be licensed and is one of four pubs still remaining in Quorn, a small town with a population of around 1070, about 40 kilometres north-east of Port Augusta. The original single-storey stone building had another level and a verandah added to it later, but these days all the action is still downstairs.

When you walk into the pub, you can check out the work of local artists: the walls are used as a gallery and you'll find artworks in the bar and the dining room.

With three other local pubs to compete with, when Nadine took over the Austral in 2009 she decided it had to offer some points of difference. The first one is that when you walk into the pub, you can check out the work of local artists: the walls are used as a gallery and you'll find artworks in the bar, the dining room and along the walls leading to the accommodation.

The other area Nadine decided to focus on was the food. 'Because Quorn has four hotels, we decided ours would offer a menu that was not your average pub meal,' says Nadine. 'We aim to provide anyone and everyone with good old-fashioned country hospitality and a great dining experience, and our food is a major contributor to our success.'

She says the menu had to be 'as local as possible, of good quality, with generous country portions and to offer good value'. She continues, 'By using an assortment of bush spices, camel meat, kangaroo, goat, farmed rabbit and barramundi we are able to offer tourists and locals a unique and interestingly topical menu.

'Our kitchen staff is always keen to try different dishes, which is reflected on our changing Specials Board, where you might find something like Rocky River barramundi dusted with bush spices and drizzled with a lemon myrtle butter, or a trio of chops – goat, lamb and pork cutlets – topped with a rich demi-glaze sauce,' she says.

A key element of the Austral's food is the dedicated schnitzel menu. Schnitzels can be kangaroo, chicken or beef, with a choice of eight toppings; all are served with chips and salad or vegetables. The Outback schnitzel is kangaroo, topped with quandong barbecue sauce, bacon, onion and cheese; the Pichi Richi has a ham, cheese and asparagus topping; and the Ned Kelly is topped with bacon, egg, onion and cheese. For those who think they can't quite manage a full schnitzel, there's a half-serve option for $10 (for all but the kangaroo).

Other dishes include steaks, burgers and, Thursday–Sunday, pizza. One of the most popular meals is the Frenched-cut rib-eye steak dressed with a choice of sauce, and which is also the base for a surf'n'turf dish.

Artwork at the Austral Hotel

The Austral kitchen has developed a great range of gourmet pies, using camel, goat and rabbit meat, which are served with chips or vegetables and are available at lunch or dinner. Gluten-free dishes are marked on the menu and there are always a couple of vegetarian options, such as quiche or cannelloni.

A 'Rug Rats' menu has plenty to tempt the kids, all for $7.50, and there are waffle cones for children large and small for $5.50. More grown-up desserts include cheesecake of the week, homemade sticky date pudding with butterscotch sauce, baked lemon-lime tart and quandong pie.

The wine list carries South Australian labels, including a section devoted to wines from the Southern Flinders Ranges, which stretch north-east of Quorn. In the bar, there's also a large espresso machine which is kept busy at all times of day, and in winter there's a fireplace to get warm beside.

On the third Sunday of every month, an 'open mic' session encourages local music talent, and on the last Sunday in April–October, the Austral Luncheon Car departs on the historic Pichi Richi Express steam train (see Nearby Attractions, right). The lunch is limited to 14 guests who get exclusive access to the first-class compartments and spacious dining saloon. The three-course meal costs $95 per person; bookings for the Austral Luncheon Car must be made through the hotel.

Accommodation at the Austral is in six former railway workers' rooms (all with ensuite, television and fridge) that open into an indoor courtyard area, and five motel rooms built at the back of the pub. Plans for the future include expansion with 15 two-bedroom units to be built on a block behind the pub.

THE AUSTRAL HOTEL

ADDRESS
16 Railway Tce, Quorn

TELEPHONE
(08) 8648 6017

WEBSITE
www.australinn.info

RATES
$65 single, $80 twin, $90 triple for motel rooms; $110 double for railway workers' rooms (1 room has extra single bed). Breakfast included in rates.

HOURS
11–12am Mon–Sat and 11am–10pm Sun.

GRUB
Lunch 12–2pm and dinner 6–8pm daily.

TOP DROP
There are 6 beers on tap, the most popular being James Squire. The wine list is exclusively South Australian, including many from the Southern Flinders region.

NEARBY ATTRACTIONS
Take a ride on the historic Pichi Richi Railway steam trains between Quorn and Port Augusta, Mar–Nov. The 40 km track weaves through deep rock cuttings, over old stone bridges and through abandoned settlements on the old Ghan line. There are several trips to choose from. During SA school holidays you can also do a behind-the-scenes tour of the Quorn railway workshops. www.ppr.org.au

MORE INFO
www.flindersranges.com

The CALEDONIAN Inn

ROBE

The Caledonian Inn, Robe

FROM THE BACK verandah of the whitewashed Caledonian Inn you can see the blue waters of Guichen Bay and smell the salt air. The pub's sheltered garden bar is a stone's throw from the beach, its backyard running down to the sands of Robe's popular Long Beach. On a calm and sunny day, it's hard to imagine that this lovely stretch of South Australian coastline, 340 kilometres south-east of Adelaide, has been the scene of terrible shipwrecks, the timbers from some being used in the building of this popular pub.

In 1857, when the Caledonian Inn was being built, shipwrecks were not uncommon along the Limestone Coast. That year alone saw the English ships *Phaeton* and *Sultana* and the Dutch *Koning Willem de Tweede* wrecked in Guichen Bay offshore from Long Beach. All were bringing Chinese immigrants bound for the Victorian goldfields – thousands of Chinese chose to walk the 150 kilometres from South Australia to the goldfields across the border, to avoid paying a tax to disembark in Melbourne. When the *Koning Willem* was driven aground by a huge and violent storm, with 15 souls lost, it was the greatest loss of life of any shipwreck at Port Robe.

From the back verandah of the whitewashed Caledonian Inn you can see the blue waters of Guichen Bay and smell the salt air.

In 1861, when the Caledonian Inn was only a couple of years old, the ships *Alma* and *Livingstone* were in Port Robe to load wool for shipping overseas. The Caledonian was the social hub of the port town, with grand social occasions being held in a large room at the inn, and a ball was held there to entertain the men from the ships. However, neither vessel would ever leave the port. One of the worst storms ever known along this stretch of coast drove the ships ashore and both were wrecked, although the wool from the *Livingstone* was salvaged. The crew of the *Alma* was saved through a dramatic rescue with rocket apparatus from a cliff-top before the vessel broke up.

The Caledonian Inn was opened in 1859 by a Scot, Peter McQueen, and it still retains many of its early features, including doors and timber from the wrecks of the *Phaeton* and *Koning Willem*: three of the ships' doors were fitted to attics overlooking the bay, and another two were used on upstairs rooms where they remain. The original roof of the Caledonian was of split palings; when an iron roof was fitted later, it was – for the sake of coolness – attached over the wooden shingles, which are still there. Despite its historic building, the Caledonian Inn was not the first pub in Robe. When Peter McQueen was allowed the hotel licence in 1858, it was the second granted for the settlement. The first had gone to the Bonnie Owl, a decade earlier. The Caledonian was however granted a Historic Inn Licence in 1975 and it is now heritage-listed.

The front bar

Six hotel rooms are still used upstairs in the old inn – with shared bathrooms for men and women – or there is a more modern choice of accommodation at the back of the hotel, some of it overlooking the beach. The hotel rooms have iron bedsteads, patchwork quilts and country-style furniture. There is a small guest lounge upstairs with a television and comfy chairs.

Stylish cottages sleep up to six

Four stylish self-contained cottages were built in the mid 1980s at the back of the hotel; beyond them is the beach. The cottages have full kitchens, baths, fireplaces and the latest entertainment systems. The upstairs bedroom in each cottage is divided in two – one side with a king-sized double bed, the other with two king-singles. There is also a double sofa bed downstairs, so each cottage can sleep up to six people. All of them are set in seaside gardens, planted with daisies and lavender, and they are just steps away from the swimming beach.

If you feel like splashing out on more expensive accommodation, you can opt to stay in Splash, the hotel's luxury beachfront retreat; it is close to the inn's back door and just across the lawn from the beach. French doors open onto a deck overlooking the

THE CALEDONIAN INN

ADDRESS
1 Victoria St, Robe

TELEPHONE
(08) 8768 2029

WEBSITE
www.caledonian.net.au

RATES
Hotel rooms: $85–$110 double or twin; extra person $25. Rates include continental breakfast in the Cellar Room 8–10am. Seafront cottages: $185–$210 for 2 people; extra person $25. Rates include continental breakfast hamper. Splash: $310 for 2 people, extra person $50, including continental breakfast hamper, except 24 Dec – 31 Jan, when flat rate of $3500 per week applies.

HOURS
Daily 10–1.30am.

GRUB
Open for lunch 12–2pm and dinner 6–8.30pm daily.

TOP DROP
Beers on tap include Carlton Draught, Guinness, Coopers Pale Ale, Coopers Sparkling, Hahn Super Dry and Cascade Light. In winter, Coopers Stout is also on tap.

NEARBY ATTRACTIONS
Victoria St has cafes, boutiques and galleries. Take time to explore the town's maritime history. A self-guided Heritage Walk takes in quaint cottages and stately homes. Don't miss the Chinese Monument, in memory of the many Chinese who made the long walk to the Victorian goldfields.

MORE INFO
www.thelimestonecoast.com
www.southaustralia.com

ocean, and there is an open fire for the colder months. Splash has a 'cook's kitchen' with stainless-steel appliances and a dishwasher, plus a separate dining room.

Splash can sleep up to eight people in three bedrooms; each room has a queen-sized bed and one has an additional double sofa bed. The bathroom has a spa bath and separate shower. Portable cots and single trundle beds are also available on request, making both Splash and the cottages great options for families.

One of the Caledonian's dining areas

The Caledonian Inn is a lovely pub with an old-fashioned feeling – no pokies and no TAB, something the licensee, John 'Diver' Atherton, is proud of. With its crackling open fires, low doorways (tall people may have to duck their heads for some), and intimate spaces, it has great atmosphere.

Enjoy a drink in the historic front bar or snuggle up in a booth in the candlelit dining room. The dining room retains a cosy feel, and seats around 50, in the booths that accommodate six diners; its menu includes fresh crayfish from local waters. Lunch and dinner is also available in the Bagatelle, Cellar Room or Provincial dining rooms. The Beach Cafe caters for the summer crowds in the walled beer garden, which has colourful mosaics, serving casual meals (and a kids' menu) and takeaways, while coffee addicts will find the locally roasted Mahalia coffee 'on tap' at all times.

'Splash', the Caledonian's luxury retreat

GERMAN ARMS *Hotel*

HAHNDORF

IN THE ORIGINAL front bar of the German Arms, a delicate mural has been painted around the entire walls, tracing the history of Hahndorf and its lovely old buildings. And what a history it has had. Behind the bonhomie of the beerhaus, the pub that wears its origins so plainly for all to see – and tourists seem to love this little slice of Bavaria in the Adelaide Hills – has not always had such a happy time of it.

Founded by German Lutherans fleeing religious persecution in their homeland in the 1830s, Hahndorf is a leafy and picturesque tourist town where the picture-postcard main street – with 90 buildings dating back to the 1800s – belies its turbulent history.

Today, when the hotel is doing a roaring trade in bratwurst, bockwurst, Black Forest cake and German beer, it's easy to forget that there was a time when things were not always so merry. Even the town of Hahndorf was wiped from Australian maps.

The German Arms, Hahndorf, opened in 1865

Many of the Lutheran refugees who came to Australia – generally from Brandenburg, Posen and Silesia in eastern Germany – settled in Hahndorf. The German Arms opened in 1839, soon after the Lutherans had begun to arrive and three years after South Australia was founded. At first, the Arms was a coffee shop, owned by Gottfried Lubasch and his wife Anna. The main road between Adelaide and Melbourne – then little more than a track – went past the front door, which was directly opposite the spelling yard for the South Australian Company's stock after their long journey from the colonies on the eastern seaboard.

It was renovated using timbers salvaged from an old woolstore in Adelaide: floors, ceilings, stairs, beams, pillars, bars and tables have all been made from this recycled wood.

Later the same year, Lubasch was granted a liquor licence and his clientele quickly expanded. Lubasch held the licence until 1849, and the German Arms remained Hahndorf's only pub until 1854, when the Australian Arms opened. In 1861 the original German Arms was destroyed by fire and the publican of the time, Thomas Ide, built a grand new establishment on the opposite side of the road, which opened in 1865 – the building that still stands today.

The outbreak of World War I changed life in Hahndorf dramatically. People of German ancestry were considered enemy aliens and some were interned on Torrens Island. The brother of local painter Hans Heysen (later one of Australia's most famous artists) was interned in Sydney – and far-sighted villagers buried some of Hans' paintings in order to save them.

The name of the German Arms came down after the hotel was raided – unsuccessfully – for guns. In 1914, the licensee Mr Fallenberg changed the hotel's name to the Hahndorf Hotel, but even that was not to last for long. The placename Hahndorf, along with others of German origin, was removed from the Australian map by an Act of Parliament in 1917. The village was renamed Ambleside, after a nearby railway station, and the hotel adopted that name too. Hahndorf's original name was restored in 1935, but the German Arms was not reinstated as the name of the hotel until 1975.

Front bar, German Arms

Time hasn't stood still for the hotel, despite its traditional exterior. In 1982 it became the first pub in South Australia to gain a Sunday trading licence and in the mid 1990s was the first to install poker machines. In 1990 it was renovated using 500-year-old timbers salvaged from an old woolstore in Adelaide: floors, ceilings, stairs, beams, pillars, bars and tables have all been made from this recycled wood. The original hotel was extended into the former bank building next door, of similar age, taking in the laneway between the two. More recently, it has been upgraded again with the addition of new bars and a gaming lounge.

German dishes are among the favourite items on the menu, which also offers standard pub fare such as schnitzels, parmigianas, beer-battered barramundi, steaks and garlic prawns. If you want to try the German-style food, go for a Bavarian mixed grill – bockwurst, bratwurst and wood-smoked kassler chop, served on red cabbage with Rhine potatoes and Bavarian mustard – or chicken krakau, which is a chicken breast filled with smoked cheese and Polish wurst, wrapped in bacon and topped with a rich cream sauce.

And what menu here would be complete without a traditional hot apple strudel on it? Other German-style desserts include a spiced Black Forest cherry tart, and beesting, a traditional German sponge with caramelised apple and chantilly cream.

The large dining areas are often packed, but it is in the front bar where you will be most likely to meet the locals, the action centring around a pool table, and fireplaces that bring added warmth on chilly days.

GERMAN ARMS HOTEL

ADDRESS
69 Main St, Hahndorf

TELEPHONE
(08) 8388 7013

WEBSITE
www.germanarmshotel.com.au

HOURS
Daily from 8.30am; front bar open 11am.

GRUB
All-day service from 8.30am.

TOP DROP
As well as Australian and German beers, you can also try German schnapps (apple, peach, plum, cherry or sour apple).

WHERE TO STAY
The Manna of Hahndorf, near the German Arms at 25 Main St, has 50 new 4-star motel rooms, including spa and family rooms; rates are $155–$215. A heated pool and spa are available at its sister motel, Hahndorf Inn Motor Lodge, 100 m away. www.themanna.com.au

NEARBY ATTRACTIONS
Hahndorf's most famous son is the painter Hans Heysen. Make a pilgrimage to Heysen's house and studio, The Cedars, on the village outskirts in Heysen Rd. The Cedars and Hans Heysen's studio are open daily except Mon (but open on public holiday Mon). Inspection by guided tour only, at 11am, 1pm and 3pm (11am and 2pm June–Aug); entry $10. The grounds and shop are open 10am–4.30pm. Tel: (08) 8388 7277.

MORE INFO
www.visitadelaidehills.com.au

HEYWARD'S ROYAL OAK HOTEL

PENOLA

TAKE A ROOM at the Royal Oak and you may well be sleeping in a room that Australia's first saint, St Mary MacKillop of the Cross, occupied. Owner John Heyward says it is certain that Mary stayed in the hotel when she returned to Penola in 1866 to found her teaching order, at the time when her maternal uncle Donald McDonald was the licensee, between 1864 and 1880.

Heyward's Royal Oak Hotel

Penola is the oldest town in the south-east of South Australia, and the Royal Oak is the oldest pub. Alexander Cameron, a Scot, founded the town in 1845, while another Scot, John Riddoch, planted the first vines in 1890, laying the rich foundations for Coonawarra's thriving wine industry. Mary MacKillop was a niece by marriage of Alexander Cameron, and is known to have stayed at the Royal Oak when it belonged to him. She may also have stayed in the slab hotel that pre-dated the current building, when Alexander Cameron held the licence in 1848–50.

With Father Julian Tenison Woods, Mary founded the religious order of the Sisters of St Joseph in Penola more than 125 years ago. A museum named after Mary but also devoted to the fascinating story of her mentor, Woods, is one of Penola's greatest tourist attractions. The poets Adam Lindsay Gordon, Will Ogilvie and John Shaw Neilson are also among Penola's famous sons. Gordon arrived in 1854 as a police trooper and reputedly enjoyed leaping his horse over the Royal Oak's hitching rail.

A heritage walk around the town takes in many of the surviving original buildings. Beside the Mary MacKillop Interpretive Centre, wander down Petticoat Lane for a glimpse of how life used to be. A statue of Alexander Cameron by South Australian sculptor John Dowie stands in the main street beside the Royal Oak. There are also art-and-craft shops, galleries, restaurants, historic homesteads and cottages to explore.

Take a room at the Royal Oak and you may well be sleeping in a room that Australia's first saint, St Mary MacKillop of the Cross, occupied.

HEYWARD'S ROYAL OAK HOTEL

ADDRESS
31 Church St, Penola

TELEPHONE
(08) 8737 2322

WEBSITE
www.heywardshotel.com.au

RATES
$55 single (or $77 in a queen room); $88 double or twin. Rates include self-serve continental breakfast in a small room (1 table inside, others on the verandah).

HOURS
Bar and reception open 10am Thurs–Sat and 11am Sun–Wed, close about 10pm–12am.

GRUB
Open for lunch 11.30am–2pm daily and dinner 6–8pm Sun–Thurs, 6–8.30pm Fri–Sat.

TOP DROP
Carlton, West End, Coopers and Guinness are on tap in the Front Bar, but this is Coonawarra wine country and you'll find a good selection on the restaurant's wine list.

NEARBY ATTRACTIONS
The Mary MacKillop Interpretive Centre, in the town's heritage precinct, is a tribute to Australia's first saint. It is next to the 1867 schoolhouse where Mary taught and the newer St Joseph's Catholic Church. Further afield, visit the World Heritage–listed Naracoorte Caves for fabulous fossils and the Bool Lagoon wetlands.

MORE INFO
www.mackilloppenola.org.au
www.thelimestonecoast.com.au

Alexander Cameron was issued one of the earliest liquor licences in South Australia, in 1848, allowing him to open the Royal Oak Hotel (although current owner John Heyward says sly grogging was probably rife before that date). The original Royal Oak was a slab building, but in 1872 Cameron built a new two-storey stone hotel.

During the construction, the Penola correspondent to the *Border Watch* reported: 'The new Royal Oak Hotel is now in full swing, the cellar walls have appeared up to the surface and a large number of men are employed ... none but teetotallers are engaged on the work.' The greater part of this building is still standing, with the addition of a balcony – with perhaps the best view in town – in the early 1900s and a tower from the top floor in the late 1990s.

The hotel is now listed by State Heritage and the National Trust. For those who want to stay, it has nine rooms – four doubles (all with beautiful queen-sized four-poster beds), four singles and one twin room. All rooms have a television, heater, bathrobes and electric blankets on the beds. They have washbasins and mirrors, but share bathrooms down the hallway; there are separate bathrooms for men and women, and the facilities have baths as well as showers. A small guest lounge, leading to the huge verandah, has tea- and coffee-making facilities, a fridge, a decanter of port and fresh fruit, while continental breakfast is served here.

Statue of Alexander Cameron

The Heyward family has owned the hotel for the past 70 years. Reginald George Heyward became the licensee in 1942 and held it until his death in 1967, when his widow Joan and son John took over. John and his wife Libby have held the licence since 1988.

'I've spent all my life in this pub,' says John Heyward. 'I was working here from the age of 15 and I've seen all sorts of people come in – governors, actors, premiers, footballers, cricketers, and even a couple of Miss Australia winners.'

Follow the tartan carpet down the stairs (or in from the street) to the dining room or lounge bar for lunch or dinner. There are three bars – the Red Lounge, the public bar and a smaller bar off the gaming room, which is tucked discreetly at the back. The dining room has changed little from the original, with a roaring log fire in winter. Above the fireplace is a clock which John Heyward believes may have been in the pub since its earliest days – it carries the name of a Penola watchmaker. Local specialties are on the menu, including Meek's special kransky sausages, smoked and served on a bed of garlic mash. You can also sip on a Mahalia of Robe coffee – cappuccino or espresso.

On summer days, head to the leafy garden bar, which seats about a hundred and contains barbecue facilities which you can use (by arrangement). There's also a play area for children.

INNAMINCKA HOTEL

INNAMINCKA

THE INNAMINCKA HOTEL sits in the Innamincka Regional Reserve, near the end of the Strzelecki Track on a gibber plain in the Sturt Stony Desert. That's just about as remote as you can get.

The Innamincka Hotel is 1065 kilometres north-east of Adelaide and nearly 500 thirsty kilometres from the next nearest pub, at Lyndhurst, so no-one who passes this way fails to stop. And that means 40000 to 50000 visitors drop in to Innamincka (population 12) every year.

In days gone by the number of visitors was lower, but the Innamincka pub has been looking after travellers since the early days of European settlement, and these days the tourists just keep coming. The Innamincka Hotel was established in 1886 and played host to the drovers and stockmen who brought cattle from the Channel Country in Queensland to the markets of South Australia. Although nothing remains of that original building, the current hotel, built in the 1970s, has been redeveloped by owners Kym Fort and David Brook (who also own the Birdsville Hotel) to reflect its character. The pub is very much a family affair, with Kym's wife Jo being the company's general manager, and David's daughter Karen providing marketing assistance.

The outback oasis of Innamincka Hotel

The Innamincka Hotel sits near the end of the Strzelecki Track on a gibber plain in the Sturt Stony Desert. That's just about as remote as you can get.

'The Innamincka Hotel is an experience in its own right, but we also help our visitors to experience outback culture and explore the fascinating history of the area,' says Jo Fort. 'Given our location, it's not surprising that tourists arrive on our doorstep hoping to find an oasis.'

And an oasis it is, from the cold beer that washes down the dust of the day's journey to the hot shower and hearty meal, and the chance for travellers to catch their breath before continuing on their outback journey.

First stop is usually the 1970s-style Front Bar, or the newer Outamincka Bar with its teak furniture, spotted-gum beams and wood finishes. Meals and snacks are served in both bars and in the beer garden, featuring fresh produce trucked in from the Adelaide markets and the Barossa Valley.

INNAMINCKA HOTEL

ADDRESS
South Tce, Innamincka

TELEPHONE
(08) 8675 9901

WEBSITE
www.theoutback.com.au

RATES
$130 single, $155 double or twin.

HOURS
Daily 10–12am.

GRUB
Daily for breakfast 7.30–9am, lunch 12–2pm and dinner 6–8.30pm.

TOP DROP
Coopers Pale Ale, XXXX Gold, Hahn Super Dry, Tooheys Extra Dry, West End Draught and James Squire are on tap, and there is a large selection of bottled beers and ciders plus an extensive wine list featuring SA wines.

NEARBY ATTRACTIONS
Visitors to Innamincka can go 4WD touring to visit historic sites associated with the explorers Burke and Wills, fish and camp beside Cooper Creek. Birdwatching and bushwalking are popular activities, as is visiting Coongie Lakes National Park.

MORE INFO
www.southaustralia.com

A cold beer washes down the dust of the day's journey

Jo describes it as 'creative Australian pub fare', combining traditional pub meals with chef's specialties such as a 450 gram Coorong Angus rib-eye steak topped with Café de Paris butter, baked potato cheddar cake and steamed greens. Specialty nights include the midweek Innamincka BBQ – choose your steak, chicken or fish, with a baked potato, damper and buffet salad bar – and the Sunday roast buffet in the Outamincka Bar, when the locals and tourists mingle over the meal, a beer or a game of pool.

If you get hungry at other times, there is cake and espresso available all day, and the pub will do takeaways and packed lunches. There are also pre-packed gourmet goods for sale.

Entertainment – if you need it – is provided by the Starlight Cinema, a huge screen just outside the Outamincka Bar where you can sit under the clear, star-studded desert sky and watch classic Australian films such as *Breaker Morant* and *Back of Beyond*. Films are screened on request, so just ask!

Accommodation is in 16 motel units (two accessible for people with disabilities) and seven huts. There is also an eight-bedroom bunkhouse with shared living area and bathroom, suitable for families, with a mix of single, double and bunk beds.

The walls of the Innamincka Hotel are papered with photographs, articles and maps that tell tales of characters and events that have helped to forge Australia's outback culture and identity. Prominent among these is the story of explorers Robert Burke and William Wills, who in 1860 set out to cross the continent from south to north. They achieved their aim, but both men perished on the return journey.

To mark the 150th anniversary in 2010 of the Burke and Wills expedition, the pub set up a permanent display that retells the story – but in an offbeat way.

'Innamincka is crucial to the story of Burke and Wills,' says Jo. 'And while acknowledging the importance of the achievement and regretting the loss of life, we also know that the story is marked by events that were avoidable, unusual and, at times, even humorous. The display focuses on the quirky aspects of the drama, bringing to life the personalities of the explorers and celebrating their determination and sheer bloody-mindedness – characteristics that have, we think, become part of our outback identity.'

The best time to visit Innamincka is during the cooler months, from April to October, but at any time of year there's plenty to see and do despite the isolation. The massive Innamincka Regional Reserve is home to more than 200 bird species and many native animals – but watch out for the world's most venomous snake, the inland taipan.

Or you could just sit in the bar with a beer.

KIMBA COMMUNITY Hotel Motel

KIMBA

AS YOU DRIVE into Kimba, especially at dusk, slow down. It's not uncommon for a large flock of pink galahs to be settled on the road. And of all places, this is not the place to be responsible for their injury or death – for just ahead of you, looking down from high, is the Big Galah.

The 8-metre-tall Big Galah is only one of Kimba's claims to fame. The other is that this small town, home to about 650 people, is the halfway point between Australia's east and west coasts. Kimba is 97 kilometres east of Wudinna and 89 kilometres west of Iron Knob, at the northern end of the Eyre Peninsula. You'll know when you've arrived by the enormous green and gold 'Half Way Across Australia' sign on the Eyre Highway.

Named with an Aboriginal word meaning 'bushfire', Kimba was proclaimed a town in 1915. It serves one of South Australia's largest wheat-, wool- and meat-growing regions. Apart from the Big Galah, standing sentinel beside the Kimba roadhouse, the massive wheat silos of one of the state's largest inland grain terminals dominate the eye as you arrive in town.

The Kimba Community Hotel Motel entrance

Publican Wally Bache dismantled the entire Yeelanna Hotel – stone by stone – moved it by rail to Kimba and rebuilt it on the site where it stands today.

Explorer Edward John Eyre discovered water near Kimba in 1839. By the 1870s the area had been opened up with pastoral leases. More settlers arrived around 1908, when the first wheat crops were sown – it is a testament to how tough life was that they referred to the area as Heartbreak Plains. Early transport was by bullock cart and camel trains, but the railway came to Kimba in 1913. Water was freighted in by rail every two weeks.

The Kimba Community Hotel is in the centre of town. A publican called Wally Bache held the licence of the Yeelanna Hotel, further down the Eyre Peninsula, from 1913 to 1924, when he decided that business might be better at Kimba. He transferred the licence and dismantled the entire Yeelanna Hotel – stone by stone – moved it by rail to Kimba and rebuilt it on the site where it stands today. Bache remained the licensee until 1926. In the days of the six o'clock swill, beer and wine were siphoned off the kegs in the cellar into flagons for patrons to take home. The hotel remained in private ownership until early 1950 when the townspeople (as the Kimba Progress Association) raised the capital to buy the lease. The freehold was bought the following year, and the hotel is still run by a community board.

The Shed at the Kimba Community Hotel Motel

Over the years the hotel has been extended, but the original stone building still dominates it, on the corner of High and Cross streets, where the entrance once was. As well as a large bar, dining area, coffee shop and souvenir store, the Kimba Hotel also has a wide range of accommodation for weary cross-continental travellers. It ranges from backpacker rooms to more up-market accommodation in the historic Old Post Office behind the pub. There are four backpacker rooms and four deluxe rooms within the hotel, and 15 motel rooms – doubles, twins and family rooms – behind the hotel building. Backpacker rooms have two single beds, television, air conditioners and shared bathrooms. Motel rooms have ensuites and televisions with Austar satellite channels; each can sleep up to four. Deluxe rooms are larger (as are their ensuites), with either a double bed or a double bed and single bed; they also have television with Austar.

The best rooms are in the Old Post Office, a stone building which was used from 1925 until 2003 as both the Kimba post office and telephone exchange. The three rooms in the building each have a queen-sized bed with an additional single bed or pull-out sofa bed.

Lunch and dinner at the hotel are served either in the bar or the dining room. Beyond the bar is another large area with tables – used for functions and at busy times – called the Shed, which aptly describes its look. Corrugated-iron walls are lined with blokey memorabilia, mostly with pub and motoring themes.

On the menu you'll find the usual run of pub grub, along with a few specialties such as a Kimba burger (rump steak, melted cheese, salad and barbecue sauce in a damper roll), a Gawler Ranges burger (with an emu patty and sweet chutney), and the Outback Grill, which has kangaroo fillet, a goat cutlet, camel sausage and emu patty served with bush chutney and wedges. For dessert? Try the quandong pie with cream or ice-cream.

Most of Kimba's major attractions are near the Big Galah. The little row of shops beside the roadhouse includes the Kimba Half Way Across Australia Gem Shop, which has locally mined Cowell jade that ranges in colour from green to jet black. There's also the Sturt Pea Shoppe, which claims to be Australia's largest commercial grower of Sturt's desert pea, the floral emblem of South Australia.

A 3-kilometre walk around the town, starting at the old post office near the hotel, takes you to 20 spots of historical significance, each marked with an informative photo board. Kimba is also a short drive from the Lake Gilles and Pinkawillinie conservation parks. The area is famous for wildflowers and you will see wildlife, including emus, kangaroos and wombats (more reasons to take care when driving, especially in the early morning and at dusk).

KIMBA COMMUNITY HOTEL MOTEL

ADDRESS
40 High St, Kimba

TELEPHONE
(08) 8627 2007

WEBSITE
www.kimbahotel.com.au

RATES
$60 double backpacker rooms; $95 double motel rooms; $120 double deluxe rooms; $140 double executive suites and Post Office. Rates include continental breakfast.

HOURS
Reception opens 7.30am, bar opens 10am.

GRUB
Breakfast for guests 7–9am. Kitchen open daily for lunch 12–2pm and dinner 6–8.30pm; the coffee shop has an all-day menu. Room service available for guests.

TOP DROP
Seven beers on tap: West End Draught, Hahn Super Dry, Hahn Premium Light, Hahn 3.5, XXXX Gold, Coopers Stout and Coopers Pale Ale.

NEARBY ATTRACTIONS
Once you have checked out the Big Galah, there are several walks around the area, and another 100 km drive will bring you to Gawler Ranges National Park. The Kimba and Gawler Ranges Museum (open Sat afternoons or by arrangement; (08) 8627 2344) is opposite the grain silos.

MORE INFO
www.kimba.sa.gov.au
www.southaustralia.com
www.eyrepeninsula.net

NORTH STAR HOTEL

MELROSE

THIS MIGHT BE among the most unusual accommodation offered at any pub in Australia: two old trucks at the back of the North Star Hotel have been converted into accommodation. Take your pick from the red truck or the green truck, climb up and feel like a gypsy for a night or two – except that these quirky caravans are not going anywhere.

Accommodation at the North Star Hotel includes these converted trucks

With Mt Remarkable as a backdrop, the historic town of Melrose, in the Southern Flinders Ranges, is about three hours' drive north of Adelaide. The North Star Hotel, which first operated from a log hut in 1854, is the oldest licensed pub in the Flinders Ranges.

Behind the two-storey stone hotel, with its modern extension and dining deck at the side, is a large backyard with a vegetable garden for the kitchen and beyond it the unique accommodation, created about ten years ago by the previous owner, David Rosenzweig.

Two old trucks at the back of the North Star Hotel have been converted into accommodation. Take your pick from the red truck or the green truck, climb up and feel like a gypsy for a night or two – except that these quirky caravans are not going anywhere.

The green truck has a queen-sized bed and fold-out sofa bed, suitable for two children, while the red truck has just one queen bed. Both are air-conditioned and have ensuite bathrooms, along with tea- and coffee-making facilities, fridges and toasters.

If you don't fancy the trucks, there are also four stylishly renovated ensuite rooms upstairs in the pub, with their own private guest lounge downstairs plus a guest kitchenette – and these rooms have little luxuries, such as bathrobes.

North Star bar

Next door to the hotel is a four-room stone cottage of similar vintage to the hotel, with a red-gum deck out the front to sit on and watch the passing parade. The cottage has a communal kitchen and living area with a microwave, kitchen table, couches and a television. Each bedroom has an ensuite bathroom, kettle and toaster, and a queen-sized and a single bed. One room in the cottage has been adapted into a disability suite. All up, the cottage can accommodate 17 people.

The North Star is – apart from being a great pub – the cellar door for Bundaleer Wines, which it stocks exclusively. The vineyard was started by old schoolfriends Graham Spurling and the late Des Meaney, and now the next generation is in charge. Graham's daughter Cate Spurling runs the North Star and Des's daughter, renowned winemaker Angela Meaney, creates Bundaleer's wines from grapes grown at the family-owned and -operated vineyard in the Bundaleer Forest, just south of Jamestown, about 70 kilometres from Melrose.

The Bundaleer range of red wines – Shiraz and Cabernet Sauvignon – is made exclusively from grapes grown at the Bundaleer Vineyard, 10 hectares that were planted in 1998. For the white wines – Chardonnay and Riesling – Angela personally selects grapes from vineyards in the neighbouring Clare Valley.

The North Star's philosophy is also to keep the food local. Anything that can't be grown in the hotel's own garden is sourced from the Southern Flinders area. 'It's not only good for our local food heroes but also for the region's economy, and it's great for the environment, reducing our carbon footprint by minimising the "food miles" that our ingredients need to travel,' says Cate.

North Star dining

North Star Hotel, Melrose

That means barramundi from the Rocky River, Bundaleer organic beef, kangaroo from Orroroo, Appila Plains bio-dynamic lamb, and free-range chicken from Riverton in the Clare Valley. Organic fruit and vegetables come from orchards near the Wirrabara Forest, pistachios from Quorn, honey, olives and olive oil from the Beetaloo Valley and Stone Hut, and Hickory's Run also provides olive oil and olives. 'Bush foodie' Lyle Dudley, who harvests wild wattle seed and quandong fruit near Wilmington, adds to the mix. Seafood is bought from S. D. Caputo & Sons, a fourth-generation family-run business that has been serving the region for almost 60 years, supplying fresh local seafood from the Spencer Gulf, including its own smoked fish.

Golden North ice-cream, from nearby Laura, is always on the dessert menu. Part of a 120-year tradition, it dates back to the 1800s when the first owner of the property, William Bowker, began supplying milk and vegetables to the miners at Broken Hill. Golden North began ice-cream production in 1923. If you get the chance, try the popular honey flavour.

The North Star's bar flows through to the dining room and out onto the deck, a lovely spot on a sunny day. This new part of the hotel has corrugated-iron walls, wooden floors and a ceiling lined with old wool bales. There's a new menu daily, with a simple pricing scheme: three courses and a glass of wine costs $40, or two courses for $35. You can be more selective: an entree is $12.50 or a main course is $28.

In Melrose, the great outdoors is the lure. The town is the meeting point of the Heysen Walking Trail and the Mawson Trail for bike riders. Or you can spend four or five hours walking to the top of Mt Remarkable and back (and then feel you have really earned your meal and glass of wine). For those not so energetic, there are less strenuous walks in Mt Remarkable National Park.

NORTH STAR HOTEL

ADDRESS
Nott St, Melrose

TELEPHONE
(08) 8666 2110

WEBSITE
www.northstarhotel.com.au

RATES
$195–$225 for hotel rooms; $160 single/double for trucks; $110–$160 per room for cottage. Extra person rate $30.

HOURS
Wed–Sun 10am–late.

GRUB
Open for lunch Wed–Sun 12–2pm and dinner Thurs–Sat 6–8.30pm. Open every day during SA school holidays.

TOP DROP
The hotel is a cellar door for Bundaleer Wines, produced in the Southern Flinders Ranges. Its wines include Shiraz, Cabernet Sauvignon, Riesling, Chardonnay, Sparkling White and Sparkling Shiraz. Among the beers on tap are Maiden Ale, King Brown and Schweinhund.

NEARBY ATTRACTIONS
Melrose is the centre for bike riding in the Flinders Ranges, with many trails around the town. Bike hire is available and you can borrow racquets and balls for a hit on the local tennis courts. There are also many walking trails in Mt Remarkable National Park, and the Heysen Trail runs through the town. A small museum features colonial furniture and farm implements.

MORE INFO
www.southaustralia.com

Overland Corner Hotel

OVERLAND CORNER HOTEL

OVERLAND CORNER

BUSHRANGERS, DROVERS, OVERLANDERS – and in modern times tourists – have all beaten a path to the Overland Corner. In the early 1800s, this was a popular and convenient resting place on the track between New South Wales and Adelaide, as well as a stopping point for paddlesteamers plying the Murray River and coach passengers between Adelaide and Wentworth. By 1855 the Overland Corner had a police station, a horse-staging building, blacksmith's forge, wheelwright's shop and a general store. The hotel came later, in 1859.

Overland Corner is a touch more than 20 kilometres from the town of Barmera. Driving from Waikerie, you cross the Murray River aboard a free vehicle and foot-passenger ferry and in a few minutes are on the other side. The Overland Corner Reserve is a 300-hectare nature reserve – which includes the hotel – managed by the National Trust of South Australia.

Wild and colourful tales of the early days of the pub abound. One visitor who was not always welcome was the daring and infamous bushranger Andrew George Scott, known as Captain Moonlight. The Irish-born adventurer became a lay preacher in Victoria but after time behind bars for a bank robbery moved on to bushranging.

The pub is listed by the National Trust

In 1879, while on the run from the New South Wales and Victorian police, Moonlight used the Overland Corner Hotel as a watering hole. His gang was said to have once locked the local constable in his own cell, re-shod their horses and then retired to the bar to quench their thirst. Moonlight would ride his horse into the bar and demand that both the back and front doors be left open to allow a quick escape if necessary! Eventually, he was captured in New South Wales and hanged at Sydney's Darlinghurst Gaol in 1880.

The Overland Corner Hotel is 'both pub and living museum'. Just 670 metres from the Murray River, it was built by the Brand brothers – William, Henry and George – for the enterprising pioneer pastoralist John Chambers, of nearby Cogdogla Station, who recognised the need for accommodation for travellers. Cogdogla was where explorer John McDouall Stuart came to select the horses he would use in his travels. A photo of Chambers, wearing a rakish eye-patch, hangs in the hotel bar today.

The hotel, the oldest building in South Australia's Riverland, was built of fossilised limestone, the walls being about a metre and a half thick. It boasts the biggest beer

The hotel, the oldest building in South Australia's Riverland, was built of fossilised limestone, the walls being about a metre and a half thick.

garden in the region, a good spot to munch on the excellent burgers and other pub grub on offer (there's a kids' menu, too). Behind the hotel the river flats that once grazed up to 30 000 sheep provide good camping spots.

Inside, the bar has a log fire burning and beyond it a small dining room with another fireplace to warm yourself. Small rooms at the back hold a pool table and lots of pioneering memorabilia – but no poker machines.

After being delicensed in 1898, the building continued to house a general store and post office, and the old post office is still set up as a museum in its original room. It also served as a schoolhouse and a private home for many years. In 1965 the hotel was purchased by the National Trust of South Australia and restored; it was relicensed in 1987.

The bar at the Overland Corner Hotel

Three walking trails start from the hotel for those who want explore the beautiful natural surrounds of the area; brochures for the trails are available from the pub. The Heritage Walk leads to the quarry, where the stone used to build the hotel was cut; the quarry walls reveal fossils of sea urchins, limpets and corals. Along the way, you'll also find a small cemetery, an old copper mine and an ochre pit. From the high ground of Banrock Viewpoint, there is a vista across the reserve, the lagoon and the river to the vineyards of Banrock Station.

The Floodplain Walk takes a track at the foot of the cliff, past a 'canoe tree', a river red gum where the ancient scar is still visible. The trail then follows the edge of a lignum swamp – keep an eye open for wildlife – to the lagoon, across an old timber footbridge, thence to the weir where there is an old pump once used for flood irrigation.

Heron's Bend Reserve, a 17-hectare reserve on the Murray River with stunning cliffs and gum trees, is the destination for the third walk. It takes you to an old stone house, the former police station (now privately owned), built in 1877 and closed in 1894. Walk past the police stables to the Heron's Bend fossil cliffs, then climb to the top of the fossilised oyster beds for more wonderful views.

Another stop worth making in the area is Devlin's Pound, on the northern bank of the Murray, off Devlin's Pound Road, 16 kilometres downstream from Overland Corner. The pound forms a natural amphitheatre enclosed by the river and cliffs and was once used as the ideal place to catch brumbies. The cattle-duffer Patrick Devlin used it in the 1890s ... and it's said that Devlin's ghost roams here.

OVERLAND CORNER HOTEL

ADDRESS

Old Coach Rd (off Barmera–Morgan Rd), Overland Corner

TELEPHONE

(08) 8588 7021

EMAIL

historicochotel@activ8.net.au

WEBSITE

www.nationaltrustsa.org.au

HOURS

Open from 11am Tues–Sun; closed Mon (except public holidays), Christmas Day and Good Friday.

GRUB

Open for lunch Tues–Sun 12–2pm and dinner Thurs–Sat 6–8pm (Tues–Wed nights by appt).

TOP DROP

Beers on tap are Hahn Superdry, Coopers Pale Ale, Cascade Light and Carlton Draught.

WHERE TO STAY

There are free camping sites overlooking the Murray River behind the hotel. If you prefer a roof over your head, about 25 km away is the Barmera Lake Resort Motel, Lakeside Dve, Barmera. www.barmeralakeresortmotel.com.au

NEARBY ATTRACTIONS

Banrock Station Wetlands and Cellar Door is a winery with a difference, committed to environmental sustainability. There are walking trails, birdwatching hides and fantastic views. www.banrockstation.com.au

MORE INFO

www.riverland.info
www.southaustralia.com

PRAIRIE HOTEL

PARACHILNA

There's a different take on 'pub grub' at the Prairie: emu fillet mignon, kangaroo fillet and camel sausage

Prairie Hotel, Parachilna

LEANING BACK AGAINST the stone wall of the Prairie Hotel, a desert lemon and lime gelato in hand and a long cool drink of your choice on the table, city life seems remote indeed. And it is ... but that doesn't mean the comforts of civilisation are wanting here. Parachilna may be a long way from anywhere much, but travellers' needs are all met at the Prairie – and then some. Word of its hospitality has travelled, making this outback pub 470 kilometres north of Adelaide a popular oasis in the South Australian desert.

You never know who you'll bump into at the Prairie, as it is often used for television and movie sets, and some of Australia's top country musicians have played here, including Lee Kernaghan, James Blundell, Jimmy Little and John Williamson – who was so taken with the pub that he wrote a song for it, 'Prairie Hotel Parachilna'.

The pub is owned by the Fargher family. Ross Fargher is the fourth generation of his family to run sheep and cattle on Nilpena Station, 35 kilometres north of Parachilna. In 1991, his wife Jane – a relative newcomer to the area, having only arrived in 1984 – took over the old Prairie Hotel and set about transforming it. The stone pub, built in 1905 by William Darmody to serve the railway station, had seen better days.

Jane has turned this formerly run-down old drinking hole into one of Australia's icons and a place where tourists turn up in droves to have a drink, and just to say they've been there. There's no town at Parachilna any more – just the pub. But that's more than enough for most people. When they do arrive, it's likely their expectations will be exceeded.

There's a hint on the roads that there's a different take on 'pub grub' at the Prairie: large signs herald the unique menu ahead. It might sound like a gimmick, but the Prairie's 'feral food' menu offers seriously good fare. The Feral Mixed Grill is the signature dish – emu fillet mignon, kangaroo fillet and camel sausage, served with grilled tomato on a bed of mash, with a red-wine pepper-leaf glaze – and it goes down a treat.

Other top choices – if you want to get into the swing of the theme – are Feral Antipasto (smoked kangaroo, camel mettwurst, emu pâté, goat cheese, bush-tomato chilli jam, chargrilled vegetables and ciabatta) and a main course red goat curry. Pub food with a feral twist includes kangaroo schnitzel, feral meat-lovers' pizza and Prairie burgers – kangaroo, emu or (for the squeamish) Coorong Angus beef. There are other, non-feral, options too, including a good old T-bone steak.

Desserts have a bush-tucker flavour to them – delights such as quandong crumble pie or lemon aspen pannacotta. And if you prefer something simpler, there's gelato (flavours include mango and macadamia, chocolate, or wild berry and vanilla) at $4 for one scoop or $6 for two.

The hotel's original six guest rooms and shared bathroom have been converted to an area offering four 'heritage' rooms (each with their own ensuite) and a small lounge for the use of house guests. Eight large new rooms have also been added to the back of the hotel, sunk a metre below ground level to keep them cool. Some have connecting doors, ideal for families. The new building has been designed to conserve and generate its own energy as there is no electricity supply to Parachilna – until 2002, the pub was powered by a 24-hour diesel generator. All the rooms are modern, but with outback flair. However, there are no televisions or phones. It's deliberate, says Jane, to 'flush you out of your rooms to soak up the environment'.

Prairie Hotel 'feral food'

Aboriginal art from the Utopia community in the Northern Territory hangs in the bedrooms and public areas of the hotel (some of it is for sale), along with work by photographer Peter MacDonald, who specialises in the stunning landscapes of the Flinders Ranges.

Smokers be warned: all smoking is banned in the Prairie Hotel. You can't even buy cigarettes at the bar and the nearest place to purchase them is 17 kilometres away in Angorichina village. Mobile phone reception is also patchy (wander up and down out the front of the hotel and you might get lucky), but you can buy wireless internet cards if you can't bear to be out of touch.

The railway came to Parachilna in 1880. A train – the longest coal train in the world, in fact – still runs through once a day on the line in front of the hotel. It is the Leigh Creek coal train, which rattles through the station and past the pub between 6pm and 8pm every day (not quite like clockwork ... but close). At 2.85 kilometres long, the train of 161 wagons, pulled by three locomotives, moves three million tonnes of coal every year between Leigh Creek, 66 kilometres north of Parachilna, and Port Augusta. A small crowd usually gathers out the front, drinks in hand, to watch it pass.

PRAIRIE HOTEL

ADDRESS
Cnr High St and West Tce, Parachilna

TELEPHONE
(08) 8648 4844

WEBSITE
www.prairiehotel.com.au

RATES
Heritage rooms $195, deluxe rooms $225, executive rooms $320. Budget accommodation (run by the hotel) known as the Parachilna Overflow is almost opposite the pub. It consists of 5 former railway fettlers' cabins for $140–$160, and 12 ATCO portable trailers $55 single, $80 double.

HOURS
Daily 8am–late.

GRUB
Breakfast served from 8am; lunch 11.30am–2.45pm; an all-day grazing menu available at other times; dinner from 6pm.

TOP DROP
The Prairie's own brew, Fargher Lager, is brewed in Mildura, and the pub also specialises in Bundaleer Wines from the Southern Flinders Ranges.

NEARBY ATTRACTIONS
The hotel runs 4WD and aerial tours to destinations including Brachina Gorge, over Lake Eyre and the usually dry salt bed of Lake Torrens. Fargher Air Safaris is run by Ross's pilot brother Ian, who also offers short scenic flights to Wilpena Pound (40 min) and the Desert Plains (75 min).

MORE INFO
www.southaustralia.com

Rising Sun Hotel

AUBURN

Rising Sun Hotel, Auburn

> Clare Valley wines and fresh produce sourced almost exclusively locally are what you will find when you stop at the Rising Sun Hotel.

CLARE VALLEY WINES and fresh produce sourced almost exclusively locally are what you will find when you stop at the Rising Sun Hotel, in the lovely village of Auburn. Paula and Ken Noack, together with their daughter Sarah and her partner, chef James Kolencik, have set about putting their own stamp on the hotel, while retaining the charm that has made it so popular.

When the Noacks bought the lease on the Rising Sun Hotel in 2010 they were determined that their first venture into pubs would be one that supported local producers. The menu, which changes often, includes a Wirreanda steak sandwich and a wagyu beef burger, as well as heartier fare such as locally grown beef and chicken schnitzels. Only seafood – Cowell oysters, barramundi and the Rising Sun's Mediterranean seafood stew – comes from further afield.

Ken, who worked for Taylors Wines in the Clare Valley for 33 years before taking on the pub, brings his vast knowledge of wine to it, which stocks only Clare Valley labels. The same 'buy local' philosophy extends to almost everything in the restaurant. 'We buy our meat from a local butcher – mainly Wirreanda beef – chicken from Riverton, oils from Auburn ... in fact everything we can, except the fish,' says Paula.

Foodies who head to the Clare Valley, one of Australia's most famous wine-producing regions, are seldom disappointed. The region is also rich in history and the lovely bluestone pub has been welcoming locals since 1851, when it was the first commercial building in Auburn. Settlers from England, Ireland and Poland moved into the area during the 1840s and the villages they built are among the prettiest in Australia. Some of South Australia's finest stone buildings are to be seen along Auburn's Main North Road and St Vincent Street, many of them listed on the National Trust and State Heritage registers. Vines were planted to the north of Auburn in the 1850s, and today the Clare Valley has more than 20 wineries.

The first licensee was Joseph Bleechmore, who owned it until 1871. The hotel grew in size to accommodate the men who drove the bullock teams working on the Gulf Copper Trail, the route between the town of Burra and the ships waiting at the head of the Spencer Gulf. Auburn was one of many towns that developed to service the route, as bullock drays laden with ore or mining supplies passed through. The drivers all needed to stop for food, a few ales and a bed for the night.

By 1860, the Rising Sun had 18 rooms, stone stables and a loft. The loft in the stables was a temporary office for the Auburn telegraph, which sent its first message on 3 June 1862. Auburn was an important commercial centre in the 1860s and 1870s, when it boasted two breweries, a foundry, gasworks, a flour mill and a shoe factory.

The existing bluestone hotel was erected in front of an earlier building in 1907, the old building later being replaced by the current accommodation. In the days before refrigeration, the barrels of beer were rolled through the verandah trapdoor into the cellar under the main bar, and the beer was then tapped into the bar.

Today there are ten rooms in the hotel, all decorated in 'old world' style. The six standard rooms, either twin or double, are in the hotel, while the other four are in the old Mews next door. The Mews' superior rooms have queen-sized beds and one of them has an extra lounge space with a wood fire and a large claw-footed tub in the bathroom. All rooms have ensuites, flat-screen televisions and tea- and coffee-making facilities. Breakfast is included, either in your bedroom or in the hotel restaurant.

Rising Sun Mews accommodation

The Mews, also built of local bluestone, were once known as the Commercial Rooms, where commercial travellers would show their wares. In World War II, the building was used as accommodation for the Auburn flax mill's workers. The front room of the Mews has also been a saddlery, a boot shop and a barber's shop.

Auburn was the birthplace in 1876 of one of Australia's great authors, C. J. Dennis, best known for *The Songs of a Sentimental Bloke*, published in 1915. He was born in the Auburn Hotel; that hotel no longer stands, but a memorial fountain and a model of the building now mark the site, on the corner of North Street, one block away from the Rising Sun. Dennis, dubbed 'the Laureate of the Larrikins', died in 1938.

Walking through the town is a great way to explore, but for something more active (and perhaps to compensate for all the good food and wine consumed), hit the Riesling Trail by bike or on foot. The 36-kilometre sealed trail was developed after the devastating Ash Wednesday bushfires of 1983, which burnt more than 6100 hectares of the Clare Valley. The railway line between Clare and Penwortham was severely damaged and eventually closed but the old rail route has been transformed into this popular trail that extends from the former Barinia siding in the north to Auburn in the south. A number of loop trails enable cyclists and walkers to explore nearby wineries along the way.

RISING SUN HOTEL

ADDRESS
Cnr Main North Rd and St Vincent St, Auburn

TELEPHONE
(08) 8849 2015

EMAIL
rising@capri.net.au

RATES
Hotel: standard room $70 Mon–Thurs, $90 Fri–Sun; Mews: superior room $115; executive room $145. All rates include continental breakfast.

HOURS
Fri–Mon 8am–late, Tues–Thurs 11am–late.

GRUB
All-day dining from 8am daily.

TOP DROP
Beers on tap include Coopers Pale Ale, Coopers Stout, Hahn Super Dry, West End Draught and Five Seeds Cider.

NEARBY ATTRACTIONS
Martindale Hall, at Mintaro (about 12 km from Auburn), is one of Australia's finest Georgian mansions and was used in the film *Picnic at Hanging Rock*. It is in near-original condition, open to the public daily and a fascinating look at how life once was lived here. www.martindalehall.com

MORE INFO
www.southaustralia.com

The STIRLING HOTEL

STIRLING

The Stirling Hotel balcony

THE LOVELY STONE exterior of the Stirling Hotel, with its iron lacework on the balcony and shady umbrellas in the courtyard at the front, heralds a pub that is well worth a stop. But for those who choose to stay overnight, the colonial charm of the old hotel does not prepare you for the straight-out-of-a-glossy-magazine style of the sleek, modern interiors. After more than a century, the Stirling stands out as one of South Australia's classiest and most comfortable hotels.

The Stirling has been catering to travellers since 1899, when it was built to replace Halfway House, a midway stop-off for those heading from Adelaide to Mount Barker. The old place was destroyed by fire, but the elm at the front survived and is still part of the streetscape. Five Rooms – for that's what the accommodation side of the business is aptly called – opened in early 2010 after a major renovation to the entire hotel. With gorgeous Art Deco mirrors, carefully chosen artwork, a king-sized bed and quirky objets d'art, large comfortable armchairs, flat-screen television, a DVD player, iPod docking station and a fully stocked minibar, it's tempting to consider staying in your room for the whole visit. The list goes on: there's a writing desk, wireless internet, fluffy bathrobes, irons and ironing boards, and tea- and coffee-making facilities (only the best brands). And then there are the bathrooms. In taking the original 12 guest rooms down to five, some have acquired massive ensuites, perfect for the large bathtubs that now have a place there (alongside the dual head rain-showers). Room Five has a spa bath. There's also a flat-screen TV on the bathroom wall – oh, and yes, the remote control is waterproof

THE STIRLING HOTEL

ADDRESS

52 Mount Barker Rd, Stirling

TELEPHONE

(08) 8339 2345

WEBSITE

www.stirlinghotel.com.au

RATES

King rooms $240 double; balcony rooms $290 double. Rates include a $50 voucher for breakfast in the bistro.

HOURS

Mon–Thurs 8–12am; Fri 8–1.30am; Sat 8–1am; Sun 8am–11pm.

GRUB

Bistro: breakfast 8–11am, lunch 12–3pm and dinner 6–9pm weekdays; 12–9pm weekends and public holidays. A limited snack menu available daily 11am–9pm. The Grill restaurant: Wed–Sat 6–9pm, Sun and public holiday Mon 12–3pm.

TOP DROP

There are 11 beers and 2 ciders on tap.

NEARBY ATTRACTIONS

Many of Stirling's beautiful English-style gardens are open to visitors through Australia's Open Garden Scheme (www.opengarden.org.au). On the 4th Sun of each month Druids Ave is closed for the Stirling Market, with local produce, plants and homemade wares.

MORE INFO

www.visitsouthaustralia.com

After more than a century, the Stirling stands out as one of South Australia's classiest and most comfortable hotels.

The beautiful Five Rooms accommodation

(they've really thought of everything!). Attention to detail was paramount when the renovation was planned, even down to electronic labelling of the light switches, so there's no confusion about which switch operates which light.

Three of the rooms have gas fireplaces and access to the balcony overlooking Stirling's pretty tree-lined main street. Each room has stunning modern artwork by Adelaide's Emma Hack; Room Four has a selection of her body art prints.

Along the corridor – which has security doors for guest-only access at the top of the lift – is a communal pantry alcove, containing an espresso machine as well as a full-sized fridge, stove, oven, microwave, washing machine and dryer (it's a nice thought, but possibly seldom used). In a drawer, you'll also find DVDs and board games. Further along the hallway is a steam room just big enough for two.

Tempting though it may be to wallow in the laid-back luxury of your room, venturing downstairs doesn't disappoint. The relaxed style carries through to the dining area and bar, and it's obvious this is a well-loved watering hole for the locals as well as those who make the 20-minute drive up the freeway from Adelaide.

Fine dining at the Grill

For formal dining, the light-filled Grill is open at weekends, but during the week everyone gravitates to the casual bistro on the other side of the main bar or to the outdoor seating on the terrace at the front of the hotel. The cuisine is modern Australian, the prices are reasonable and the service is slick but friendly.

At the Grill, the menu offers steaks (from a 250 gram Clare Valley sirloin to a 500 gram Angus aged beef T-bone) with a choice of four sauces – sparkling shiraz jus, green peppercorn, smoked tomato chutney or mushroom – along with other delectable dishes. The bistro menu is simpler, with burgers, salt-and-pepper squid and other pub staples. Gourmet pizzas are available in the evenings and can be ordered to take away.

The main bar has two pool tables, a video jukebox and plasma screens, as well as live entertainment every Friday and Saturday from 9pm, and Sundays from 3pm. Happy hours are 5.30–6.30pm Monday to Thursday and 9pm–12am on Friday and Saturday.

Stirling is home to some of South Australia's most beautiful homes, built as summer houses by Adelaide's wealthy in the 1800s to escape the heat of the plains. There are also galleries, boutiques, country markets and wineries to explore in the area. The best times to visit are spring and autumn, when the tree-lined streets are alive with colour.

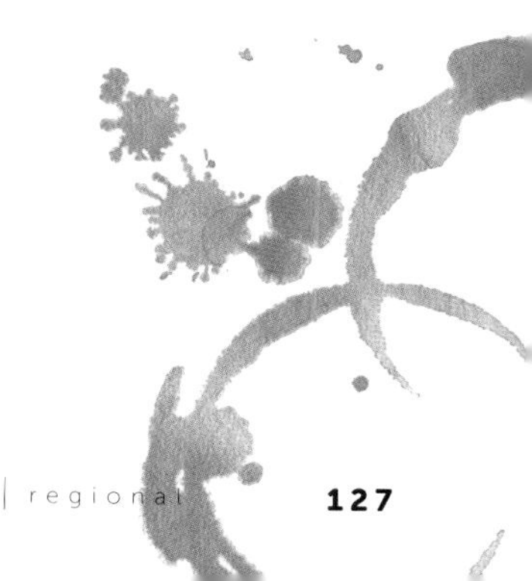

TUMBY BAY HOTEL

TUMBY BAY

Tumby Bay Hotel

KIDS DANGLE FISHING lines from the pier, grey nomads pull their vans and trailers into the parking bay specially designed for them along the foreshore, seagulls call and fish and chips on the beach is almost compulsory at Tumby Bay.

A 10-kilometre crescent of white sand runs the length of this lovely bay on the eastern side of the southern Eyre Peninsula, about 600 kilometres from Adelaide and 50 kilometres from Port Lincoln. A walking path dotted with memorials, playgrounds, barbecues and park benches to sit on and drink in the view extends along the foreshore, while the backdrop to the township is rolling farmland and the Koppio Hills. Overlooking it all is the imposing Tumby Bay Hotel. Its size – and its red roof – sets it apart and it's been part of the scenery in this seaside town since 1904, when it was built for an early pioneer of the district, Mr Mortlake of Yalluna Station.

Overlooking it all is the imposing Tumby Bay Hotel. Its size – and its red roof – sets it apart and it's been part of the scenery in this seaside town since 1904.

Explorer Matthew Flinders was the first to sight Tumby Bay, in 1802 on his voyage of discovery around Australia. He later named it after the small village of Tumby in Lincolnshire. Settlers arrived in the 1840s and a jetty was built in 1874 to ship grain, but was later demolished and replaced with the current jetty in 1908, at about the same time the Tumby Bay Hotel was going to add a second storey. Sydney F. Potter was the first in a long line of line of publicans, including members of the Dunn family, who ran the hotel from 1955 to 1976.

Much of the hotel's history has been lost, but photographs exist and many are displayed on the walls in the foyer and dining room. The original hotel was only one storey but in around 1908 the second floor, with its ornate wrap-around balcony overlooking the bay, was added. What is known is that the Front Bar of the pub has been serving customers for more than a century without changing too much at all. The bar itself is made from recycled wood from the original Tumby Bay pier.

The Front Bar extends out onto the street, with a sheltered pergola area (there are blinds to shade patrons from UV rays) providing a place to sit with a view of the jetty. Or you can head through the large restaurant to the beer garden. Families love this area – the restaurant has a 'play pen' for toddlers in one corner, while the beer garden has an enclosed grassy area for kids.

The Tumby Bay Hotel has many of the usual pub entertainment options. There's a pool table, televisions in the bar and a menu that offers lots of deals, including a seniors' lunch menu. The normal menu has daily specials (curry or braise, pasta and roast of the day) and Thursday is Schnitzel Night (all schnitzels are under $11). Friday nights offer special steak and seafood menus, and the à la carte menu includes Cowell oysters among the usual line-up of pub grub. Kids aren't forgotten here either, with most of their meals priced at $7 and some fun desserts, like Frog in the Grass: ice-cream with a chocolate frog and lime topping.

Recent and ongoing renovations have transformed the upstairs accommodation into smart, modern suites. There are nine rooms; six of them have doors opening onto the balcony, but all overnight guests have access to this pleasant spot to sit and catch the sea breeze while looking out on the bay.

Six of the bedrooms have ensuites – four are double rooms, the remaining two are family rooms with two bedrooms. The other three rooms have a shared bathroom down the hall. All are newly furnished, with large well-appointed bathrooms, flat-screen televisions, tea- and coffee-making facilities and air conditioning. There's even room service.

There's additional accommodation in four two-storey seafront apartments adjacent to the hotel (and even closer to the foreshore). Each has a kitchen with dishwasher, dining area, lounge with television and DVD player, laundry, secure undercover parking and a two-person spa. There are paved areas outside and upstairs balconies which have stunning views. A small grassy area out the front is great for those with kids.

The township of Tumby Bay, population 1350, extends along the tree-lined foreshore, with the long pier stretching 347 metres out into the bay. It's a popular spot for hopeful fishers – people and birds. Pelicans and gulls swoop, while everyone from kids to old men casts a line in to try their luck. The calm waters of the bay are also popular with scuba divers, for the visibility is excellent and there is abundant marine life. Those who want to go further can head out to the nearby Sir Joseph Banks Group of Islands.

A feature on the foreshore is the tiny Rotunda Art Gallery, home to the Tumby Bay Art Group, which is decorated with a colourful mural by Elliston artist Siv Grava depicting the history of the town. It is open Monday–Wednesday 10am–12pm. There is another local attraction on Berryman Crescent, where a 70-metre boardwalk winds through Australia's most southerly stand of mangroves, with interpretive signs explaining their importance to the environment, ecology and birdlife of the area.

Coopers Stout

TUMBY BAY HOTEL

ADDRESS
1 North Tce, Tumby Bay

TELEPHONE
(08) 8688 2005

WEBSITE
www.tumbybayhotel.com.au

RATES
$100 double, $120 family room (sleeps 4). Seafront apartments $160 double, $30 per extra person.

HOURS
Daily 9am–late.

GRUB
The hotel does not open for breakfast (even for guests) but the Little Jetty Cafe (tel: (08) 8688 2364) across the street is open daily from 9am and the local bakery opens at 7.30am. The hotel serves lunch daily 12–2pm, dinner 6–8pm Mon–Wed and 6–8.30pm Thur–Sun.

TOP DROP
Beers on tap are Hahn Super Dry, Hahn Premium Light, Coopers Pale Ale, Coopers Stout, West End Draught and Hahn 3.5.

NEARBY ATTRACTIONS
Take a stroll out on the pier or on the mangrove boardwalk at Berryman Cres. Visit the C. L. Alexander National Trust Museum (tel: (08) 8688 2760) housed in an old timber schoolroom on West Tce, open Wed 10–11am and Sun 2.30–4.30pm, or by appt.

MORE INFO
www.tumbybay.com
www.tumbybay.sa.gov.au

Western Australia

Opposite (clockwise from top): Yanchep Inn; The Esplanade Hotel, Busselton; Palace Hotel, Kalgoorlie; Sail & Anchor Hotel, Fremantle.

Yanchep Inn

Hotel
Reception
Café & Bar

The BRASS MONKEY

NORTHBRIDGE

The Brass Monkey, Northbridge

SINGLETS AND 'SUITS' sit at the bar together. That's the kind of pub the Brass Monkey is. Backpackers head here for the great deals on beer, pizza and pub grub, but you're just as likely to be rubbing shoulders with businessmen or theatregoers.

This rambling old Northbridge institution has been part of the scenery on William Street since 1897, when it was the Wentworth Hotel – a major renovation in 1988 came with a new name, the Brass Monkey. It's the kind of place that people come back to when they haven't been in Perth for years ... just to have a beer and see if the old place has changed. And the good news is that it hasn't. Or at least not for the past couple of decades.

It might be easy to get lost inside the Brass Monkey, with its many bar areas, but it wouldn't be for long. Right in the heart of Perth's nightlife district, the Brass Monkey is a beacon for friendly locals who'll point you to where you need to be. That might either be upstairs on the Federation-style balcony overlooking the bustle of William Street, in the Sports Bar watching the latest game on the huge plasma screens, or in the sophisticated tapas and wine bar.

It's the kind of place that people come back to when they haven't been in Perth for years ... just to have a beer and see if the old place has changed.

With its corner location on James and William streets, this is a pub with several different personalities. Come in through the glass-fronted bar on William Street and you'll find yourself in a very smart bottleshop-cum-cafe. Enter from James Street, through the courtyard with its palms and stainless-steel furniture and then you'll be in the enormous Main Bar, all brass fittings, wooden panelling and floors, with hand-crafted beers on tap. In the Sports Bar – it can be noisy – fans can watch their favourite teams from the comfort of a chesterfield on a mega-screen linked to Bose surround-sound speakers.

It all flows into one, swirling around the pizza counter and the pool tables. If you're hungry, there are $15 daily specials from 12–9pm. They are advertised on the blackboard outside, offering the same dish for each day every week ... so if it's Thursday try the

The Brass Monkey courtyard

Brass Monkey burger, on Friday it's chilli mussels with garlic bread, and on Saturday chicken parma with chips and salad.

In the GrapeSkin, it's a cooler scene. Stylish cocktails, bubbles, a glass of red with tapas (or something more substantial), live jazz or a DJ. While you're relaxing, others may be just popping in off the street to buy a bottle from the huge range on the other side of the polished marble bar.

Upstairs there's a table-service lounge bar with chesterfields and an open fire in the winter, and the balcony, a perfect spot in summer. The upstairs à la carte restaurant, BrassGrill, serves a selection of char-grilled Western Australian beef, pork, chicken and local seafood, complemented by an extensive Australian wine list.

For theatregoers, the Brass Monkey also teams up with the Black Swan State Theatre Company to offer special meal deals for patrons heading to the new State Theatre Centre of Western Australia, just a couple of minutes' walk away on William Street.

The Brass Monkey's bars have comfy chesterfields

THE FACTS

THE BRASS MONKEY

ADDRESS
209 William St, Northbridge

TELEPHONE
(08) 9227 9596

WEBSITE
www.thebrassmonkey.com.au

HOURS
Mon–Tues 11–12am, Wed–Thurs 11–1am, Fri–Sat 11–2am, Sun 11am–10pm.

GRUB
GrapeSkin Kitchen open Wed–Sat 12–10pm, Sun–Tues 12–9pm; GrapeSkin Lounge Bar & Cafe Mon–Thurs 12pm–12am, Fri–Sat 12pm–1am, Sun 12–10pm; BrassGrill Restaurant & Lounge Bar Wed–Sat from 6pm; Upstairs Lounge & Balcony Bar Wed–Sat from 5pm.

TOP DROP
A range of Australian beer (Beez Neez, Boag's, Little Creatures, Crown Lager, Bohemian Pilsner and Redback Original).

WHERE TO STAY
Quest on James has 1-, 2- and 3-bedroom modern apartments, each with a balcony or patio area, a few blocks from the Brass Monkey. Rates start from around $269 for a 1-bedroom apartment. www.questapartments.com.au

NEARBY ATTRACTIONS
Northbridge is home to several of Perth's major cultural attractions, including the Western Australian Museum, the State Library of WA, the Art Gallery of WA and the Black Swan State Theatre Company.

MORE INFO
www.westernaustralia.com
www.wavisitorcentre.com

ROSE & CROWN

GUILDFORD

The Georgian-style Rose & Crown, Guildford

> The spirits of convicts and previous publicans roam the corridors and cellar; the most notorious is the bushranger Moondyne Joe, who local legend tells hid in the hotel briefly before being captured in the Houghton Winery cellars.

THE WATCHFUL EYE of Thomas Jecks looks down from above the fireplace on the wall of a cosy lounge at the pub that he opened in Guildford in 1841, when the colony of Western Australia was barely a decade old.

The Rose & Crown is the oldest hotel in Western Australia and the third-oldest licensed hotel in Australia. Jecks opened a general store on the site in 1839 and two years later extended the business to include a licensed inn. The beautiful heritage-listed Georgian-style hotel is made of local handmade bricks and still retains many of its original features.

A major renovation by current owners Mark and Tracy Weber, who bought the hotel in 2004, has brought new life to old walls but without sacrificing any of its history. The best place to get a real feel for how it might have been in its early days is take the narrow stairs past the heavy wooden, jail-like door down to the convict-built cellar.

Leather lounges, a swish new bar and moody lighting can't disguise that this must once have been a very eerie place. Thick hand-sawn jarrah beams overhead (one inscribed with the year 1837), handmade nails, brick floors and walls and the blocked-off entrance to a tunnel reek atmosphere. The tunnel, leading from the cellar to the shores of the nearby Swan River, is something of a mystery but is believed to have been used to bring in stores (perhaps among other, less legitimate uses). The cellar also has an old well sunk in the floor.

A portrait of founder Thomas Jecks in a lounge at the Rose & Crown

The mood is lighter in the spacious 1841 dining room, where daily specials keep patrons coming back for more. One such is the Taste Plate ($30), with chicken nori rolls, a mild coconut fish curry with jasmine rice, mini vegetable stacks, almond-crusted ricotta and apricot bake. Among other specials there is always a grill of the day, plus market fish, a pasta dish, a wok of the day, a soup of the day and a choice of two desserts.

Rose & Crown frontage

A single-storey east wing was added in 1890 and was originally used as the bar, restaurant and lodging quarters for weary travellers. In the 1970s when the motel accommodation was built and the hotel was renovated, this area became a restaurant and ballroom space. Today it is a trendy gathering place for locals and visitors as a restaurant and wine bar – aptly named the Posh Convict.

The stables, built directly behind the hotel with Dutch gable ends and a small turret, were constructed in about 1880 and were once used to stable camels trekking to the goldfields and as accommodation for single men.

It is said that the spirits of convicts and previous publicans roam the corridors and cellar of the main hotel building. Among the resident ghosts are said to be an old man in period clothing, who smokes roll-your-own

ROSE & CROWN

ADDRESS
105 Swan St, Guildford

TELEPHONE
(08) 9347 8100

WEBSITE
www.rosecrown.com.au

RATES
Motel: $120 Sun–Thurs, $160 Fri–Sat and public holidays for queen room; $135 Sun–Thurs or $185 Fri–Sat for triple room. Hotel: Emerald $160–$200, Ruby $180–$220, Sapphire $220–$270, Gold $270–$300. Weekend rates include breakfast.

HOURS
Daily 11.30am–late.

GRUB
Open for breakfast weekends 8–10.30am; devonshire tea 10am–12pm and 3–6pm daily; lunch 12–3pm daily; dinner 6–9pm daily.

TOP DROP
There are 9 beers on tap, including Guinness, Becks, James Squire Amber Ale, Redback Original, Cascade Light and several drops from Little Creatures. You'll also find Matso's ginger beer and Monteith's apple and pear ciders.

NEARBY ATTRACTIONS
Visit Woodbridge House, an 1800s National Trust property in nearby West Midland. Take a self-guided heritage walk of Guildford (map from visitor centre) or browse in the James St antiques shops. A craft market is held at the Guildford Town Hall on the 3rd Sun of every month.

MORE INFO
www.swanvalley.com.au

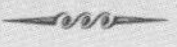

Convict-built brick walls in the cellar bar

cigarettes. Another is believed to be a publican who was killed in the cellar by a falling beam; but the most notorious is the bushranger Moondyne Joe, who local legend tells hid in the hotel briefly before being captured in the Houghton Winery cellars.

Upstairs are four opulent suites – two on each side of the hallway – which have been renovated and updated, with spa baths, plasma televisions and iPod docks. With their aptly rich names, the Sapphire, Emerald, Ruby and Gold rooms are colour-themed and furnished with antiques, but each has its individual style. All but the Emerald Room have spa baths, and the Gold Room has a king- rather than queen-sized bed. The Sapphire Room has a four-poster bed and – like the Gold Room – has doors opening onto the slightly sloping heritage-listed verandah at the front of the hotel.

There are also 25 modern motel rooms centred around a swimming pool. All rooms have queen-sized beds, ensuites, television, air conditioning, fridge and free wireless internet access.

The large beer garden and its lovely gardens are home to the first rose bush ever planted in Western Australia and a dragon tree thought to be more than 150 years old.

Period touches in the opulent suites

SAIL & ANCHOR HOTEL

FREMANTLE

HOLDING TRUE TO its passion for handcrafted beer – despite the closure in 2010 of the brew-house that made it famous – the Sail & Anchor is one of Fremantle's liveliest pubs and a must-visit for beer aficionados. The brewing tanks are still in place, but no longer can you sit with a beer and watch the brewers going about their work to produce the drop you are drinking.

Originally the Freemasons Hotel, the pub was redeveloped and renamed in 1984 by Phil Sexton and his partners in the Matilda Bay Brewing Company. It was Australia's first pub brewery and fast developed an international reputation for its handcrafted beer.

The rejuvenation of the Sail & Anchor was timely. By 1987, when Fremantle was the base for Australia's successful challenge for the America's Cup, the pub was hugely popular and became a haunt for yachties and their supporters, who filled the bars and spilled out onto the upstairs balcony overlooking Fremantle's 'cappuccino strip' along South Terrace.

Sail & Anchor Hotel is one of Freo's liveliest pubs

The Sail & Anchor team are passionate about their beer and you won't often find mainstream or mass-market brands here.

Matilda Bay Brewing – and the Sail & Anchor – was bought by Carlton United Brewers in 1990, and the pub continued to pump out its popular range of boutique beers, winning many awards as it did so. The most notable success was the India Pale Ale, which is served under hand-pump, along with popular brands Redback and Beez Neez. Another change of ownership, however, resulted in the closure of the hotel's brewing operations in early 2010. The house beers are now made under contract by Feral Brewing Company in the Swan Valley.

However, the Sail & Anchor team under manager Matthew Marinich (described by one colleague as a 'beer jedi') are still passionate about their beer, and in 2010 the pub won

SAIL & ANCHOR HOTEL

ADDRESS
64 South Tce, Fremantle

TELEPHONE
(08) 9431 1666

WEBSITE
www.sailandanchor.com.au

HOURS
Mon–Tues 11am–11pm, Wed–Thurs 11–12am, Fri–Sat 11–1am, Sun 10am–10pm. Lounge Bar open Fri 4pm–12.30am, Sat 12pm–12.30am, Sun 12–6pm.

GRUB
Daily 12–9pm.

TOP DROP
The signature beer is Sail & Anchor India Pale Ale, but there are plenty of other handcrafted beers on tap to try, including Brass Monkey Stout, Fremantle Pilsner and Sail Blonde Wheat Beer.

WHERE TO STAY
The Esplanade Hotel is an 1897 colonial hotel with 300 rooms, close to the harbour, which has been modernised recently. Room rates start around $200 a night. www.esplanadehotelfremantle.com.au

NEARBY ATTRACTIONS
Most of Fremantle's attractions, including the Fremantle Arts Centre, Fremantle Prison, the Roundhouse and the Shipwreck Galleries, are within walking distance of the Sail & Anchor. Don't miss the wonderful Western Australian Maritime Museum at the western end of the harbour; www.museum.wa.gov.au/maritime

MORE INFO
www.fremantlewa.com.au

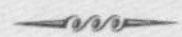

The Main Bar at the Sail & Anchor

Beer Venue of the Year for Western Australia. Showcasing small-output handcrafted beers from Western Australia and around the world is still vitally important to the pub, and you won't often find mainstream or mass-market brands here.

The Sail & Anchor is one of Australia's most awarded small breweries. Against competitors from around the world it has won a plethora of gold, silver and bronze awards over the years. It also won three silver medals and one bronze at the 2009 Australian International Beer Awards for its India Pale Ale, Brass Monkey Stout, Chilli Beer and Sail Blonde Wheat Beer.

There is plenty of beer to choose from

Walk in off the street and you'll find yourself in the Main Bar, with its original wooden floors and wrap-around bar. Beyond that is the leafy beer garden, and upstairs is the Lounge Bar with a cocktail menu and laidback couches, leading out to the wrap-around balcony. The extensive menu offers a wide selection from nibbles to light meals, or filling traditional pub grub, as well as pizzas, kebabs, tapas and steaks (all grain-fed Western Australian beef). On Wednesday nights from 7.30pm singer–songwriters claim the stage in the Green Room, and there's also music on Friday and Saturday nights with local DJs.

Special events see the Sail & Anchor inundated with tourists and locals. One of the biggest is the annual Fremantle Festival in November, when the streets are closed to traffic and the party rages. Much of the action, including the big street parade, is on South Terrace, with the pub at the heart of things. To coincide with the festival, the Sail & Anchor runs a month-long 'Novembeer' showcase of Australian craft beer. This includes ales from around 25 breweries, and the pub features about 60 on tap throughout the month. There are free tastings, special keg tappings, beer tapas and merchandise on sale.

The Sail & Anchor has a reputation for its handcrafted beer

A game of pool, or the action on the big screen

CASTLE HOTEL

YORK

The impressive, rambling Castle Hotel, York

IF IT'S MONDAY night at the Castle, the ghost of Basil Craig may well be restless (and so might you, if you're looking for a quiet night). Monday is karaoke night and it's a hit with the locals. But when the music's finished and everyone's gone home, the occupants of Room 20 in this historic pub might still feel a presence: the spirit of Basil Craig, a member of the family who owned and ran the hotel from 1850 until 1990, is said to haunt the room.

The Castle is an impressive rambling place, right on the main street of one of Western Australia's interesting heritage-listed towns. It is the oldest pub in inland Western Australia, and one of only three surviving pubs in York.

Samuel Smale Craig used ticket-of-leave men from the York Convict Hiring Depot to build the elegant Georgian two-storey brick hotel.

A smaller hotel was built on the site by John Henry Monger and sold to the Craig family in 1850. In 1853, Samuel Smale Craig used ticket-of-leave men from the York Convict Hiring Depot to build the existing elegant Georgian two-storey brick hotel; in 1862, he extended it along Avon Terrace. Samuel Craig died in 1869 and for the next 50 years the pub was run by women – his widow Mary, and later by Emily, widow of their son James. It was Emily who built the Federation-style wing facing South Street in 1905. After World War I, Emily handed over the business to her son Basil, who ran it until after World War II (and who's apparently never wanted to leave).

Situated 97 kilometres from Perth along the Great Southern Highway, in the Avon Valley, York was first settled in 1831, just two years after the establishment of the Swan River Colony. With the discovery of gold at Southern Cross in 1889, the town boomed as all travellers to the goldfields passed through York – it is now classified as an historic town by the National Trust.

Like most of York's historic buildings, the hotel has maintained its heritage by not changing its exterior. Inside, it has been upgraded and maintained, air-conditioned to deal with the heat and has added modern facilities like a swimming pool for guests staying in the hotel rooms and in the modern motel units at the back, adjacent to the large garden bar.

There are 24 motel rooms and 24 pub rooms, including two family suites (the one in the hotel has a spa and a fireplace). All rooms have an ensuite, fridge, tea- and coffee-making facilities, colour television and reverse-cycle air conditioning. Hotel rooms have an LCD screen for DVD players.

Behind the accommodation wings are two old stable blocks in the courtyard. These are the only part of the hotel that was damaged in the 6.9 magnitude earthquake that hit York in 1968.

During renovations in 1989, one of the dining-room walls was stripped of old paint, revealing a coat of arms, the insignia of the Order of the Garter, the highest order of English chivalry, with the motto: *Honi soit qui mal y pense* (Shame on him who thinks this evil). The history of that coat of arms and how it came to be in the pub remains a mystery.

The hotel has traditional interiors

During the late 19th century, the Castle Hotel was the venue for a large banquet attended by influential members of the York Agricultural Society on the eve of the annual York Agricultural Show. The show has been running for more than 165 years and is still held every September at the York Racecourse on Spencers Brook Road.

The menu in Craig's Bistro ranges from wood-fired pizza to steaks or garlic prawns and of course meals for the kids on the 'Little Buggers' menu – the usual mix of chicken nuggets, fish and chips, cheeseburgers, bangers and mash, steak and chips or spaghetti bolognaise for $12.50. Pizzas can be ordered at dinner Thursday–Sunday or for lunch on weekends in the Garden Bar courtyard, where there's a pool table and jukebox.

There may be plastic flowers and paper doilies on the tables, but the surroundings are finer, with pressed-metal ceilings and walls. Licensee Nicky Worthing, whose family owns the pub, says much of the lovely old dinner service, historic photos and other treasures that helped tell the story of the hotel were removed by a previous management.

On Sunday nights, the bistro has a self-service ('once only', instructs the barmaid) roast of the day for $17.50; on other nights the menu is à la carte. A barbecue area is also available for overnight guests to use.

In the Shearer's Bar you'll find a mix of locals and visitors, and if you time it right you might hear some daring stories from the skydivers who come to jump at Western Australia's largest skydiving centre, Skydive Express on Spencers Brook Road, about 10 kilometres out of town.

CASTLE HOTEL

ADDRESS
97 Avon Tce, York

TELEPHONE
(08) 9641 1007

WEBSITE
www.castlehotel.com.au

RATES
Hotel: $100 single, $120 double or twin, $160 executive spa suite (sleeps 2 adults and 2 children). Motel: $125 single, $140 double or twin, $160 family suite (sleeps 2 adults and 2 children), $170 executive spa suite. Extra adult $15, extra child $10. Seniors' discount of 10 per cent. All rates include self-serve continental breakfast.

HOURS
Open weekdays from 12pm, weekends from 11am.

GRUB
Breakfast for guests daily 7.30–10am. The bistro open for lunch weekdays 12–2pm, weekends 12–2.30pm, and dinner from 6pm daily.

TOP DROP
There are 12 taps in the bar, serving a range of Swan and Carlton beers.

NEARBY ATTRACTIONS
Drop into the magnificent York Town Hall on Avon Tce (the main street), which is also the visitor information centre. Other buildings worth visiting are the Old Gaol and Courthouse (1895) and the Residency Museum (1843), in York's oldest house. The York Motor Museum has a collection of veteran, classic and racing cars.

MORE INFO
www.yorkwa.org
www.york.wa.gov.au

CAVES HOUSE *Hotel*

YALLINGUP

Caves House Hotel, Yallingup

YALLINGUP MEANS 'PLACE of love' in the language of the Wardandi indigenous people, and as if to prove it honeymooners have been heading to Caves House Hotel for more than a century. As soon as you step inside, it's easy to see why. This is a warm, charming and romantic hotel, stylish and comfortable at the same time, luxurious without being over the top.

Yallingup is 292 kilometres south of Perth and is surrounded by the ruggedly beautiful Leeuwin–Naturaliste National Park. As well as having some of the best surfing breaks in Australia, Yallingup also has a protected lagoon for swimming and snorkelling. Caves House is the perfect place to stay for those who want to do nothing at all, as well as those who prefer to get out and about.

The hotel is set in 4.5 hectares of sweeping gardens, a short distance from Yallingup beach and within easy reach of the Margaret River vineyards. A ten-minute walk through the gardens and along a bush path brings you to the reason Caves House was built in the first place – the Ngilgi Caves. The hotel was established by the Western Australia government to cater for tourists flocking to see this natural wonder, which should be a 'must' for all visitors.

A ghost called Molly roams the hotel (she loves Room Six), waiting – so they say – for her lover to come home from sea.

The original Ngilgi Cave was discovered in 1899 by Edward Dawson, who became its first guide when it opened to the public. The cave system, which now has stairs and boardwalks to a depth of 37 metres in the main Show Cave, is a spectacular display of stalactites, stalagmites, shawls and other natural formations.

By mid 1902, the cave system was such a popular attraction the government decided to build accommodation for visitors. Caves House was completed in early 1905, a two-storey timber building with an iron roof. It had nine single and three double bedrooms, dressing rooms with toilets and bathrooms and a smoking room.

The first hotel was badly damaged by fire in 1930. The present Caves House was built in 1938, with a striking Tudor-baronial exterior and Art Deco interior. In 1993 it was classified by the National Trust. In recent years, the hotel has had a major refurbishment and in 2008 it won a Heritage Council Award for outstanding conservation and/or

interpretation of a place listed in the State Register of Heritage Places. Historic photos are displayed throughout, along with a marvellous collection of old movie posters.

Caves House has always been a favourite wedding and honeymoon destination and it is not unusual to find your fellow guests are celebrating their anniversaries at the place in which they honeymooned as long ago as 50 or 60 years before. It's an equally popular spot for surfers who like to hang out on the jarrah deck at the side of the Long Bar.

Some regulars come for miles for the 'Sunday sessions' of live music that have been running since the 1960s. Surfboards hang from the ceiling and walls of the Long Bar (named for the classic polished long counter-top, as well as for the local long-board surfers). Plasma televisions on the walls show the latest sporting events, and there are eight-ball tables and dartboards.

The menu in Caves Bistro offers a wide selection, using fresh local produce where possible, including seafood, steak, poultry, salad, pizza and many other traditional bistro styles, as well as a kids' menu. Meals are ordered at the bar and can be eaten either in the bistro dining room, at a table in the bar (both have fireplaces) or outside on the deck that extends into the garden bar.

The hotel bedrooms are comfortable and peaceful

The hotel has many moods that reflect each season. Sitting by the fireplace in the front guest lounge in winter, it feels like someone's living room, but a summer afternoon in the garden bar with the music raging produces a very different vibe.

In the recent refurbishment, the bedrooms were made larger and all now have a marble-tiled ensuite bathroom, while some have an adjacent sitting room. The choice ranges from heritage standard rooms to deluxe spa rooms with double spa baths, some with balconies and views of the garden and ocean, or luxury spa suites which also have a lounge area. The Injidup Suite – the honeymoon suite – has a separate lounge with open fireplace, marble ensuite with double spa bath, a large balcony overlooking the gardens and ocean, and a king-sized bed.

While couples can luxuriate in the comfort of the hotel, if you're with a larger party or have brought the family, there's ideal accommodation for you too. Seashells Yallingup, built within the Caves House grounds, is a complex of 40 resort-style one- and two-bedroom apartments, each with its own large balcony.

And if Caves House is not romantic enough already, a tale of lost love comes with it. A ghost called Molly roams the hotel (she loves Room Six), waiting – so they say – for her lover to come home from the sea.

CAVES HOUSE HOTEL

ADDRESS
Yallingup Beach Rd, Yallingup

TELEPHONE
(08) 9750 1500

WEBSITE
www.caveshousehotel.com.au

RATES
Caves House Hotel: deluxe spa suite $260, luxury spa suite $290, Injidup Suite $400. Seashells Yallingup: 1-bedroom apartment $260, 2-bedroom $375 ($30 surcharge applies Fri–Sat nights).

HOURS
The Long Bar open from 11am Mon–Sat and from 12pm Sun.

GRUB
The bistro open for breakfast 8–11am, lunch 12–3pm and dinner 6–9pm daily.

TOP DROP
Among the beers on tap expect to find Hahn Super Dry, Hahn 3.5, Teds, James Squire Golden Amber, James Squire Amber Ale, Becks, Heineken, Swan Draught, Coopers and Carlton Dry, as well as Five Seeds cider.

NEARBY ATTRACTIONS
Ngilgi Cave has semi-guided tours (you set your own pace but guides are on hand to answer questions) 10am–3.30pm daily. Access is on boardwalks through several of the most impressive chambers. Adventure tours, involving crawling and climbing by torchlight, run daily and take 2–3 hrs. www.geographebay.com

MORE INFO
www.geographebay.com
www.westernaustralia.com

The ESPLANADE Hotel

BUSSELTON

The Esplanade Hotel, Busselton

SATURDAY NIGHT IS a big night at the Esplanade Hotel in Busselton, the night when the cool crowd turns out to sip cocktails in the glitzy Gold Bar or lines up at the bistro for a family meal.

On Sunday mornings a regular turn-out shows up for Church in the Pub, and the walls ring with the sound of gospel music.

But on Sunday mornings this sprawling hotel really shows its point of difference. That's when a regular turn-out – about a hundred people – shows up for Church in the Pub, and the walls ring with the sound of gospel music.

'In this business, we found we couldn't get to church ourselves, so we decided we could bring the church to us,' says Glennys White, who has owned the Esplanade with her husband Lance since 2005. So at 9.30am on Sundays, the congregation gathers in Dallys Room at the pub for a service led by Christian surfer Noel Kara, of the Down South Gospel Church.

Dallys Room, like the other function and dining rooms at the hotel, is named for one of the White children. The others are Courtney, Maddison and Ryan – and it's not unlikely you might find one of their namesakes serving behind the bar, for this is very much a family-run pub. The family-friendly feeling is obvious in other ways too, most notably the grassy playground with colourful slides and climbing frames, carefully fenced from the road and next to the front beer garden.

Despite its name, the Esplanade Hotel is not on the esplanade. It is one block back from the Busselton beachfront and jetty, separated from Geographe Bay by a park and carparking area. Glennys White says she's not sure how that came to be – perhaps a change in the streetscape since the original hotel was built in 1898.

With 37 rooms, the hotel is a popular weekender for people from Perth, a 218-kilometre or easy two-hour drive away, and no matter how busy it gets the Whites have a reputation for never turning anyone away. 'Even when the town is full, we can usually find a place for someone, if they don't mind being on a rollaway in one of the empty meeting rooms, and I've even been known to take people home with us,' says Glennys.

The Esplanade Hotel's Gold Bar

There are rooms in the hotel as well as a modern complex of smart motel rooms at the back. The hotel rooms are basic, mostly with shared bathrooms down the hall, but have televisions, fridges and air conditioning. Room 35, which has five beds in it, is the only one with a private bathroom, but it can be noisy as it is directly above the main bar.

The Gold Bar

The motel rooms offer more space and privacy, and include a couple of two-bedroom family apartments which can sleep up to seven and have their own kitchen. There are also two apartments in the hotel, each with two bedrooms, suitable for families. The hotel offers free wireless internet access to guests, and the motel rooms have all you need, right down to a kettle, toaster and iron.

THE ESPLANADE HOTEL

ADDRESS
Marine Tce, Busselton

TELEPHONE
(08) 9752 1078

WEBSITE
www.esplanadehotelbusselton.com.au

RATES
Hotel: $60 single, $80 double. Motel: standard room $80 single, $110 double; superior room $110 single, $140 double; family room (sleeps 4) $220.

HOURS
Sun–Thurs 10am–11pm, Fri–Sat 10–1am.

GRUB
Daily for lunch 12–2pm; dinner Sun–Wed 6–8pm and Thurs–Sat 6–8.30pm.

TOP DROP
There are 14 international and local beers on tap, including Emu Bitter, Swan Draught, Kilkenny, Guinness, James Squire, Hahn, Tooheys, Boag's and XXXX Gold, as well as a large selection of cider. Wines are mainly from WA.

NEARBY ATTRACTIONS
The 1.8 km Busselton Jetty, the longest timber pier in the Southern Hemisphere, is 2 min walk from the hotel. It has an underwater observatory at the end, 8 m below sea level; if you don't want to walk to the end you can catch the Jetty Train. There is an interpretive centre in the jetty boatshed. www.busseltonjetty.com.au

MORE INFO
www.westernaustralia.com and www.geographebay.com

The Esplanade hosts some of Busselton's biggest parties and events, with bands and DJs in the pergola in the garden bar (with heaters in the winter), and live music on Thursday, Friday and Saturday nights. You might also catch theme nights or special events – like the Ralph Swimwear Model Search or a visit from a *Cleo* Bachelor of the Year (actor Firass Dirani was a hit). Major events on the local calendar include the week-long Festival of Busselton in late January, and the annual Half Ironman in May and Ironman Western Australia Triathalon in December.

WA wines dominate the list

The large Sports Bar, which opens onto a small terrace, has a stage for bands, three pool tables, a jukebox, and 12 flat-screen televisions showing sports all day. The blackboard bar menu has pub grub, with nothing priced over $15 (steak and chips is $12.95).

More sophisticated is the Gold Bar & Lounge, which opens out onto the Gold Bar Beer Garden. With red and black couches and armchairs, the room is accented with gold; this is the place for a quiet daiquiri, margarita or 'shaken special'.

In the bistro, the lines at the bar to order meals can be long on busy nights, but the food is good and the atmosphere congenial. The blackboard menu is extensive, with all the usual pub grub items as well as curries, seafood, pasta and risotto and more. Any main course costing more than $20 also comes with soup and salad. In summer months, there's pizza as well.

And if you happen to see the ghostly figure of a man in a top hat, you won't be the first. He might just have wandered in from the old pioneer cemetery next door to the bottleshop.

A playground makes the Esplanade family friendly

MARGARET RIVER HOTEL

MARGARET RIVER

Guest room at the Margaret River Hotel

The unusual names of the gourmet wood-fired pizzas are all surfing points along the Margaret River coast – Huzza, Injidup Point, North Point, South Point, Redgate, Smiths, Lefthanders and Boodjidup.

IN THE 1970S the Margaret River Hotel was considered a hangout for surfers, musicians and hippies. It had moved on from the days when guests had their shoes polished for them, and indulged in formal four-course dinners in the evening. Today, things are different again. Still very much a 'local', the hotel has had a facelift that includes elegant and comfortable guest rooms upstairs and a smart restaurant with a wood-fired pizza oven warming up a corner.

But some things stay the same. The relaxed vibe is obvious from the minute you drive along Margaret River's main street and see the patrons at the open Corner Bar, suitably named for its location at the junction of Willmott Avenue and Bussell Highway. This is still the most popular drinking hole in town, the place to meet and to watch the passing parade.

Locals and visitors alike also like to gather in the beer garden (heated in winter) to catch up with friends, watch sport on the big screen or shoot some pool. On Thursday, Friday and Saturday nights there's live entertainment.

Margaret River township was settled in the 1850s, taking its name from the river named by pioneer John Bussell, but it was not gazetted until 1913. In 1922 about a

MARGARET RIVER HOTEL

ADDRESS
125 Bussell Hwy, Margaret River

TELEPHONE
(08) 9757 2655

WEBSITE
www.margaretriverhotel.com.au

RATES
Hotel: economy room from $105 double, standard room from $120 double, family room (sleeps 3) from $145, spa room from $170 double. Motel: double room from $120, triple room from $145, king room with spa from $170. Rates $30 higher per night in peak season. Extra person rate $25.

HOURS
Wine Bar open daily 12pm–late; Corner Bar open Mon–Sat 12pm–12am, Sun 12–10pm.

GRUB
Bistro open for lunch from 12pm daily, dinner from 6pm. Breakfast not available but there are lots of cafes along the main street.

TOP DROP
Eleven beers are on tap: Little Creatures, Carlton Draught, Coopers Pale Ale, Coopers Mild, James Squire Golden Ale, Tooheys Extra Dry, Swan Draught, Boag's Draught, Pure Blonde, Stella and Guinness, plus Bulmer's cider.

NEARBY ATTRACTIONS
There are more than 100 wineries and cellar doors to visit in the Margaret River region. There are great beaches, fishing, diving and surfing, as well as caving, forest walks, horseriding, walking trails along the river and more.

MORE INFO
www.margaretriver.com

hundred settlers, mainly from England, moved to the area to open up new farming land. Built in 1936 by Bernard McKeown, the Margaret River Hotel was the first pub in town. The front lounge was added in 1961 and the bar was extended as Margaret River's popularity as a destination for tourists and wine lovers grew. The hotel was sold by the McKeown family in 1972 and since then has undergone further extensions and renovations.

Margaret River Hotel

After a big day of touring, or taking the 277-kilometre three-hour drive from Perth, the hotel is a welcoming spot to arrive. It offers traditional country-style accommodation with a contemporary feel, from standard and economy ensuite rooms to a deluxe spa room and a family room. For those staying overnight, there is a small guest lounge upstairs with an open fireplace and the latest magazines to browse through.

Economy rooms are small, with a double bed; standard rooms are a little larger with a queen-sized and king single bed, or a king-sized bed. Spa rooms have a king-sized bed, an open fireplace and a double spa bath in the ensuite. The family room is two rooms with an adjoining door: one has a queen-sized bed and the other has two singles, while both rooms share an ensuite bathroom and a balcony. All rooms have a television, tea- and coffee-making facilities, hairdryer, iron and a telephone (and in the family accommodation, each bedroom has these amenities).

As well as the 11 hotel rooms, there are also 35 large and modern motel rooms behind the hotel, across the carpark. All these have reverse-cycle air conditioning, a television, microwave, toaster, tea- and coffee-making facilities, an iron and a hairdryer.

On the highway street-front, away from the Corner Bar, is the small Wine Bar which leads into the bistro – meals are not served in the bar at night. The bistro's large à la carte menu has traditional pub specials such as veal parmigiana, bangers'n'mash, chilli mussels, and beef and ale pie, as well as some 'MRH house specials' which include a Thai green chicken curry, chargrilled sirloin steak, surf'n'turf and Mount Barker chicken (braised in Moroccan spices with sweet potato ragout, eggplant, preserved lemon chutney and yoghurt).

If you are wondering about the unusual names of the large range of gourmet wood-fired pizzas, they are all surfing points along the Margaret River coast – Huzza, Injidup Point, North Point, South Point, Redgate, Smiths, Lefthanders and Boodjidup. And, of course, the wine list – as you would expect – is extensive, with more than 40 varieties from the Margaret River wine region to choose from.

One of the great things about this pub is its location right on the main street. Walk outside and you are in the heart of the action, with cafes, restaurants, shops, galleries, wine bars and more.

MUNDARING WEIR
HOTEL

MUNDARING WEIR

WHEN JENS JORGENSEN bought the run-down old Mundaring Weir Hotel in 1984, there were rusting car bodies on the lawns, the patrons were mostly bikie gangs, and it was on the verge of closing down.

'It's more than 20 years since I last served a patch,' he says now, surveying the two-storey brick pub, with its sweeping gardens and 2000-seat amphitheatre at the back. 'It's a family pub now.'

The amphitheatre has been a key part of the revival of this fantastic pub in the heart of Mundaring State Forest, surrounded by jarrah trees, about 45 minutes from Perth's city centre. About a year after buying the hotel, Jorgensen hit on the idea of holding a concert.

'We hired David Helfgott; part of the idea of having a classical music concert was to discourage the bikies from coming and to attract a new kind of crowd,' he says. It was a huge hit, attracting around 800 people, and Helfgott has returned every year since, along with dozens of other top acts at what are now locally famed concerts. Other big-name artists who have appeared include Marianne Faithfull, flautist Jane Rutter, the Platters, Kate Ceberano, Gerry and the Pacemakers and the Black Sorrows.

Mundaring Weir Hotel

The amphitheatre has been a key part of the revival of this fantastic pub in the heart of Mundaring State Forest, surrounded by jarrah trees.

The hotel was built in 1898 by Fred Jacoby on the first piece of freehold land in the area. The original one-storey building, which is still there behind the later addition, was called the Reservoir Hotel. It housed the local post office in a room next to the bar.

C.Y. O'Connor, the engineer responsible for Western Australia's goldfields water supply pipeline, used the hotel as his office when he visited the weir site, often staying overnight in one of the upstairs rooms rather than travelling back to Perth at night. The 560-kilometre pipeline – the lifeline for the goldfield towns – starts at Mundaring Weir, on the Helena River, and runs to Kalgoorlie. It is the world's longest freshwater pipeline, pumping an average of 90 million tonnes of water each day since it opened in 1903.

The ballroom-sized dining area at the Mundaring Weir Hotel

MUNDARING WEIR HOTEL

ADDRESS
Mundaring Weir Rd, Mundaring

TELEPHONE
(08) 9295 1106

WEBSITE
www.mundaringweirhotel.com.au

RATES
Cottages: $110 Sun–Thurs, $125 Fri and $135 Sat.

HOURS
Mon–Sat 9am–5.30pm; Sun 8am–7pm.

GRUB
Breakfast and lunch available daily, dinner only Fri–Sat nights. Coffee shop open Sun and public holidays for lunch, coffee and refreshments.

TOP DROP
Beers on tap include Swan Draught, XXXX, Hahn Light, Boag's, Heineken, Becks, Guinness and Kilkenny. About 60 per cent of the wine list is local labels, including Hainault, Galafrey and Hartley Estate.

NEARBY ATTRACTIONS
Several bushwalks of varying lengths go past the hotel. The 2 km Golden Pipeline loop around Mundaring Weir and No. 1 Pump Station Museum has interpretive signage to explain interesting points. The museum is 5 min walk from the hotel; open Wed–Sun and public holidays 10am–4pm.

MORE INFO
www.goldenpipeline.com.au

When the weir was being built, sly grog was being sold on the construction site and the local police were keen to get alcohol under control. Jacoby needed a bigger hotel to accommodate the construction workers and the visitors arriving to watch the weir's progress, and the issuing of a licence to him helped stem the illicit booze. A two-storey building was added to the hotel and it was renamed the Goldfields Weir Hotel in 1906.

During World War II, the weir was considered a military target and guards were posted. The hotel's roof was painted black and part of the cellar was made into a bomb shelter with access from the ballroom above (the shelter is now the kitchen for the cafe).

The big family day at Mundaring Weir is Sunday, when the hotel is packed with people and a bush band plays 2–5pm. There's a playground for kids, face painting and a swimming pool that's open to all. Lamb on the spit is the specialty on Sundays (at $12.50) or you can have burgers, filled baguettes, curry, or steak and Guinness pie with beer-battered chips and salad. Wood-fired pizza ($19.30) from the cafe comes with a range of toppings, including hot and spicy, smoked salmon, chicken bruschetta, vegetarian, baked ham and pineapple, or continental (cacciatore sausage, red onion, roasted capsicum, sun-dried tomato, olives, fetta, mushrooms and mozzarella).

Inside, the hotel is warm and inviting, with a large front bar leading to a lounge bar with a fireplace. Downstairs, there's a ballroom-sized dining room with leadlights and terrazzo floors, and everywhere you look there are antiques, artwork and collectibles adding to the interest. Throughout the rambling building there are 20 fireplaces: 'We use about two tonnes of wood a week in winter,' says Jorgensen.

After lunch, take a walk to the weir – it's worth it. You can walk across the dam wall, or head down to the No. 1 Pump Station at the foot of the weir, which has a 41.5-metre-tall chimney, the original boilers and steam engines. It is now a National Trust museum and interpretive centre.

If you're really energetic, take one of the walking tracks that pass the hotel. Apart from the short track to the weir, there is also the 15-kilometre Kalamunda Track and the Bibbulmun Track, both with interpretive signage by the National Trust.

The hotel has ten motel rooms, styled like brick cottages, which run down the sloping garden beside the amphitheatre, overlooking either the pool or the forest. There are twin and double rooms, some with bunk beds, allowing up to four people to a room. Each has a kitchenette and an open fireplace with wood supplied (but they also have heaters).

The NEW NORCIA HOTEL

NEW NORCIA

A SEAT ON the wide verandah of the New Norcia Hotel is the perfect place to contemplate one of Australia's most unusual towns. Laid out before you is a Spanish Benedictine village set in the West Australian bush. Black-robed monks stroll along the dusty roads and work in the orchards.

You are not dreaming. This slice of Spain, the creation of Benedictine missionaries, was built in 1846 and is still going strong. New Norcia has frescoed chapels, one of the finest and largest post-Renaissance religious art collections in Australia, and a grand hotel built to accommodate a Spanish royal family who never arrived.

Apart from the monastery guesthouse, which takes up to 24 visitors, the only place to stay in town is the imposing New Norcia Hotel. When the monks thought a Spanish royal visit to New Norcia was imminent in 1926, they built this grandiose hotel, but sadly the royals never came. The building was later used as a hostel for parents of the children boarding at the town's colleges.

The imposing New Norcia Hotel

Laid out before you is a Spanish Benedictine village set in the West Australian bush. Black-robed monks stroll along the dusty roads and work in the orchards.

It has been a hotel since 1955, but only the sweeping central staircase, soaring pressed-metal ceilings and grand Iberian facade hint at its early splendour. Nevertheless, it still has the feel of an Aussie pub. Lunch and dinner are served either in the bar or the dining room – and Sunday night is pizza night. An open fire is lit in the dining room and the guests' lounge during winter.

The 15 guest rooms are small, but open on to the huge verandah. Only one has an ensuite bathroom, air conditioning and a television; the others share a bathroom down the hallway. Every room has electric blankets for chilly nights, a ceiling fan, a refrigerator and tea- and coffee-making facilities.

Just 132 kilometres north of Perth, about two hours' drive, with a population of around 70 (when everyone's in town), New Norcia has 27 heritage buildings – the whole town is classified by the National Trust. It is still home to eight monks, and has one of only

The Latin 'Salve' welcomes visitors

six Benedictine monasteries in Australia – there are three for men and three for women.

In the cemetery you will find the tomb of Bishop Rosenda Salvado, the founder of New Norcia, who died in 1900; the white unnamed crosses in the cemetery are the Aboriginal people who are buried here. With fellow Benedictine Dom Joseph Serra, Salvado's original vision was to create a self-sufficient village, but after many local Aboriginal people were killed by introduced diseases in the 1860s, the monks concentrated on educating Aboriginal children who came from all over Western Australia.

The best way to hear the amazing story of New Norcia is to take a guided tour. Highlights include the monks' own chapel within the monastery and the beautifully frescoed interiors of St Ildephonsus' and St Gertrude's college chapels, not otherwise accessible to the public. Much of the monastery is closed to visitors, but the tour does show you the orchards and gardens and a glimpse of the men-only courtyard.

The Museum and Art Gallery is full of relics from the monks' past: old mechanical and musical instruments, artefacts from the days when New Norcia was an Aboriginal mission, gifts to the monks from the Queen of Spain, and an astounding collection of paintings by Spanish and Italian artists, dating back to the 1400s. A more recent painting, by Australian artist Pro Hart, records the 1847 'miracle of New Norcia' – the saving of the town from a bushfire.

New Norcia's modern history has not been untroubled. Over the bar you may hear first-hand tales of the famous New Norcia art heist. In 1986, thieves cut 26 of New Norcia's collection of paintings in the Museum and Art Gallery from their frames in a daring daylight robbery. All but one were later recovered and returned, but it took 20 years for their restoration to be complete.

Head upstairs to 15 guest rooms

Visitors can join the monks for 15-minute prayers in the monastery chapel five times a day (noon and 2.30pm are the most convenient for daytrippers), or for mass in Holy Trinity Abbey Church at 7.30am Monday–Saturday, 9am Sunday, or at 5.30pm for vespers. If you are staying overnight it is worth getting up early for mass.

New Norcia's traditional crafts of breadmaking and olive oil production have been revived in recent years. The monastery's 8336 hectares includes old olive groves, planted in the 1860s with seedlings from Europe. And don't go home without tasting the famous New Norcia nut cake, straight from the monastery's 120-year-old wood-fired oven.

THE NEW NORCIA HOTEL

ADDRESS
New Norcia

TELEPHONE
(08) 9654 8034

WEBSITE
www.newnorcia.wa.edu.au

RATES
$75 single, $95 double, $22 extra person per night, including continental breakfast.

HOURS
Mon–Thurs 11am–10pm; Fri 11–12am; Sat 10–12am; Sun 10am–9.30pm.

GRUB
Breakfast 7.30–9.30am daily, lunch 12–2pm weekdays, 12–2.30pm weekends and public holidays, dinner 6–8pm daily.

TOP DROP
New Norcia Abbey Ale, a traditional monastic ale developed by brewmaster Chuck Hahn of Malt Shovel Brewery, is available exclusively from the New Norcia Hotel. There is also a New Norcia range of wines and ports, including Shiraz, Cabernet Merlot and Chardonnay, a Liqueur Muscat and two ports.

NEARBY ATTRACTIONS
The European Space Agency's Deep Space Satellite Dish is 10 km south of New Norcia, off Great Northern Hwy. The dish is not open to the public but at the New Norcia Space Room you can learn about ESA missions through scale models, DVD presentations and display panels.

MORE INFO
www.westernaustralia.com

ORA BANDA INN

ORA BANDA

THERE ARE KIDS playing in the grassy garden, the Australian and Eureka flags are flapping on the flagpole out the front and a trickle of cars is turning up for Sunday lunch at the Ora Banda Inn. It's hard to imagine that this, just a little more than a decade ago, was one of the most notorious crime scenes on the Western Australia goldfields. Step into the bar, though, and in the pressed-metal wall you can still see the scars of the bomb blast that ripped the hotel apart in 2000.

Ora Banda Inn

The story goes like this: on a moonlit night in October 2000, Gypsy Jokers bikie gang member Billy Grierson was shot dead while sitting around a campfire outside the Ora Banda Inn, which was owned by retired police officer Don Hancock and who became the main suspect. Days after Grierson's death, two explosions blew apart the front of the historic hotel in what was believed to be a revenge attack. About $200 000 worth of damage was done to the hotel.

The Ora Banda Inn was one of the most notorious crime scenes on the Western Australia goldfields. Step into the bar and in the pressed-metal wall you can still see the scars of the bomb blast that ripped the hotel apart in 2000.

About a month later, on 5 November, more bomb blasts rocked the tiny township, this time at the general store adjacent to the pub and at the gold battery. A house belonging to Don Hancock was burnt to the ground. Hancock and another man died a year later in a Perth car bombing. Gypsy Joker Sid Reid later admitted planting the car bomb in retaliation for Billy Grierson's shooting. He was convicted of murder and in 2002 was sentenced to life in prison with a minimum term of 15 years. No convictions were made in relation to the attacks on the Ora Banda Inn.

Since then, things have been quiet at the pub. After being closed for two years, it reopened, closed again for another 18 months, and has now had another reincarnation under current owners Michael and Rhonda Lucas, who took over in 2006.

'The previous owner, Barry Foote, did the renovations and he left part of the damage there so that people could see what it had done,' says Rhonda Lucas. It's a talking point, and there's also a book of newspaper clippings about the dramatic events at the hotel kept on the bar for anyone to browse through.

Ironically, these incidents put Ora Banda on the map and the tiny pub on the outskirts of Kalgoorlie became a tourist attraction. During the week, the tourists come, while at weekends the crowd is likely to be from Kalgoorlie, just 70 kilometres (the last 10 kilometres is dirt road) south.

'There aren't many pubs you can take kids to in Kal,' says Rhonda, 'so we get a lot of families who come out here for the day.'

The Ora Banda Inn is a great bush pub, with two beer gardens (smoking and non-smoking) that have barbecues, a small fountain and gardens. Inside, the dining room has fireplaces, a collection of old bottles and a few armchairs; a pool table is situated in the lounge area, behind the front bar.

'It's a quiet day if we do less than 100 lunches,' says Rhonda, while on Easter Sunday 2011, the Lucases and their staff served 233 meals. That's a record for a 'normal' day; on Ora Banda Day, a special event in mid September, a crowd of 4500 came through the doors over the course of the day.

ORA BANDA INN

ADDRESS
Cnr Johnson and Gimlet sts, Ora Banda

TELEPHONE
(08) 9024 2444

WEBSITE
www.orabanda.com.au

RATES
Motel units: $110 double, including continental breakfast; caravan park: $25 double for a powered site, $15 for an unpowered site.

HOURS
Weekdays 12pm–late; Sat 11am–late; Sun 11am–8pm.

GRUB
The kitchen is open weekdays 12–7.30pm; Sat 11am–7.30pm; Sun 11am–7pm.

TOP DROP
Beers on tap are James Squire Golden Ale, Hahn Super Dry and Extra Dry, Hahn Premium Lager, XXXX Gold. Only Western Australian wines are stocked.

NEARBY ATTRACTIONS
Next door to the pub is the old Government Battery which used to process ore for the local prospectors. It is leased to the Ora Banda Inn and there are plans to turn it into a museum in the future.

MORE INFO
www.kalgoorlietourism.com

Ora Banda Day is the Thursday of the week-long Kalgoorlie Race Round. It's a big family day, with helicopter rides, two-up, food stalls, show bags, face painting and a jumping castle for the kids, a foot race with $300 in prize money, a toilet-seat throwing contest and pony club events on the racetrack opposite the pub. During the day, a shuttle bus runs between Ora Banda and Kalgoorlie every 15 minutes.

Beer garden decoration at the Ora Banda Inn

In 2011, Ora Banda – the town and the pub – celebrated its centenary. To be more precise, it's really only the pub, as the town has dwindled to two occupied houses over the past 25 years or so. In its heyday, the mining town with the Spanish name (it means 'band of gold' and was named for the underground wealth that brought a rush to the area) was home to about 2500 people. The original town was pegged in 1896 but it later was moved about 3 kilometres up the road to the spot where the Ora Banda Inn now stands.

During World War I, Ora Banda held the distinction of sending more men to the war than any other town in Australia, per head of population. In appreciation, the town received an Honour Roll and a German machine gun. Both were later lost – the Honour Roll in a fire, the artillery simply 'mislaid'. In 1996, a replica Honour Roll was unveiled and a tree was planted along Gimlet Street for each soldier on it.

PALACE HOTEL

KALGOORLIE

IT WOULDN'T BE the first time a young man has fallen in love with a barmaid ... and nor will it be the last. But few have left such a tangible reminder of their love as a young mining engineer in Kalgoorlie did in the late 1890s.

The romantic tale of a 22-year-old engineer and the barmaid he wooed before leaving to return to his native America is still told in the Palace Hotel, where the poem the lovelorn young man wrote to the object of his affection is displayed on the lobby wall.

Do you ever dream, my sweetheart, of a twilight long ago,

Of a park in old Kalgoorlie, where the bougainvilleas grow?

The romantic tale of a 22-year-old engineer and the barmaid he wooed is still told in the Palace Hotel ... the young man, Herbert Hoover, went home to marry his college sweetheart – and to become the 31st president of the United States.

Its significance, of course, is all the more important because the young man, Herbert Hoover, went home to marry his college sweetheart – and to become the 31st president of the United States in 1929. Hoover's romantic gesture is framed for all to see, alongside the massive and ornate 'Hoover mirror'. Hoover was a regular guest at the Palace when he worked in the goldfields for several years, and when he left he had the elaborately carved mirror built and shipped from America to the hotel as a gift.

Palace Hotel, Kalgoorlie, entrance

In Kalgoorlie there's not quite a pub on every corner – but there are pubs on three of the four corners at the intersection of Hannan and Maritana streets. As well as the Palace there is the Exchange Hotel and the Australia (closed at the time of writing). The Palace, built in 1897, was one of the grandest hotels in a town renowned for its impressive architecture and its many pubs – it was designed to be the most luxurious hotel in Western Australia outside Perth.

Stained-glass windows in the lobby cafe

Getting to Kalgoorlie today is still a trek, but a worthwhile one; the city is nearly 600 kilometres east of Perth, about an eight-hour drive in an almost straight line. The other options are to fly or take the Prospector train from Perth, or the Indian Pacific from Perth, Adelaide or Sydney.

The two-storey Palace Hotel, built from locally quarried stone, was the first pub in the town to have electric lighting and fresh water piped to the bathrooms. It is a landmark in Kalgoorlie's main street and although the grandeur may have faded a little, the Palace still welcomes guests from around the world.

The sweeping staircase, impressive lobby and beautiful stained-glass windows of the large lobby cafe hint at its one-time luxury, and the upstairs Balcony Restaurant is one of the best places to eat in town – but the Palace also caters to the other side of Kalgoorlie's nightlife, offering a topless barmaid service in the Gold Bar. Known colloquially as 'skimpies', they are as much an attraction as the other entertainment in the Gold Bar – live bands, touring DJs and karaoke. The bar is divided in two, so you won't walk into the front bar and see the girls (not in this pub, anyway); for that you need to go around to the other, back side of the bar.

The hotel's reception is in the bustling Hoover Cafe, where the dining tables share space with chesterfield lounges, and artwork on the walls tells the history of the goldfields.

The Palace Hotel is on a prominent corner

Palace Hotel lobby and staircase

In the bar section, a large mural depicts mining scenes. There's wi-fi access too, so laptops on the tables aren't unusual.

The wide first-floor verandahs are a feature of the Palace – and they have been the setting for many public speeches delivered to crowds in the streets below – but only 'balcony rooms' and the Balcony Bar & Restaurant have access to them. So book a table there for dinner, and if it's Saturday night you can be assured of plenty to see as you look down on the street and over to the pub across the way.

For those who stay, there's a choice of rooms. The most expensive are the balcony rooms – but it may be worth paying that extra, as some of the cheaper, internal rooms have no windows.

Kalgoorlie may not awaken the romantic in you, but a visit is sure to be memorable.

Beer taps, Palace Hotel

PALACE HOTEL

ADDRESS
137 Hannan St, Kalgoorlie

TELEPHONE
(08) 9021 2788

WEBSITE
www.palacehotel.com.au

RATES
Rooms with shared bathroom: $50 single, $75 twin or double; budget rooms with ensuite: $55 single, $65 double, $75 twin; standard doubles $85–$90; balcony rooms: single $110, queen $130; standard single $75–$85; standard family room (1 double and 2 single beds) $120; Hoover apartment (1 bedroom, plus lounge area with sofa bed) $160; 2-bedroom suite $260; Apartment 143 (5 queen bedrooms) $500.

HOURS
The Gold Bar open from 6pm Tues–Sat.

GRUB
The Hoover Cafe open Mon–Sat 8am–5pm (until 6pm Fri). Breakfast 8–11am, lunch 11am–3.30pm. Closed Sun and public holidays. The Balcony Bar & Restaurant open from 5pm Mon–Sat.

TOP DROP
Hahn Super Dry, XXXX Gold and Swan Draught are on tap.

NEARBY ATTRACTIONS
Drive to the Super Pit lookout on the Goldfields Hwy for a look at Australia's largest open-cut mine. Kalgoorlie's other famous attraction is Questa Casa, one of the world's longest operating brothels; open for guided tours at 2pm daily (book at visitor centre).

MORE INFO
www.kalgoorlietourism.com

YANCHEP INN

YANCHEP NATIONAL PARK

Kangaroos graze on the lawns of the Yanchep Inn

WESTERN GREY KANGAROOS graze on the lawns outside the Tudor-style Yanchep Inn, koalas doze in the nearby gum trees and endangered Carnaby's black-cockatoos swoop overhead at dusk. It's an idyllic setting – and quite a surprise to find a 'pub in the park', for the Yanchep Inn is planted firmly inside the 2799-hectare Yanchep National Park, just 45 minutes' drive north of Perth.

Built in 1936 from local jarrah and limestone, the Yanchep Inn quickly became a popular meeting place. It was the brainchild of conservationist Louis Edward Shapcott, a public servant who became secretary to the Western Australia premier and was later chairman of the State Gardens Board. When the board took over the management of Yanchep in 1931, he worked for the establishment of a national park and in 1935 applied for a publican's licence and to build a hotel on 2 acres (0.8 hectares) near the south-eastern corner of Loch McNess (now called Lake Wagardu). With 16 bedrooms, two lounges, a dining room and a large verandah across the front of the building and down two sides, the hotel opened on 12 December 1936 and was immediately booked out for Christmas and New Year.

Western grey kangaroos graze on the lawns outside the Tudor-style Yanchep Inn, koalas doze in the nearby gum trees and endangered Carnaby's black-cockatoos swoop overhead at dusk.

Petrol rationing during World War II brought a quieter time to both the park and the inn, and the park was closed for a time. In 1942, the inn was taken over by the RAAF and became a rehabilitation unit for servicemen. After the war, the inn reopened to visitors and became known as a 'honeymoon hotel' but several decades later it fell on hard times and closed in late 1996. Major renovations were carried out and it reopened the following year. The Yanchep Inn is now heritage-listed by the National Trust.

The fountain rockery at the front of the hotel was built just before World War II, and in the 1980s members of the RSL erected a small stone memorial to those who gave their lives in World War I, World War II, Korea, Malaysia, Borneo and Vietnam. At the back of the hotel there is a large light-filled atrium with a soaring ceiling and bi-folding glass doors that open out to the beer garden and views of the lake.

The Yanchep Inn is very close to several of the park's main attractions, including the 240-metre elevated boardwalk that runs through a koala habitat. There are viewing platforms for close-up views of the many koalas who live here, and information boards. There is also a 2-kilometre walking trail around the freshwater lake, great for birdwatching.

Yanchep Inn's Tudor Manor Restaurant

After a drink in the Guards Bar – named by former long-time publican (1973–89) and Welsh Guard John Hearne – have dinner in the Tudor Manor Restaurant, which has a warm atmosphere enhanced in winter by the log fire. Not surprisingly, given the proximity to the seaside village of Two Rocks and to Yanchep beach, seafood features on the menu, including a 'chef's selection' seafood platter of oysters, mussels, smoked salmon and whatever else is freshly available ($84 for two).

The à la carte menu also has a selection of seafood, steak and pasta dishes, and there's a bar snacks menu with burgers, nachos, toasted sandwiches, an all-day breakfast, ploughman's lunch, fish and chips and more. On Sundays, the specialty is a carvery roast, when two courses – soup and the roast – cost $21.50.

There are 37 rooms in the hotel. These are basic but clean and comfortable, with bathrooms down the hallway, and most of them open on to the verandah. There is a small guest lounge with a television and tea- and coffee-making facilities.

Like so many self-respecting pubs, there are ghosts at Yanchep. Reports of beds being turned back then remade, and of lights, showers and switches being turned off and on, of footsteps in the hallways ... all these have been attributed to ghosts called Charlie (1948), George (in the late 1970s) and Henry. In 1997, the manager Brenda Greening called in a pastor to bless the inn – and since then things have apparently been quieter.

If you'd prefer to avoid potential spooks, or if it is winter (the hotel rooms have no heating and can be very cold), there are other options for overnight stays. Next door to the hotel is a block of 14 modern motel units, built in 2007, which overlook Lake Wagardu. Four older motel units are also available: these have ensuites, television, reverse-cycle air conditioning and tea- and coffee-making facilities.

Access to Yanchep National Park (and the hotel) requires a permit. The cost is $11 for a vehicle with up to eight passengers and it can be bought at the entrance to the park.

YANCHEP INN

ADDRESS
Yanchep National Park (off Wanneroo Rd)

TELEPHONE
(08) 9561 1001

WEBSITE
www.yanchepinn.com.au

RATES
Hotel: $45 single, $70 double Sun–Fri; $62.50 single, $105 double Sat (with breakfast). Lakeside motel: $140 single, $170 double standard room; $150 single, $190 double spa room; $160 single, $210 double corner spa room (more on Sat). Motel: $80 single, $105 double (more on Sat).

HOURS
Daily 8–12am.

GRUB
Daily 8am–8pm.

TOP DROP
A full range of local and imported beers, with 16 on tap including Coopers, Boag's, Hahn, James Squire, Swan Draught, XXXX Gold, Tooheys, Becks, Little Creatures Pale Ale, Guinness and Peroni, plus Strongbow Draught cider.

NEARBY ATTRACTIONS
Yanchep's attractions include the Crystal Caves, Aboriginal Experience and Koala Boardwalk. The latter two are adjacent to the hotel. The Crystal Cave runs 45-min tours 5 times a day. The Aboriginal Experience runs weekends at 2pm and 3pm. Visit McNess House visitor centre for more information and bookings. There are also 9 walking trails and a golf course within the park.

MORE INFO
www.dec.wa.gov.au

Northern Territory

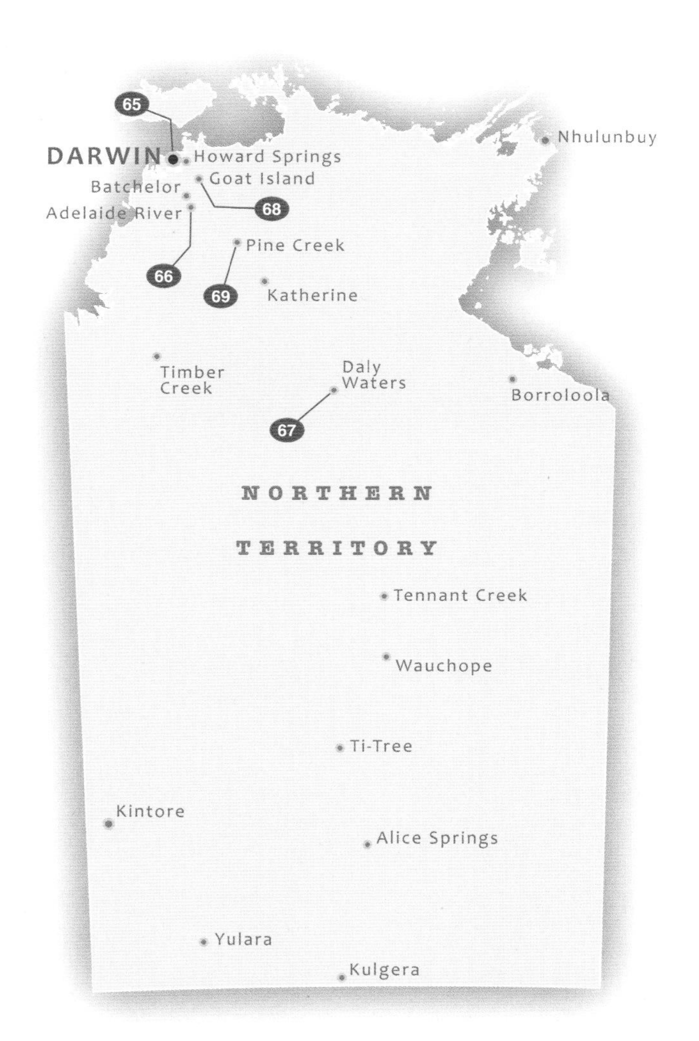

Opposite (clockwise from top): Trophy wall, Daly Waters Historic Pub; Lazy Lizard Tavern, Pine Creek; bar deck, Goat Island Lodge; jumping crocodile, Adelaide River.

NIPPON GINKO
The Royal Bank of Scotland
ONE POUND
LIMA RIBU RUPIAH
SINGAPORE

The VICTORIA Hotel

DARWIN

The Victoria Hotel, Darwin

BY DAY, THE sandstone walls of 'The Vic' provide a cool oasis in the heart of Darwin's Smith Street Mall. By night – especially in the Dry when backpackers are flocking to the Top End capital – the bars heave with party-goers and music pounds upstairs.

Since the day Ellen Ryan opened the doors of her hotel, in September 1890, it has been one of Darwin's best known and most popular places for a drink. She probably wouldn't be surprised. The woman who built the Vic (originally called the North Australia Hotel) and the driving force behind it for more than 25 years was, by all accounts, a colourful character who established pubs all over the Top End. Ellen arrived in Darwin in 1873, three years after the settlement was founded on the back of gold discoveries in the Northern Territory, and moved to the goldfields near Pine Creek. Realising there was a lucrative market for 'liquid gold', within a few weeks she had leased the area's first pub, the Miner's Arms.

Cyclone Tracy was not the first time the Victoria Hotel had been hit by a cyclone: during a storm in 1897 a ceiling had cracked and a bedroom full of furniture fell through into the billiards room.

Ellen Ryan became one of the Territory's wealthiest women, owning land and several mining leases. In 1888, as the gold rush began to slow, she applied for a licence for a two-storey hotel to be built in Darwin's Smith Street. Since then, it has had a colourful and somewhat chequered history – like the city it stands in.

In the old cellar, a few steps down from the bar, the stone walls are hung with framed photographs and documents tracing the story of Darwin and the pub. This is the only part of the original hotel still intact, and provides a small area with barrel tables for your drinks while you check out the walls.

In the early days of aviation, pioneering pilots were among the guests at the Vic, including Qantas founder Hudson Fysh, who stayed in 1919 while building the Darwin airstrip for competitors in the England–Australia air race. On 10 December 1919 Ross

and Keith Smith, with their mechanics, sergeants Bennett and Shiers, completed the first flight from England to Australia in less than 30 days – having taken 28 days – and were toasted at the Vic.

The Vic has further links with aviation. Goldminer Christina Gordon, the licensee of the hotel at the time, became a passenger on Qantas' first commercial flight from Darwin in 1926, while on 28 June 1937, aviators Amelia Earhart and Fred Noonan stayed at the Vic during their intended round-the-world flight. Three days later their plane disappeared off Papua New Guinea and no trace was ever found of them.

For two decades from 1946, the hotel was owned by the Lim family, descendents of Chinese miners. Alec Fong Lim, later a popular Lord Mayor of Darwin, returned from boarding school in Adelaide when he was 19 to help run the pub. In those days, after World War II, the patrons were a mix of bank clerks, public servants, stockmen, buffalo hunters and miners.

When Darwin was flattened by cyclone Tracy on Christmas Day 1974, the damage was enormous. It was not the first time the Victoria Hotel had been hit by a cyclone: during a storm in 1897 a ceiling had cracked and a bedroom full of furniture fell through into the billiards room.

As Darwin rebuilt after cylone Tracy, Smith Street became a pedestrian mall and the rebuilt Victoria Hotel became a tavern. In 2005 it was remodelled again with industrial-style design, using cement, steel and sharp angles, but softened with handmade teak furniture, giving it the look that remains today.

It's a great escape from the heat on the street, whether you head to the air-conditioned Banjo's Bar, or relax on the front or back verandahs with a drink. Upstairs, the young crowd hits the nightclub dance floor to DJs or local and interstate bands. There's also a cavernous pool room, and an area where you can play electronic games or poker machines.

Pub meals include a buffet offering roasts, fish and chips, curries and more for $5 – which must make the Vic a contender for the cheapest meals in town. Other offerings on the menu include local wild-caught barramundi and 'buffalo bangers' with vegetables and mash. Pizza lovers aren't forgotten either.

Crocosaurus Cove, Darwin

THE VICTORIA HOTEL

ADDRESS
27 The Mall, Darwin

TELEPHONE
(08) 8981 4011

WEBSITE
www.thevichotel.com

HOURS
Mon–Sat 10am–6pm (later in the Dry).

GRUB
Meals Mon–Sat 11am–5pm (later in the Dry).

TOP DROP
Jugs of Carlton Draught and Boag's are the most popular orders here.

WHERE TO STAY
Darwin's options include the lovely Moonshadow Villas. The self-contained villas, with 2 bedrooms and 2 bathrooms, are in lush gardens around a plunge pool; rates are $215–$699 per villa per night. www.moonshadowvillas.com The Vibe Hotel Darwin Waterfront, overlooking the city's new man-made lagoon, has double rooms from $170. www.vibehotels.com.au

NEARBY ATTRACTIONS
Two blocks away, on Mitchell St, test your mettle in the 'cage of death' at Crocosaurus Cove as you are lowered into the territory of several huge crocodiles. For adventures of a gentler kind, take a daytrip to Litchfield National Park or explore the interesting Museum and Art Gallery of the Northern Territory.

MORE INFO
www.travelnt.com

ADELAIDE RIVER INN

ADELAIDE RIVER

Charlie the water buffalo looms over the bar ... he was the buffalo star of the 1986 hit movie *Crocodile Dundee*.

Charlie the water buffalo has pride of place in the bar

CHARLIE THE WATER buffalo looms over the bar at the Adelaide River Inn, his presence a drawcard for tourists' cameras. In life, Charlie was used to the cameras ... he was the buffalo star of the 1986 hit movie *Crocodile Dundee*. Remember the scene where Mick Dundee (played by Paul Hogan) 'hypnotises' the buffalo until he drops to the ground? That's Charlie, who died in 2000 and now has pride of place in the 303 Bar.

For many years, Charlie wallowed in a waterhole beside the pub, a popular attraction for tourists who would pose sitting on his back. He is probably as much photographed in death as he was in life. And there are photographs, movie posters and other memorabilia around the bar to tell the story of how he rose to fame (he also had a small part in *Crocodile Dundee II*) as well as Charlie toys to take home – among other souvenirs.

The township of Adelaide River, 112 kilometres south of Darwin and about 200 kilometres north-west of Katherine, on the Stuart Highway, developed slowly following completion of construction of the Overland Telegraph Line in 1872. The township, which today has a population of about 250, is near the headwaters of the Adelaide River, which flows north to the Timor Sea about 50 kilometres north-east of Darwin.

The town grew as it became a popular overnight stopover for travellers and prospectors heading to Pine Creek following the discovery of gold there in the 1870s, but its heyday was during World War II, when it became one of the most strategically important places in Australia. Adelaide River played a major role in Australia's war effort, being the location for a huge military base, with a hospital and army camps. By the end of 1942 there were 5000 military personnel stationed in the town and surrounding areas.

Adelaide River Inn

After the Japanese bombing of Darwin in 1942, Australian and American military headquarters were relocated from Darwin to Adelaide River. The town is now the site of the third-largest war cemetery in Australia, the burial place for 434 service personnel. A civil cemetery alongside it is for 64 civilians killed during the bombing raids. The cemetery opened in February 1942, soon after the first air raids on Darwin.

The Adelaide River Inn began life as refreshment rooms, built in 1942 by Eileen Gribben, when the town was booming with the military influx. In 1951 Eileen transferred the licence of her property to some relatives, the Fawcett family, who renamed it the Adelaide River Hotel. Today the pub forms the heart of the Adelaide River Resort complex.

There is a large, lush beer garden out the front, overhung by tropical shade trees and a big expanse of lawn with tables and chairs; it's very appealing, so in general hardly anyone is found inside the small 303 Bar, except when it's very quiet or to buy their drinks.

There's a pool table, big-screen television and live music from resident regulars and visiting performers. Digger's Bistro serves country-style pub meals, with snacks and burgers also available. The main menu has a range of fish, seafood, chicken and steak dishes, but the pub's specialty is local wild-caught barramundi – battered, crumbed or grilled – with chips, for $19.50. Blackboard specials change daily, usually offering seasonal dishes. An all-day breakfast costs $6–$12, Friday is pizza night (dine in or takeaway) and Sunday is roast night; a kids' menu is also available. There's undercover outdoor seating for 100 people – and the kids all usually end up playing on the grass.

For those who want to break a journey here, there's a choice of accommodation set a short distance across the extensive gardens, away from the pub. The 23 budget rooms each have a small television, fridge, a double or queen-sized bed plus a single bed, fan and air-conditioning, and ensuite. Fourteen more modern cabins each have their own kitchen and bathroom, and a small deck at the front, with chairs and an overhead fan. There are also five motel-style rooms and a caravan park. The complex has a large fenced tropical pool and amenities include a guest laundry.

Note: If you are looking for any of the several 'jumping crocodile' cruises that operate on the Adelaide River, be aware that despite their names, they are not located near the township, but are reached off the Arnhem Highway, on the way to Kakadu National Park.

ADELAIDE RIVER INN

ADDRESS
106 Stuart Hwy, Adelaide River

TELEPHONE
(08) 8976 7047

WEBSITE
www.adelaideriverinn.com.au

RATES
$75 for budget rooms;
$95 for motel rooms;
$125 for self-contained cabins.

HOURS
Daily 7am–11pm.
Closed Christmas Day.

GRUB
Digger's Bistro open daily 7am–8pm (hours subject to change seasonally).

TOP DROP
A wide range of tap and bottled beers, including boutique beers. Some cocktails and shooters available upon request.

NEARBY ATTRACTIONS
The Adelaide River War Cemetery is in Memorial Dr, which runs alongside the Adelaide River Inn. The cascading Robin Falls, on Dorat Rd off Stuart Hwy near the Adelaide River township, is a good place to swim; the falls are reached via a short walk through surrounding bush. Mt Bundy cattle station, about 3 km from Adelaide River township on Haynes Rd, offers station tours and horse treks. www.mtbundy.com.au

MORE INFO
www.visitnt.com

DALY WATERS
HISTORIC PUB

DALY WATERS

Daly Waters Historic Pub

BRAS HANGING ABOVE the bar have helped make this one of Australia's most talked about pubs, but a young barman confesses he's never actually seen any female patrons leave one! The bras, the lone parking meter out the front and the mock traffic light – 'Australia's most remote' – all signal that a sense of humour is a handy thing to have when you drop into the Daly Waters pub.

One of Australia's best known outback drinking holes, the Daly Waters pub is about 600 kilometres south of Darwin on the Stuart Highway, a good stopping point for those taking a through-the-Centre road trip. Thirsty travellers have been breaking their journeys here since 1930, while the Daly Waters airstrip was a stopover for early aviators, as well as being a war-time bomber base.

Visit in the Dry (April–September), the tourist season, and treat yourself to the pub's specialty, Beef & Barra, a barbecued dish with hot damper and a choice of salads. All the barramundi served here is wild, caught by local commercial fishermen – none of that imported or farmed stuff, thank you. It's caught off the coast and in the rivers of the Territory.

All the barramundi served here is wild, caught by local fishermen off the coast and in the rivers of the Territory.

Beef & Barra nights are hugely popular and in the Dry, the busiest time, bookings are essential; the pub runs three sittings to accommodate as many as possible – at 6.30pm, 7pm and 7.30pm. The extensive menu includes everything from homemade burgers to rib-eye steaks and warm Greek lamb salad, while there's a 'Monster Menu' for kids.

During the Dry, there's also free nightly entertainment. The regular performer for many years, Frank the Chook Man and his 'wild wedge-tailed eagles', retired recently, so there are now two new regulars – rock'n'roller Steve Staples, who is followed by Chilli, billed as songwriter, balladeer, poet, spinner of tall yarns, a champion bull-rider and rodeo clown, who does an Australiana show that goes down a treat. Travelling musicians are sometimes persuaded to join in.

With the Daly Waters population now standing at nine – although it's surrounded by cattle stations – the pub is the only business in town. The population swells in the tourist season, and you never know who you might find propped up at the bar.

Robyne Webster and Lindsay Carmichael have owned the pub since 2000. They followed in the footsteps of the founders, pioneers Bill and Henrietta Pearce, whom Robyne describes as 'incredible people'. The Pearces, who settled in the area in about 1914 and built a shop at Daly Waters in the 1930s, became renowned for their hospitality. But the story of Daly Waters and its important place in Australia's history goes back much further.

In 1861, after making two previous attempts, John McDouall Stuart successfully crossed the continent from south to north. He named Daly Waters, a place where he found much-needed fresh water, in honour of the then governor of South Australia, Sir Dominic Daly. The water source was vital for cattle drovers, and Daly Waters became the last watering hole for thirsty cattle and cattlemen before they set out on the Murranji Stock Route.

A decade later, the telegraph line followed Stuart's route, with a station at Daly Waters. One of the original telegraph poles, dating back to around 1878, now stands outside the pub, after having been found a few years ago in nearby bush.

Bill and Henrietta Pearce's shop became the Daly Waters pub, and they continued running it throughout World War II. The aerodrome at Daly Waters became a base for Hudson and Mitchell bombers, Kitty Hawks and a fighter squadron, and played a vital role in the defence of northern Australia. After the war it became an essential refuelling stop for international aircraft, with a heavy flow of air traffic.

The Pearces were responsible for feeding passengers and refuelling the aircraft in those early days of international flights. Their fascinating story is told in the book *Two at Daly Waters* by Elizabeth George, published in 1945 and which Robyne has had reprinted and sells at the bar, to preserve the history of the pub and the area.

If you are planning to stay overnight, there are a few accommodation choices, all basic but very clean. Seven pub rooms, behind the outdoor eating area and backing on to the caravan park, run off a long corridor with a shared bathroom at the end of it. Each is different, some with a double bed, while some are singles or twins. All are air-conditioned and have overhead fans and a few pieces of furniture. Otherwise, the motel rooms have an ensuite, television and fridge, as do the cabins, which also have small verandahs overlooking a grassy, park-like area. In addition, there are some backpacker rooms with bunks and shared bathrooms. The caravan park has powered and unpowered sites.

A saltwater swimming pool is open 7am–10pm (towels available at the bar) to cool off in, and there's also a kids' toys and games area.

Bras above the bar

DALY WATERS HISTORIC PUB

ADDRESS
Stuart St, Daly Waters

TELEPHONE
(08) 8975 9927

WEBSITE
www.dalywaterspub.com

RATES
$20 per person for backpacker rooms; $60 double pub room (with shared bathroom); $95 double motel room with ensuite; $115 cabin with ensuite. Extra person rate $15.

HOURS
Daily 7am–11pm (later in the busier months).

GRUB
Breakfast 7am–2pm; lunch 9am–2pm; snacks 2–6.30pm; dinner 6.30–8.30pm.

TOP DROP
Draft beer on tap is XXXX Gold, Tooheys New and Extra Dry, Coopers Pale Ale, NT Draught and Hahn Light. House wines – red, white and sparkling – are McWilliam's Select Series, and there's an extensive wine list.

NEARBY ATTRACTIONS
Drive out to the old aerodrome's WW II aircraft hangar, which is heritage-listed and has a display telling the story of Daly Waters' role in the war. On the way, detour to the Stuart Tree, where explorer John McDouall Stuart carved his initial 'S' in the trunk on his third attempt to cross the Centre. For birdwatchers, there's a list of 88 local species to spot.

MORE INFO
www.travelnt.com

GOAT ISLAND LODGE

GOAT ISLAND

On the deck at Casey's Bar

CASEY'S BAR AT Goat Island Lodge, built on a 10-hectare island in the Adelaide River, is one of the most unique outback pubs you'll find. For a start, you can only get there by boat or helicopter. If there are other boats moored at the jetty when you drop in for a pub lunch, it's a sure sign that buffalo or barra burgers are probably already sizzling on the grill.

Danish-born publican Kai Hansen presides over the kitchen, Casey's Bar and four rooms at Goat Island Lodge, the only building on the island, which is 22 kilometres from the Adelaide River boat ramp. 'You got me, and Denmark got Princess Mary,' says Hansen, who's been in Australia since 1972. 'Australia got the cheaper deal.'

You can fish from the lodge's barge or the pontoon, before returning to have your catch cooked for you. And if today's not your lucky day there's a choice of 'beef, buff or barra' burgers on the menu – just don't get Hansen talking while he's cooking or your lunch might get a little overdone!

The roomy elevated deck at Casey's Bar – named after the resident crocodile who comes up on the riverbank most evenings, but which is safely out of her reach – is adorned with hand-carved wooden furniture and lots of pot plants. Entertainment is provided by Hansen's pooch Hot Dog, who 'sings' to his harmonica. Casey is fed regularly, her favourite dish from the kitchen being caramelised potatoes.

Casey the resident crocodile comes up on the riverbank most evenings and is fed regularly, her favourite dish from the kitchen being caramelised potatoes.

'You don't have to be crazy to live out here, but it helps,' says the exuberant Hansen – nicknamed 'Happy' – as he spins tales of life on this tiny island in the middle of nowhere, where he has lived since 2001. The changing seasons bring challenges for him, including isolation and floods, plus visiting crocs and other creatures.

It might be isolated, but there are benefits too, he says. 'There are no traffic lights, no rates to pay! It's the only freehold island in the Northern Territory.'

It's also a birder's heaven, with bright flashes of colour in the trees that surround the lodge alerting visitors to the photo opportunities in the overhanging tree canopy. Among the species regularly spotted are whistling kites, azure kingfishers, lemon-breasted flycatchers and the beautiful wet-season visitors, crimson finches, who come to nest. Some years there have been more than 50 of their nests around the bar and accommodation area.

Goat Island Lodge is perfect for those who want to get away from it all. But if you think that 'lodge' is synonymous with 'luxury' then this is not the place for you. The four rooms are clean and comfortable but very basic. They are all air-conditioned, with

Goat Island jetty

ensuites, and have private balconies at the back which provide beautiful bushland and river views.

The lodge sleeps a maximum of 16 guests. There are two family rooms, each with one queen-sized and two single beds; two 'fishos' rooms each have four single beds.

The menu matches the casual accommodation. The kitchen blackboard declares it to be 'not the best, but good enough' – and that's true. As well as 'the best hot dog north of the South Pole', the snack menu offers a choice of burgers, including barra, buffalo, camel and kangaroo (the latter only if ordered at least two hours ahead). For something more substantial at dinner, there are steaks, more barramundi, chilli buffalo sausages and the special chicken à la Goat Island. All are served with caramelised potatoes, salad and vegetables.

The blackboard also admonishes those who might not find any of this to their liking: 'You can order anything else that you feel like, BUT due to our 12 secret herbs and spices, it will look and taste like the rest of the bloody menu'.

The raised open deck under overhanging shade trees is the perfect place to enjoy the changing moods of the tidal river. The deck's furniture was carved by a former resident woodworker called Kris, who shaped the unusual tables and chairs and the sculptures that you'll see here and there with his chainsaw, using wood from the leichhardt trees that grow on the island. In a corner of the deck is a spa, another popular spot for relaxing with a drink and letting the world pass by.

A leisurely hike around the island's meandering 2-kilometre walking track is best done at the start or end of the day, when it is coolest. The island is bush-covered, with huge trees and native bamboo growing up to 20 metres high in some areas.

One of the liveliest times to visit Casey's Bar is for Melbourne Cup Day, when chook races are held to raise money for charity. In 2010, Hansen's fun event – featuring entrants with names like Croc Bait and Centrelink – attracted 35 visitors and raised $7500 through race bets and an auction. At other times, the entrants may be pecking around at your feet.

How to get to Goat Island? If you don't have a boat and can't afford the helicopter ride, Hansen will bring his own boat to pick you up at the Goat Island pontoon, near the boat ramp on the southern side of the Adelaide River bridge on the Arnhem Highway.

THE FACTS

GOAT ISLAND LODGE

ADDRESS
Goat Island, in the Adelaide River; postal: PO Box 100, Virginia, NT 0822

TELEPHONE
(08) 8978 8803

WEBSITE
www.goatisland.com.au

RATES
$120 double; $150 triple; $180 quad share.

HOURS
Whenever you arrive.

GRUB
Whenever you are hungry.

TOP DROP
Most mainstream beers, including XXXX and VB, but don't expect anything out of the ordinary.

NEARBY ATTRACTIONS
The Adelaide River boat ramp is the departure point for several Jumping Croc cruises – but this is only an option if your children are over 4. Also well worth a stop on Arnhem Hwy is the Window on the Wetlands interpretive centre, which is free, open daily 8am–7pm.

MORE INFO
www.travelnt.com

LAZY LIZARD *Tavern*

PINE CREEK

Lazy Lizard Tavern bar

IF THE MUDBRICK walls of the Lazy Lizard Tavern seem strangely familiar, it's probably because they bear a striking resemblance to the tall termite mounds that dot the landscape as you drive through the Northern Territory. There's a reason for this: the bricks that the pub is built from were handmade from termite mounds collected by its creator and first owner, Rod Haines, in the mid 1990s. 'You probably wouldn't be allowed to do that now,' says current owner Bruce Jenkins, 'but back then ...'

The tavern is set in over 1.6 hectares of gardens, including a caravan park, in the heart of Pine Creek, a sleepy town that's home to about 350 people, just off the Stuart Highway 230 kilometres south of Darwin. Around the open-air bar – or, if it's hot (which it usually is), in the swimming pool that is situated to one side of the bar – you'll find locals ready to chat.

Pine Creek is one of the Northern Territory's oldest towns, the only surviving settlement from the gold-rush era of the 1870s and still a mining community. Today its location at the junction of the Kakadu and Stuart highways makes it 'the gateway to Kakadu' and it is a regular stopping point for tourists from all over Australia and overseas. The Lazy Lizard is pet-friendly too, but four-legged friends need to be kept on a leash.

> The mudbrick walls of the Lazy Lizard Tavern were handmade from termite mounds collected by its creator and first owner, Rod Haines, in the mid 1990s.

The tavern is a striking setting for a cold beer on a hot day. As well as the termite-mound walls, the building is constructed of ironwood timber pillars, beautifully carved by a former patron to feature animals and birds of the Northern Territory: cockatoos, kookaburras, kangaroos and more. Large wrought-iron wagon-wheel 'windows' were created by Canadian–Australian Earl Gayno. The walls are hung with colourful lizard sculptures, and with the work of resident artist Bolda Hunter, who has shared the traditional lifestyle and culture of the local Jawoyn people for more than 20 years. Bolda was taught and guided by senior Jawoyn elders, to whom he is related by marriage, and his art has been exhibited nationally and internationally. He often uses the Lazy Lizard as his studio, so visitors can watch him working. Bolda also runs spear- and didgeridoo-making workshops in the hotel grounds.

For those interested in local history, old mining tools add interest. The Lazy Lizard also has an upright piano and a pool table to keep visitors entertained. Live music and karaoke are part of the mix from time to time.

Birds flock to the property's lush gardens: about 25 species have been recorded here. Among them is the gouldian finch, returning to the Territory in good numbers after being on the brink of extinction. Early risers are likely to spot the yellow and blue hooded parrot at the end of the Dry. Other species to look out for are the partridge pigeon, red-collared lorikeets, blue-faced honeyeaters, red-winged parrots, northern rosellas, galahs and the great bowerbird, the crimson or blood finch, the masked finch and the zebra finch. The best months for birdwatching are August–October, as many international birders are discovering.

If you're stopping for a meal, there's a fairly extensive pub-fare menu – schnitzels with varying toppings, barramundi and chips, hot dogs, burgers and steaks – plus weekly specials on the blackboard, including a Sunday roast. The weekend lunch menu has nothing priced over $16. Pizzas with all the usual toppings, including an Aussie of ham, bacon, egg and onion, cost $20 for large or $12 for small. A kids' menu offers steak, schnitzel, fish and nuggets, all with chips and all for less than $10.

Make sure you leave room for dessert, which is something of a feature at the Lazy Lizard, with offerings such as Black Forest cake, cheesecakes and homemade ice-cream in ten different flavours including mango, Turkish delight, strawberry and white chocolate, banana and passionfruit, and more. The pub sells small tubs of this delicious ice-cream for $4. The coffee, too, is surprisingly good for such a remote spot: there's a selection of espressos, made from arabica beans.

Lazy Lizard sculptures

Travellers who want to break their journey can stay in the caravan park adjacent to the pub. It has 24 powered sites, 60 tent sites and three self-contained one-bedroom cabins, with more accommodation planned. There's a small shop, where daily road and weather reports are available, along with basic supplies and fuel.

You can explore the Pine Creek Railway Precinct, where the original 1888 station building is now a museum. There's a restored 1877 Beyer, Peacock steam engine and carriage, which operated from 1890 to 1943 between Darwin and Pine Creek. Next to it is Miners Park, which has an outdoor display of machinery from old mines in the area.

The Pine Creek National Trust Museum building is the oldest surviving prefabricated structure in the Territory, and tells the story of the goldminers, the local Chinese community, the buffalo hunters and the creation of the Overland Telegraph Line.

LAZY LIZARD TAVERN

ADDRESS

299 Millar Tce, Pine Creek

TELEPHONE

(08) 8976 1019

WEBSITE

www.lazylizardpinecreek.com.au

RATES

Powered sites $25 per night for 2 people; $6 per extra person. Unpowered camp sites $17 for 2 people, $6 per extra person. Campsites cannot be booked in advance. If you'd rather have a roof over your head, cabins cost $100.

HOURS

The bar opens at 10am daily and closes at 2am (or earlier if it is quiet).

GRUB

The bistro is open 12–2pm for lunch daily, and 6–9pm for dinner Tues–Sun. A range of snacks is available at other times. Mon (chef's day off) only pizza and specials are available.

TOP DROP

There's no beer on tap here, but it's all on ice. The most popular drop is XXXX Gold.

NEARBY ATTRACTIONS

Umbrawarra Gorge, 22 km SW of Pine Creek, has steep red cliffs with a stream running between them, and secluded swimming holes with sandy beaches. There are great views from the cliff-tops.

MORE INFO

www.travelnt.com

Queensland

Opposite (clockwise from top): Birdsville Hotel; The Spotted Cow, Toowoomba; Breakfast Creek Hotel, Albion; The Blue Heeler Hotel, Kynuna.

METROPOLITAN

REGIONAL

ESTABLISHED
1884
BIRDSVILLE HOTEL

RUM CK
Delicious Sparkling
FOUREX

GAMING LOUNGE
GREAT STEAKS
BEER OFF THE WOOD
PUBLIC BAR
(TAB/GAMING/KENO)
SUBSTATION no41 BAR
(SUPERB COCKTAILS)
COFFEE @ THE CREEK

The Spotted Cow
MILK
PINT
Fine Culinary Delights

BREAKFAST CREEK *Hotel*

ALBION

Breakfast Creek Hotel, Albion

The Substation No. 41 bar, created in the shell of a derelict electricity substation next to the hotel, makes the most of its exposed brick walls and soaring ceilings. Its 15-metre-long wooden bar is just the place to sip the latest cocktail.

A VISIT TO Brisbane, for many people, is simply not complete without a steak and a beer 'off the wood' at the Creek. The Breakfast Creek Hotel is quintessentially Queensland, famed for its beer garden, its massive steaks and its beer.

Built in 1890 and listed by the National Trust, the Renaissance-style pub is fondly known as the Brekky Creek – or simply the Creek. It is arguably the most famous watering hole in Queensland and the best loved in Brisbane. A $4.5 million renovation and restoration in 2002 gave a contemporary spin to the old place but took nothing from its appeal. With five bars, the tropical Beer Garden and the Spanish Garden steakhouse, there are plenty of choices for patrons – and each bar and restaurant has its own special atmosphere.

The Creek is famous for serving beer 'off the wood'. In 1977, a plan to change from wooden to steel kegs met with fierce opposition from patrons; a petition signed by hundreds and a deputation to the brewery led by unionists and wharfies who were among the regulars ensured that the wooden kegs remained. Today, the Private Bar is the home of the 'beer off the wood' and every day at midday you can watch the tradition of spiking the keg. This bar is a favourite spot for Brisbane businessmen, with its gentlemen's club atmosphere, extensive wine list, old fireplace and verandah.

Spanish Garden steakhouse

The public bar is, however, the heart of the Brekky Creek. Prop yourself up at the original island bar and have a look at the historic photos of the pub hanging on the walls. You will hear about the interesting clientele who have sat here before you, among them small-time criminals, journalists, politicians, wharfies and jockeys – Eagle Farm and Doomben racecourses aren't far away – or maybe you'll even meet some of them.

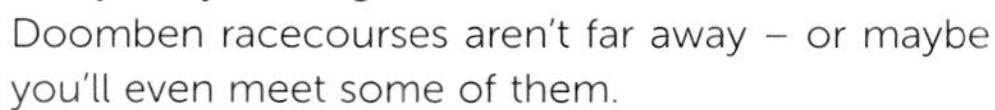

The newer Substation No. 41 bar, created in the shell of a derelict electricity substation next to the hotel, makes the most of its exposed brick walls and soaring ceilings. Its 15-metre-long wooden bar is just the place to sip the latest cocktail. DJs play here on Friday, Saturday and Sunday nights with a mix of lounge, house and retro tunes. There are 16 beers on tap, but if you can't decide, just go for the Substation sampler, which gives you a taste of four premium or craft beers.

The Spanish Garden steakhouse has been pulling in the crowds since 1968; the early idea of serving Mexican food here was soon ditched for barbecues and the Spanish Garden has never looked back. With shady green alcoves it is perfect on a summer day, when everyone is tucking into a steak. Line up and choose your own aged fillet from the chilled cabinet and watch it being chargrilled in the open kitchen. All the steaks are served with an Idaho baked potato topped with bacon sauce (or chips), coleslaw, salad, a bread roll and a choice of mushroom, pepper or chilli sauce. Don't eat red meat? There are

Substation No. 41

BREAKFAST CREEK HOTEL

ADDRESS
2 Kingsford Smith Dr (at Breakfast Creek Rd), Albion

TELEPHONE
(07) 3262 5988

WEBSITE
www.breakfastcreekhotel.com

HOURS
Public bar 10am–late; Staghorn Bar 11.30am–late; Substation No. 41 and Private Bar 12pm–late.

GRUB
Beer Garden open Mon–Wed 11.30am–2.30pm and 5–9pm, Thurs–Sat 11.30am–3pm and 5–9.30pm, Sun 11.30am–9pm. Spanish Garden open Mon–Wed 12–2.30pm and 5–9pm, Thurs–Fri and Sun 12–3pm and 5–9.30pm, Sat 5–9.30pm (closed for lunch on Sat).

TOP DROP
Among the 16 beers on tap are Big Helga, Fat Yak, James Squire, Tooheys Extra Dry, XXXX Gold, Carlton Draught and Stella Artois.

WHERE TO STAY
The Emporium Hotel, one of Brisbane's newest and smartest hotels, is a couple of km from Breakfast Creek. It has 102 rooms and suites, from about $280. www.emporiumhotel.com.au

NEARBY ATTRACTIONS
Newstead House, Brisbane's oldest surviving home, is just across the road from the Breakfast Creek Hotel. Built in 1846, it is now a house museum. www.newsteadhouse.com.au

MORE INFO
www.visitbrisbane.com.au

Public bar

plenty of other options, including barramundi, chicken and oysters.

The subtropical Staghorn Bar is the heart of the beer garden, with large timber decks that separate the dining area from the bar. With seating for more than 500 people, it is noisy and fun, and somewhere you never know who you might run into. The Staghorn Bar is the place to watch the latest sport, with lots of plasma screens and a choice of games.

The Breakfast Creek Hotel was built in 1890 by a former Lord Mayor of Brisbane, William MacNaughton Galloway, whose initials appear on the facade. Five years later, Galloway fell to his death from a second-floor window of the hotel (the coroner found that he was drunk at the time), and his ghost is said to roam the original parts of the building. Later, members of the Cavill family leased the hotel for more than 70 years until 1998, establishing its popularity with their faithful clientele.

The Creek was a trend-setter among Brisbane pubs, introducing the first beer-garden dining in the late 1940s or early 1950s, the outdoor kitchen where customers could choose their own steaks from a cabinet in the early 1960s and the city's first drive-through bottleshop, also in the 1960s.

With its location on the main route to Brisbane's airports from the city, the Brekky Creek is often a 'must' for visitors either arriving or leaving. This might account for visits from famous faces such as Mikhail Gorbachev, Russell Crowe, Greg Norman and Powderfinger – or they might just have heard about the steaks!

Choose your own steak

CLEVELAND POINT

THE NAME SAYS it all for this historic Queensland pub. Built in 1851 the Grand View – the GV to the locals – has views across Moreton Bay to North Stradbroke Island and on a sunny day it's hard to beat for location.

This 'grand old lady of the bay' is Queensland's oldest licensed hotel. Since it is only 30 minutes from Brisbane's CBD it's a popular spot for weekend lunches, with a large outdoor restaurant in a garden setting with lots of grassy areas, a shaded children's playground and live music.

Grand View Hotel, Cleveland Point

The name says it all … the Grand View – the GV to the locals – has views across Moreton Bay to North Stradbroke Island.

The Grand View Hotel was built by Francis Bigge in 1851, the year after Cleveland was proclaimed a township, and it was originally named the Brighton Hotel. It was a much-needed hotel in the area and quickly became popular for its bayside location, sea breezes and beautiful scenery. The first 'government road' – little more than a track – connecting Cleveland Point (at the time called Emu Point) and Brisbane had been surveyed in 1840, so it was possible for the citizens of Brisbane to reach the hotel via the Cleveland Point Road (now called Old Cleveland Road).

In 1855 Bigge leased the Brighton Hotel to John Cassim, who ran it until 1860 when he built the Cleveland Hotel on land adjacent toward the point. Francis Bigge returned to England in the early 1870s leaving Andrew and Mary Goodall in charge and in 1878 they bought it from him. Some time before the turn of the century, the hotel was remodelled for the last time, probably when the rail link between Brisbane and Cleveland opened. But hopes that Cleveland would become Brisbane's premier resort town were dashed when the rail line was extended to Tweed Heads in 1903, giving city folk easy access to the beaches of Southport and Coolangatta.

GRAND VIEW HOTEL

ADDRESS
49 North St, Cleveland Point

TELEPHONE
(07) 3286 1002

WEBSITE
www.gvh.com.au

RATES
$90 double for the Shamrock Room; $100 double for the Brighton Room. Rate includes continental breakfast.

HOURS
Mon–Wed 10am–11pm; Thurs–Sat 10–12am; Sun 10am–10pm.

GRUB
Emu Point Garden Restaurant open for lunch Mon–Thurs 12–2pm, Fri–Sat 12–3pm, and for dinner Tues–Thurs 6–8.30pm and Fri–Sat 6–9pm; open Sun 12–8pm. The Verandah Restaurant open Fri–Sat for dinner 6–9pm.

TOP DROP
The beers on tap include XXXX Bitter, XXXX Gold, Hahn Premium Light, Carlton Draught, VB, Boag's Draught, James Squire, Guinness and Old Speckled Hen.

NEARBY ATTRACTIONS
Drive to the old hexagonal lighthouse at the end of Cleveland Pt. Built in 1865, it is the only remaining timber lighthouse in Moreton Bay. Towards Brisbane, the Black Swamp Wetlands has abundant wildlife. Easy, paved paths lead through it; there is a platform for birdwatching and at dusk the flying fox colony – about 100 000 strong – disperses.

MORE INFO
www.more2redlands.com.au/explore
www.queenslandholidays.com.au

The upstairs verandah has stunning views

The hotel's name was changed to the Grand View Hotel in 1910, and while it may not have the lure of the Gold Coast, it has continued to be a favourite spot for many people for its quiet charm.

As well as the laid-back Emu Point Garden Restaurant, the upstairs of the heritage-listed hotel also contains the Verandah Restaurant for more formal dining and those stunning views. Fresh local seafood – scallops, oysters, Moreton Bay bugs, lobster and mussels – is a feature of the menu, along with premium cuts of meat and fresh market produce.

In the lounge bar, there are comfy couches and the walls are lined with photographs of some famous (and not so famous) faces. The portraits seem a puzzle but the link between them – many of them autographed – is that they are all authors who have taken part in the Grand View's regular literary lunches. The list reads like a who's who of Australian writers, among them journalist George Negus, actor and writer Graeme Blundell, travel writer Ann Rickard, novelist Di Morrissey, William McInnes, Tracey Wickham ... the list goes on.

Other regular events include monthly wine dinners, live entertainment, poker and trivia nights and special seasonal dining events, as well as sport on the big screens. There's also the Vegas by the Bay gaming room, where free coffee and croissants are provided for players 10–11am daily.

The Grand View Hotel's two bed-and-breakfast heritage rooms have been furnished in the style of the hotel's early days and have access to the verandah. The Brighton Room has a queen-sized bed and an ensuite, and the Shamrock Room has a queen bed and a single bed with a bathroom along the hallway. A continental breakfast is included, but on Sunday mornings an à la carte breakfast is also available in the Emu Point Garden Restaurant.

The NORMAN HOTEL

WOOLLOONGABBA

PROUDLY DECLARING ITSELF 'Brisbane's Worst Vegetarian Restaurant' has not hurt the Norman Hotel one little bit. It may be a gimmick, but after a fire in 2009 closed the hotel for a month, that reputation helped rebuild it as committed carnivores headed back here in droves.

There were no injuries when the fire broke out during a busy Friday lunchtime service, and nor was there damage to the historic public bar, but the closure was the catalyst for a new addition to the pub, Norman's Bar.

The Norman Hotel, Woolloongabba

The juicy steaks at the Norman Hotel turn first-time visitors into regulars. Sourced from Australia's top meat suppliers, they are ranged in a chilled cabinet where you can browse as if it's your personal butcher shop and choose exactly which cut you'll have grilled and served up to you.

There are several places to eat in. Take your pick from the large open Grill Court and Fountain Court, the beer garden or the new Norman's Bar, which is also the spot to watch the game on the huge 264-centimetre plasma screen – the first of its size in a Queensland pub – or for a drink before heading to a match at the Brisbane Cricket Ground, the Gabba. The Sports Bar, tucked in a corner of the heritage-listed part of the hotel, also has live sport action and is a favourite with the locals.

Norman's Bar is the spot to watch the game on the huge plasma screen – or for a drink before heading to a match at the Brisbane Cricket Ground, the Gabba.

The Norman stands on the corner of Ipswich Road and Qualtrough Street, the latter named after Elizabeth Qualtrough who sold her land to Robert Heaslop in 1885 so he could build his grand hotel. In the late 1880s, Queensland was beginning to develop its own distinctive architecture and the hotel, designed by John Nicolson, was completed in 1889, the same year that Brisbane's Central Station opened.

THE NORMAN HOTEL

ADDRESS
102 Ipswich Rd, Woolloongabba

TELEPHONE
(07) 3391 5022

WEBSITE
www.normanhotel.com.au

HOURS
Daily 11am–late.

GRUB
Open for lunch 12–2.30pm daily (until 3pm Fri–Sun), and for dinner daily 5.30–9pm (9.30pm Fri–Sat).

TOP DROP
There are around 20 beers on tap, including XXXX Gold, VB, Hahn Super Dry, Hahn Light, Tooheys New, Fat Yak and James Squire.

WHERE TO STAY
The Hotel Chino at Woolloongabba is a new boutique hotel with 66 guest rooms and apartments, from $185 per night. It is about 1 km from the Norman Hotel, 2 km from the Brisbane Cricket Ground and 4 km from the Brisbane CBD. www.hotelchino.com.au

NEARBY ATTRACTIONS
The Brisbane Cricket Ground – the Gabba – runs tours every Thurs at 10.30am with a duration of 1–1.5 hrs; they give you a first-hand look at player facilities, media rooms, the Members' Dining Room with all its memorabilia, the Gabba's indoor and outdoor practice wickets, and sometimes access to the main field. Tours cost $16. www.thegabba.com.au

MORE INFO
www.visitbrisbane.com.au
www.queenslandholidays.com.au

Norman's Bar

Heaslop named his hotel after Sir Henry Norman, the newly appointed governor of Queensland. Norman, who had relocated to Queensland from Jamaica, was a well-liked and respected governor who had many places in Brisbane named after him.

From 1896, Heaslop leased the hotel before selling it to the brewing company Perkins & Co in 1900. Perkins & Co, which acquired a number of other Brisbane pubs in the same year, was known for its beers featuring the letter X, referring to the strength of the alcohol content. It produced the Perkins XXX Bitter Ale, XXXX Bitter Ale (introduced in 1924) and even a XXXXXX beer. Perkins & Co leased the Norman to a number of licensees until 1928, when the brewer was taken over by its biggest rival and became part of Castlemaine Perkins.

With the exception of minor renovations and the construction of wartime air-raid shelters, the Norman Hotel remained relatively unchanged until the late 1980s, when it was bought by the Cavill family, who owned it until 2006. Today the Norman is part of the Australian-owned Independent Pub Group.

Indoor dining

The Cavills extended the hotel onto some adjoining land, adding the beer garden and outdoor dining area. The air-raid shelters and old stables were removed and in 1988 the steakhouse opened, beginning a new era and resulting in new fame for the old hotel. As its popularity and reputation grew, the Norman soon gained the title of 'Brisbane's Worst Vegetarian Restaurant' – a tag that stuck and has become the key marketing platform for the hotel.

The hotel runs the Norman Express, a minibus service between the pub and the CBD (within a 5-kilometre radius) on weekdays and to all Suncorp Stadium home games of the Queensland Reds rugby team.

THE PLOUGH INN

SOUTH BRISBANE

WHETHER YOU ARE upstairs on the elegant iron-lace trimmed verandah, dining under the front awning, or in the slick new beer garden with its deck, the Plough Inn offers some of Brisbane's best views. And don't the patrons know it, flocking to this historic pub for big events like New Year's Eve and Brisbane's River Fire – or perhaps just because it's a balmy Queensland night.

If location is everything, then publican Daniel Costigan certainly knew what he was doing when he built the Plough Inn in 1885 to replace an earlier pub of the same name. A century later, the pub was one of five buildings to survive the clearing of old docklands to make way for Brisbane's hosting of World Expo 88. The Plough closed while the redevelopment went on around it, emerging for the opening of the six-month event after a half-million-dollar facelift and with a new lease on life.

The Plough Inn and its covered beer garden

In the redevelopment of South Bank Parklands after the heady Expo days were over, the Plough Inn once again became a central part of a 'new' Brisbane, and it hasn't looked back. On weekends, the place is packed with diners and drinkers and its proximity to all that the Parklands has to offer makes it a great place for watching the world go by.

One of the city's oldest buildings, the Plough Inn still retains many of its original features, giving it character and charm.

The Plough's views of the city skyline, the Parklands and the river could be the best from any pub in Brisbane. One of the city's oldest buildings, the Plough Inn still retains many of its original features, giving it character and charm, but recent makeovers have also brought it smartly into the 21st century.

The newly built beer garden next to the original building is one of the most popular places to be, with live entertainment at the weekends and the chance to sit in the sun (but with sail shades to keep off the rain and the worst of the heat). There is counter service for meals, you can eat inside or outside, and the bar staff are always happy to give advice on new beers that are being showcased.

THE PLOUGH INN

ADDRESS
Stanley St Plaza, South Brisbane

TELEPHONE
(07) 3844 7777

WEBSITE
www.ploughinn.com.au

HOURS
Mon–Thurs 11am–10.30pm, Fri–Sat 10–12am, Sun 10am–11pm.

GRUB
Open for lunch 11am–3pm Mon–Thurs, 11am–4pm Fri–Sun and for dinner 5–9pm Mon–Thurs, 4.30–9.30pm Fri–Sat and 4.30–9pm Sun.

TOP DROP
Beers on tap include Carlton Draught, Carlton Midstrength, VB, Pure Blonde, Pure Blonde Naked, Pure Blonde White, Asahi and Hoegaarden.

WHERE TO STAY
Rydges South Bank Brisbane has 304 guest rooms and 64 1-bedroom suites, from around $180 per night, and is located just behind South Bank Parklands. www.rydges.com/southbank

NEARBY ATTRACTIONS
The Plough Inn is in the heart of South Bank Parklands, a stone's throw from the swimming lagoon and beach, and a few minutes' walk to the Queensland Art Gallery, Queensland Gallery of Modern Art, Queensland Museum and the Wheel of Brisbane. On Fri nights and weekend days, the South Bank Lifestyle Markets fill the Stanley St Plaza outside the pub's front door.

MORE INFO
www.southbank.net.au
www.ourbrisbane.com

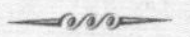

The lounge bar

Inside the original building the recently renovated Sports Bar has several LCD screens and is a popular place for fans to meet before heading off to a match at Suncorp Stadium or the Gabba, or to stay and enjoy the game in comfort. It has 11 beers on tap, and the bar is full of sporting memorabilia.

For a quieter spot, there's the lounge bar, or head upstairs to the Heritage Bar, a replica of the bar in the Sydney Cricket Ground Members' Stand. It is open from lunchtime on Friday for the weekend and has the best views of the city and the South Bank swimming lagoon.

A traditional steakhouse menu offers a large range of cuts and styles, along with pub favourites and house specialties such as hickory barbecue pork ribs, smoked in-house and served in two sizes. You will need the bib provided – these ribs can get messy! Chef's specials on Monday and Tuesdays are a 400 gram rump or T-bone steak or a full serve of pork ribs for $22. Another signature dish is the fresh mussel pot, served in several ways, with fresh bread and chips. If you love mussels, Thursday night is the night to be at the Plough, when the chef tries out new recipes with them and the 'mussel madness' price is $20 for all types. You might find yourself eating them with creamy smoked salmon, baby spinach and parmesan, or as a Thai red curry with wilted bok choy. Fans of the 'parmy' should head here on Wednesday nights for live entertainment and $17 parmigianas – traditional, gamberoni or Sicilian – for $17.

South Bank Parklands is a magnet for families – especially in the summer when the lagoon and man-made beach are crowded – and the Plough Inn caters for all: its kids' menu has a fixed price of $9 for the under-tens.

The REGATTA HOTEL

TOOWONG

THE FLOOD MARKERS on the wall of the Regatta Hotel chronicle the reality of life by the Brisbane River. To varying degrees, the elegant pub on Brisbane's Coronation Drive went under water in 1887, 1890, 1893 and 1974. Now there's a new marker needed for 2011. Famous for many reasons, the Regatta once again felt the force of nature when the Queensland floods of February 2011 rushed into the basement floors and put the pub out of action for a short time.

It's not the first time that patrons have been without their beloved riverside hotel. In fact, the first flood to hit the Regatta Hotel, in January 1887, was before the first customer had even set foot inside the building.

The original Regatta Hotel had been built in 1874 by Lawrence Howard Healy. It was a small single-storey timber building, with a dirt floor and an iron roof. In 1882, it was sold to William Winterford, who had grander things in mind. In 1886 he tore down the building and began replacing it with the imposing three-storey edifice that still pulls in the crowds today.

The Regatta Hotel, Toowong

Antique rowing boats are displayed around the hotel; the boat hanging in the verandah of the main bar is from Brisbane's oldest rowing club, the Commercial Rowing Club.

A year later, the first flood came. Then, in March 1890, the river rose 45 centimetres higher than it had in 1887, and in January 1893 the water level rose once again, to flood the cellar bar, the public bar and rise one-third of the way up to the first floor. Another flood two months later reached the first-floor balcony – and was the last that the Winterford family had to endure.

The next major deluge was the 1974 Australia Day flood, when the water level reached two-thirds of the way up the public bar and which saw kayakers paddling through it to order. In the equally devastating floods of January 2011, although the pub was only closed for a few days, the restoration and renovation work continued for about nine months.

But its proximity to the river has always been integral to the Regatta – even its name reflects this. Antique rowing boats are displayed around the hotel; the boat hanging

THE REGATTA HOTEL

ADDRESS
543 Coronation Dr, Toowong

TELEPHONE
(07) 3871 9504

WEBSITE
www.regattahotel.com.au

HOURS
Daily 10am–late.

GRUB
Daily for breakfast 6.30–10.30am, lunch 11am–2.30pm and dinner 5.30–9pm.

TOP DROP
The Regatta has about 30 different beers available, including local, craft, premium and imported labels.

WHERE TO STAY
The Jephson Hotel is 3 blocks from the Regatta, and has a variety of queen, twin, family and spa rooms, and 1- and 2-bedroom apartments, from $199.
www.jephsonhotel.com.au

NEARBY ATTRACTIONS
Catch a CityCat at the ferry terminal across the street from the Regatta and travel the length of the Brisbane River. One way will take you to the University of Queensland campus, the other to the city centre, South Bank Parklands and further to New Farm Park or the trendy suburb of Bulimba.

MORE INFO
www.visitbrisbane.com.au
www.queenslandholidays.com.au

in the verandah of the main bar is the Fred Winters Four from Brisbane's oldest rowing club, the Commercial Rowing Club. Rowing was at its peak around 1913, attracting huge crowds of spectators from all walks of life in a way that rivalled going to the horse races. The Toowong Rowing Club's boatshed, next to the hotel on Coronation Drive, was a popular venue for dances but was washed away in the 1974 floods. It was replaced by the Regatta's Boatshed Restaurant in 1992.

Entrance to the Regatta

Floods aside, the Regatta also holds an iconic place in Australian pub history. On a Wednesday afternoon in March 1965, two Brisbane feminists, Merle Thornton and Rosalie Bognor, made headlines when they walked into the Regatta's public bar and ordered a lemonade each. In the 1960s, it was illegal for women to enter the public bar of any hotel. When they were refused service, Thornton and Bognor chained themselves to the foot rail of the bar. The police were called, but while they searched for a bolt-cutter, the 40 or so men in the bar bought the ladies beers while their husbands handed out protest materials detailing the discrimination women faced in Queensland hotels. Despite the publicity, their protest was in vain and the law did not change for another few years. To avoid any repetition of the stunt, the foot rails were removed from the Regatta's public bar! But the pub now has a Thornton Room, named after Merle.

The Regatta promises a great night out

With $8 million being spent on restoring, refurbishing and rejuvenating the Regatta in 2011, its long history as a favourite watering hole for Brisbane looks set to continue, whatever nature throws at it. And ironically, one of the best ways to get to the Regatta is on the river. The hotel has its own ferry terminal across the street, with Brisbane's CityCats making regular stops.

STORY BRIDGE *Hotel*

KANGAROO POINT

TRADITION FEATURES STRONGLY at the Story Bridge Hotel. Not only is the third generation of the Deery family at the helm but one of the strangest traditions of Australia Day is still going strong at the hotel 30 years after it began.

Built under the pylons of its namesake bridge, the hotel is now one of the last remaining family-owned and -operated hotels in Queensland. Built in 1886, the pub was originally called the Kangaroo Point Hotel but changed its name in 1940 to coincide with the opening of the Story Bridge, an event that saw 600000 people turn out to walk across it. The pub's classic Queenslander-style architecture is now rare, with the hotel one of only seven three-storey hotels remaining in the state from this period.

Thousands of people head to the hotel on Australia Day to race cockroaches with numbers painted on their backs.

The Story Bridge Hotel, Kangaroo Point

Beside the Story Bridge

The Shelter Bar

In 1967 the Deery family, headed by Barrie Deery, bought the hotel, which was patronised mainly by workers from local industries around Kangaroo Point. By the 1970s the neighbourhood had changed, becoming more residential, and there was a need for a more 'village-pub' style. In 1978 Barrie Deery therefore decided to restore the hotel to its former glory, but it was a plan that took many years to bring to fulfilment as he battled red tape and regulations.

Meanwhile, the annexe at the back of the hotel – a bottleshop converted from an old World War II bomb shelter – underwent further extensions and established itself as one of the most original and well-known venues in town for its live entertainment.

The hotel also became home to two great special events: the Australia Day Cockroach Races and the National Festival of Beers every September. Both have put the Story Bridge Hotel on the map nationally, with the cocky races even making it into *The Guinness Book of Records* in 2010 as the 'Oldest Roach Races'.

It is undoubtedly one of the world's weirdest race meetings. Thousands of people head to the hotel on Australia Day, as they have since 1981, to race cockroaches with numbers painted on their backs and names like Cocky Balboa, Ita Buttroach, Osama Bin Liner and Sir Roach-a-Lot. Up for grabs is the Story Bridge Hotel Annual Australia Day Cockroach Races Cup, a $3000 prize for Best Dressed, and the 'Miss Cocky' Pageant crown. The unusual race day is a charity fund-raiser. Entrants pay $5 per cockroach to enter, and in 2010 the day raised almost $20 000.

'The cockroach races began out of a conversation from two locals sitting at the old Story Bridge Hotel's Bombshelter Bar discussing who had the biggest cockroaches in their suburb,' says Richard Deery. 'To settle it, it was suggested by one of the Deery family that both of them should bring the cockroaches from their respective suburbs to the pub on Australia Day and these questions would be answered.'

Story Bridge Hotel

The first restoration of the pub was completed in 1994 and in 2003 the Bombshelter Bar was finally retired as plans were made for yet another extensive renovation. The new-look hotel has a more contemporary style, with a new bar and 'urban beer garden', but all of it still under the bridge and with Barrie Deery's children Richard and Jane now at the helm.

The new bar, called the Shelter, is positioned between the pylons of the bridge and makes the most of the balmy Brisbane climate with its outdoor areas. It also has five plasma screens so patrons need never miss a second of the latest sporting event. The big nights are Friday and Saturday, and crowds also turn out for the Sunday session at the Outback Bar & Grill, which carries on the pub's 50-year tradition of live jazz sessions on Sunday afternoons from 3pm.

A true landmark, 'The Bridge' frequently plays host to the rich and famous but has retained the laidback atmosphere it has always had.

Views of the city from the upstairs verandah

STORY BRIDGE HOTEL

ADDRESS
200 Main St, Kangaroo Point

TELEPHONE
(07) 3391 2266

WEBSITE
www.storybridgehotel.com.au

HOURS
Mon–Thurs 10–12am, Fri 10–1.30am, Sat 8–1.30am, Sun 8–12am.

GRUB
Breakfast weekends 8–11.30am. Deery's Restaurant open daily for lunch 12–3pm and dinner 6–10pm. Bar snacks 12–10pm daily. Pizza Corner open until 11pm Fri–Sat.

TOP DROP
There are 26 beers on tap, the most popular being XXXX Gold. Boutique beers always available, such as the Lord Nelson Three Sheets and Moo Brew from Tasmania.

WHERE TO STAY
The Point is a boutique hotel at Kangaroo Point with a mix of hotel rooms and 1- and 2-bedroom apartments from $362 per night. www.thepointbrisbane.com.au

NEARBY ATTRACTIONS
Take the Story Bridge Adventure Climb to a platform that's 80 m above the river. You can climb during the day or at twilight, and at dawn on Sat. It's safe and easy, and you'll be rewarded by 360-degree views of the city, river and Moreton Bay. www.storybridgeadventureclimb.com.au

MORE INFO
www.visitbrisbane.com.au
www.queenslandholidays.com.au

The APOLLONIAN Hotel

BOREEN POINT

The Apollonian Hotel, Boreen Point

THE APOLLONIAN HOTEL looks so perfect in its park-like setting that it's hard to believe it hasn't been there forever. But that's the case. This historic pub on the Sunshine Coast was built at the height of the 1860s gold rush in Gympie and was moved to the village of Boreen Point on the shores of Lake Cootharaba more than a century later.

Gold was discovered in Gympie in 1867 and within a short time an English comedian and vocalist named Robert 'Billy' Barlow had built Barlow's Apollonian Philharmonic Music Hall Hotel, taking its name from the Greek sun god Apollo, also the god of theatre and music. Through several changes of name and owners, the Apollonian stuck until it became simply the Apollonian Hotel.

Early in 1879, the existing Apollonian Hotel was built of hoop pine, with cedar windows and doors. In 1890 the hotel was leased to Richard Henry Cox, father of the gifted soprano Mabel Cox. The lease was held by the Cox family for 31 years before Mabel's brother Richard – later the mayor of Gympie – was able to buy the freehold. The pub remained unchanged and intact, but in 1987 was moved to the pretty village of Boreen Point, about 52 kilometres south-east of its first home, where its walls still ring with music on a regular basis.

Sunday lunch is particularly special, with a wood-fired spit-roast prepared in the rustic bush kitchen and served with platters of salad, hot potatoes and damper.

Set on about 1.2 hectares, with rolling lawns down to the street and rainforest gardens all around it, the wide cool verandahs are a popular spot for families, especially at weekends. Sunday lunch is particularly special, with a wood-fired spit-roast (pork or beef) prepared in the rustic bush kitchen and served with platters of salad, hot potatoes and damper. There's a slightly more limited menu than usual on Sundays for those who don't want the roast, and live music plays in the shady beer garden until 4pm.

On other days, there are hearty counter meals and you can either eat in the large dining room – there's a fireplace in winter – or under the verandah awning with its trailing

Restored railway quarters accommodation

bougainvillea and views of the lawns. Try the signature Apollonian chunky meat pie with chips and salad or a side of mushed peas. The kids' menu has meals for $7, but make sure they leave room for dessert because they won't want to pass up the Frog in the Lake (green jelly and ice-cream with a Freddo frog).

BYO-instrument 'muso' nights are held every second Tuesday, all comers are welcome to play, and since 2000 the Apollonian Hotel Folk Club has seen local and visiting musicians presenting anything from traditional jazz to gospel, classic rock and a capella music.

Accommodation is in restored railway quarters on the far side of the gravel carpark, with ten budget rooms sharing kitchen and bathroom facilities. There are five double rooms, four with queen beds and one room with a double bed, and five bunk rooms with two double bunks in each. The communal kitchen has a large fridge, gas stovetop, toaster and kettle. As all tap water is from a bore, drinking water is provided in the fridge.

A short distance down the street is the shore of Lake Cootharaba. This part of the Sunshine Coast is only 20 minutes' drive from the busy beaches and boutiques of Noosa Heads, but seems a world away. Lake Cootharaba is a saltwater lake about 10 kilometres long and 5 kilometres wide, part of the Noosa River system and the Great Sandy Region. Campers, boaties and families who enjoy the quieter spots of the Sunshine Coast come here.

Lake Cootharaba is a popular spot for sailing and Boreen Point has been home to the Lake Cootharaba Sailing Club since 1946. The Apollonian Hotel is a major sponsor of the sailing club, which conducts several large regattas each year. The Apollonian All-Boats Regatta is held every August to kick off the sailing season, and there are other big events in November and December and at Easter, creating a colourful spectacle on the water.

THE APOLLONIAN HOTEL

ADDRESS
Laguna St, Boreen Point

TELEPHONE
(07) 5485 3100

WEBSITE
www.apollonianhotel.com.au

RATES
$35 single; $50 double; $60 twin; $70 triple share; $75 double and two singles. Weekly rates $210, or $150 for a single guest.

HOURS
Daily 10–12am.

GRUB
Daily for lunch 12–2pm and dinner 6–8pm.

TOP DROP
Guinness and Tooheys New are on tap.

NEARBY ATTRACTIONS
Explore more of the Noosa River and lakes system on a cruise from Noosa. For walkers, the Elanda Circuit in the Great Sandy National Park at Lake Cootharaba (via Lake Flat Rd) offers several tracks ranging from a 5.1 km circuit via historic Mills Pt, to longer walks up to 12 km to Fig Tree Pt and Harry's Hut.

MORE INFO
www.sunshinecoastvisit.com.au
www.queenslandholidays.com.au

BIRDSVILLE HOTEL

BIRDSVILLE

Birdsville Hotel

IT'S THE PHOTO that almost every visitor to Birdsville has taken of themselves: standing under the sign on the deep wooden valance of the Birdsville Hotel's verandah, grinning widely, having finally made it to this iconic outback pub. It's what the owners of the pub, Kym Fort and David Brook and their families, call 'an outback version of a flag poked into the snow after a hard climb to the top of Mt Everest'.

The hotel looks much the same as it was when patrons were predominantly drovers taking cattle south and when horses were hitched to the verandah posts. The verandah, with an awning of corrugated iron supported by timber posts and decorated with the wooden valance bearing those much-photographed words 'Birdsville Hotel', has been restored with respect for the original.

One of the pub's busiest times is the first weekend in September when the annual Birdsville Races attract nearly 6000 visitors to join the locals for this iconic outback horseracing event.

There's just something special about the Birdsville Hotel, says Kym Fort's wife Jo. 'It's an atmosphere that evokes the spirit of a particular type of Australian and a particular approach to life. Our manager, Brian, is fiercely proud of the way the hotel is the ultimate level playing field. Everyone is welcome. Everyone is treated well. Everyone is expected to treat everyone else well. It's a simple approach. And people seem to like it very much.

'Today's visitors are usually on their way to or from somewhere a long way from anywhere else! While they're here, they revel in the stories and characters of the outback and we encourage them to get to know and understand a place and people that are a vital part of that inheritance.'

Birdsville is 1600 kilometres west of Brisbane, on the edge of the Simpson Desert where temperatures reach the mid-40 degrees Celsius in summer and are around 35 degrees in winter. To the south of Birdsville is the legendary Birdsville Track, mapped as a stock route in 1905 from Marree in South Australia and now a major touring route for outback travellers. Before Federation in 1901, Birdsville was a collection point for a toll on all stock and supplies entering South Australia from Queensland. It was a thriving community then, and today still has a population of about 110.

Birdsville was originally established to service surrounding pastoral holdings and then became an administrative centre and marshalling point for cattle. Back then, stockmen and drovers gathered at the Birdsville Hotel; today the bar sees a mix of business people, contractors, tourists and local landowners. 'We delight in being the place where all these very different people can relax and share their stories, where the decor is a hotchpotch of conversation starters, where visitors learn about Australia and Australians,' says Jo.

The Birdsville Hotel has two large bars, two dining areas, a beer garden and 27 modern motel units. The original sandstone building dates back to 1884, and since buying it in 1980, Kym and David have redeveloped and renovated without the hotel losing its character.

Visitors can dine in the Green Lizard bar, the dining room, the beer garden or have a 'countery' at the Front Bar. Friday is BBQ night in the beer garden, Saturday is buffet night when the chefs 'get creative', and Sunday is roast night. 'We'll leave a meal for guests arriving late,' says Jo. 'We won't let our visitors go to bed hungry.' They'll also provide a packed lunch for daytrips to nearby attractions.

Locals and tourists mingle in the bar

Over many, many years, the pub has built up a collection of stories, signs, photos, paintings, trophies, mementos and all sorts of oddities that now adorn its walls. One wall is crammed with hats of all types and in all conditions that belonged to people who have lived and worked in Birdsville. To get their hat on the wall, the person has to have achieved one year of unbroken service. On another wall are the hats and memorabilia of patrons who have died but left their mark on the Birdsville community.

There are also many art works, mostly of outback images and characters, including works by local artist and Blue Poles Art Gallery owner Wolfgang John, and by local indigenous artists. One special piece is a depiction of the Birdsville Hotel in the company of a tiny pink elephant, painted by Australian artist Pro Hart in the 1970s.

'We're always looking to forge links with the history of the hotel,' says Jo. 'We have commissioned a talented outback artisan to create three magnificent benches for the verandah, exactly where photographs show similar seating was placed in the early days of the hotel's existence.'

One of the pub's busiest times is the first weekend in September when the annual Birdsville Races attract nearly 6000 visitors to join the locals for this iconic outback horseracing event. But at any time of year, the experience of staying at Birdsville is never forgotten. 'There is a lot to see and experience around Birdsville, and we encourage our visitors to stay a while to check it all out,' says Jo.

BIRDSVILLE HOTEL

ADDRESS
Adelaide St, Birdsville

TELEPHONE
(07) 4656 3244

WEBSITE
www.theoutback.com.au

RATES
$130 single, $155 double or twin.

HOURS
Daily 10–12am.

GRUB
Open daily for breakfast 7.30–9am, lunch 12–2pm and dinner 6–8.30pm.

TOP DROP
Beers on tap are XXXX Gold, Hahn Super Dry, Carlton Draught and Hahn Premium Light.

NEARBY ATTRACTIONS
The excellent Wirrarri Visitor Information Centre is also the town's library and sometime art gallery. Visit the Frontier Services Museum, the famous Birdsville Racecourse, or try a camel pie at the Birdsville Bakery.

MORE INFO
www.queenslandholidays.com.au

THE BLUE HEELER HOTEL

KYNUNA

The Blue Heeler Hotel, Kynuna

THE BROLGAS ARE dancing in the dusty space between the front verandah of the Blue Heeler Hotel and the highway. They are bold and unafraid of people, walking right through the open door and into the bar if they are not chased out, and scavenging for any dropped scraps. It is a daily event and one that the locals don't bat an eyelid at ... but for the tourists it's a great novelty and the cameras click furiously.

The Blue Heeler is the lone pub in the tiny town of Kynuna, an 1860s staging post for Cobb & Co coaches that once boasted three hotels. It was built in 1889 and was originally called Absolon's Hotel.

Kynuna is most famous for its links with Banjo Paterson and 'Waltzing Matilda'. Folklore has it that the owner of nearby Dagworth Station, Bob MacPherson, told Paterson the story of the suicide of Samuel Hoffmeister beside the Combo Waterhole, 13 kilometres upstream on the Diamantina River, in September 1894. Hoffmeister was reportedly one of the shearers on strike involved in the burning down of the Dagworth woolshed. It is said he had a last drink at the Blue Heeler Hotel and then killed himself at Combo Waterhole.

This story, together with others that Paterson heard while he was visiting at Dagworth, inspired him to write 'Waltzing Matilda'. His fiancée, Christina MacPherson, adapted a popular Scottish tune, 'Craiglea', to become the original music for 'Waltzing Matilda'. In the Blue Heeler's dining room an upright piano stands ready for someone – anyone – to play a tune. No prizes for guessing which is the most attempted!

The brolgas are dancing in the dusty space between the front verandah of the Blue Heeler Hotel and the highway. They are bold, walking right through the open door and into the bar.

Guillotine window, a link with Banjo Paterson

In the pub, a sign declares this to be the site of the first performance of the unofficial Australian anthem, but some people contest this version of history. The town of Winton, 166 kilometres along the Matilda Highway, also makes that claim to fame, naming the North Gregory Hotel as the pub where it took place.

Travellers who stop at the Blue Heeler often leave a piece of themselves on the walls, on which messages, names and dates – along with the odd original verse – are scrawled with marker pens, covering almost every inch of it. There are also hats, shirts and other mementos pinned up.

The narrow main bar runs between a pool room and the dining room. In the pool room, beyond the red felt of the table, is a large brick fireplace donated by R. M. Williams for the pub's centenary (the Blue Heeler sign that glows neon on the roof of the pub is another relatively recent addition, a 99th birthday gift from the XXXX brewery).

A guillotine window between the bar and the dining room is a direct link with Paterson's stories of his time here. He wrote in *Golden Water* how the MacPhersons passed champagne through the window to the union shearers after the burning of the woolshed, in a gesture that ended the conflict. That was in September 1891, when the pub was known as Mick Fahey's Kynuna Hotel.

THE BLUE HEELER HOTEL

ADDRESS
Hulbert St, Matilda Hwy, Kynuna

TELEPHONE
(07) 4746 8650

RATES
Motel rooms $95 per night, trailers $55 per night.

HOURS
Daily 10–12am.

GRUB
Open daily for breakfast 7–9am, lunch 12–2pm and dinner 6.30–8.30pm.

TOP DROP
There are 4 beers on tap: VB, XXXX Gold, Hahn Premium Light and Tooheys New.

NEARBY ATTRACTIONS
A little further along the highway at McKinlay, 104 km SE of Cloncurry, is another famous outback pub, the Walkabout Creek Hotel, which was built in 1900 and was known as the Federal Hotel until it found fame in the hit Australian movie *Crocodile Dundee* in 1986. After the movie the pub adopted its 'stage name' permanently.

MORE INFO
www.mckinlay.qld.gov.au
www.queenslandholidays.com.au

Brolgas on the verandah

The pool room with its brick fireplace

Combo Waterhole Conservation Park is 16 kilometres from Kynuna, the last 5 kilometres on an unsealed road, off the Matilda Highway (the old Landsborough Highway). A lovely 2.5-kilometre walking track loops through the bush to the waterhole on the Diamantina River. There are picnic spots under the coolibah trees and interpretive signs with appropriate verses from the song. The path takes you through the dry channels of the Diamantina and crosses historic stone-walled overshots built by Chinese labourers in 1890 to trap the water. The waterhole is brown and murky, but the birdlife is prolific – pink galahs, whistling kites and waterbirds – and it's a very peaceful spot.

Back at the pub, if you feel like resting before tackling the rest of the highway, there is basic accommodation at the back of the hotel. Six motel-style rooms have ensuites and in 2011 underwent a complete renovation with new beds and bedding, flat-screen televisions (with satellite reception) and air conditioning. There are also ten single-bed trailers and a caravan park next door.

As for the brolgas, as dusk nears they simply fly away into the distance, in the direction of the river and the waterhole. But tomorrow's visitors can be almost certain they'll be back.

CORONES HOTEL

CHARLEVILLE

The extraordinary and expansive Corones Hotel, Charleville

THE LEGEND OF Harry Corones lives large in Charleville. The man who built the outback town's extraordinary pub is remembered every day in tours of the 'living museum' that give an insight into a dream that has lived on long after he has gone.

A single-storey hotel built around 1895 on the corner of Wills and Galatea streets and called the Hotel Norman was bought in 1924 by Harry Corones, who set about an ambitious task of creating his dream hotel in four stages, to enable him to continue trading throughout the five years it would take. In those days, timber hotels were often destroyed by fire, something Corones knew only too well, as this had been the fate of his former hotel, the Charleville, on two occasions. The new hotel would be built to last, the first two stages being of reinforced concrete, the third and final stage of brick.

By the end of 1926 the new hotel was two-thirds complete and it was the talk of the district 'from Roma to Eulo and out to the far west and north', according to the local newspaper. 'In every way the new Hotel Corones will be an example of hotel architecture and comfort scarce equalled in the Southern Hemisphere, and will undoubtedly be a great centre for all western men,' it reported. The building was completed in 1929, had cost £50 000 and stretched almost an entire block of Charleville's main street.

It was the ultimate in luxury, with copper-topped tables, deep leather lounges and chairs, a writing room and telephone booth, a dining room that seated 150, and a private bar which gave exclusive service and was screened from the public bar by a French-polished oak partition with mirrors. The public bar was deemed modern and luxurious and a courtyard formed an entrance to the ballroom.

Upstairs all guest rooms opened onto the verandah, some with their own bathrooms, and there was also an upstairs smoking lounge. Corones Hall, a function room on Galatea Street, was in demand for exclusive balls, parties and banquets; today it is the pub's bottleshop.

The building was the ultimate in luxury, with copper-topped tables, deep leather lounges and chairs, a writing room and telephone booth, a dining room that seated 150, and a private bar.

CORONES HOTEL

ADDRESS
33 Wills St, Charleville

TELEPHONE
(07) 4654 1022

WEBSITE
www.hotelcorones.com.au

RATES
Motel rooms: $79 single, $89 double; hotel: $60 single, $70 double for hotel ensuite rooms; $85 single, $95 double for heritage suites; $40 per person for backpacker rooms.

HOURS
Daily 11am–late.

GRUB
Open for dinner 6–8pm daily.

TOP DROP
XXXX Bitter, XXXX Gold, Carlton Draught, Carlton Midstrength, Cascade Light, Cascade Blonde and VB are all on tap.

NEARBY ATTRACTIONS
Clear outback nights and a low horizon combine to make stargazing a great experience at the Charleville Cosmos Centre and Observatory. Visitors can also visit the National Parks Research Station, home of the Save the Bilby Fund, where seasonal Meet the Bilbies tours are held. The Charleville Heritage Trail is a guide to the town's many heritage buildings.

MORE INFO
www.charlevilletourism.com.au
www.queenslandholidays.com.au

Corones Hotel has richly decorated interiors

For more than 30 years the Hotel Corones was 'The Leading Hotel of the West', used by wealthy local graziers, commercial travellers and tourists to the outback town about 760 kilometres west of Brisbane. It hosted famous names, including aviator Amy Johnson, singer Gracie Fields and the Duke and Duchess of Gloucester. During World War II when American servicemen occupied the local aerodrome and hospital, 'Poppa' Corones did a roaring trade, with dances being held every night in Corones Hall. In 1959, Queensland's centenary year, Charleville's civic welcome to its royal visitor, Princess Alexandra, took place in front of the hotel.

Within a few more years, though, the grand hotel was being eclipsed by a new style of modern accommodation, the motel, and the drought years of the 1960s saw its decline. Harry Corones died in 1972 but his oldest son, Peter, and his wife Mary continued the family business for another ten years.

New owners Doreen and Bob Bishop built a motel at the back of the hotel in 1990, the same year that a disastrous flood which engulfed Charleville damaged the ground floor of the hotel. Restoration work extended to converting some of the guest rooms to bathrooms, and the hotel now has 50 rooms for overnight guests. In 1993, the hotel was listed by the National Trust of Queensland.

Brett and Jackie Tanzer bought the hotel in 2006 and operate it both as a local pub and as a tourist attraction. While the fabulous interiors and historic displays may attract some, for others the lure is the bar with its four large-screen televisions and the beer garden with its generous shade sails to protect from the Queensland sun.

Corones Hotel offers several options for overnight guests, from single hotel rooms to motel rooms with king-sized beds, flat-screen televisions and air conditioning. The heritage rooms have ensuites and period furniture, with double beds. One of these rooms has a second bedroom with three single beds, and some open onto the balcony. Basic pub rooms are available in singles, doubles, twin singles, and a double with an additional single bed, and some have ensuites. Most of these rooms open onto the magnificent verandah.

The daily tours – at 2pm – are led either by Jackie or by former licensee Carl Aschoff, who ran the pub in the late 1970s and knew the Corones family. Tours cost $15 and include afternoon tea with Jackie's own scones 'made to a recipe it has taken me five years to perfect'.

'The tours are just a way of keeping the magic alive,' says Jackie. 'To make sure that the mythology of both the man and his hotel continues.'

CAIRNS COURTHOUSE *Hotel*

CAIRNS

THE PRISTINE WHITE facade of the old courthouse, with its official coat of arms above the front door, lends a sense of importance to this elegant building in the heart of Cairns. You might almost expect to see bewigged barristers hurrying in and out, but the bench seats and tables under shady sun umbrellas give the game away. This lovely old courthouse building is now a popular pub with a beer garden out the front.

Exterior of Cairns Courthouse Hotel

After a long history and several years lying empty and in disrepair, the former Cairns courthouse opened its doors as one of Far North Queensland's swishest pubs in 1998.

The building dates back to the post-World War I era, as a Queensland government job-creation initiative for returned servicemen. It took more than two and a half years to build, with the Cairns community attributing the slow progress of the building to the use of casual 'day labour'. Some of the joinery was made in government workshops in Brisbane and shipped to Cairns but the remainder of the timber – including the impressive silky oak fittings in the courtroom – came from the Cairns hinterland. By November 1921 the new courthouse, which had cost more than £13500, was completed and it was used for the first time on 17 January 1922.

The pristine white facade of the old courthouse, with its official coat of arms above the front door, lends a sense of importance to this elegant building in the heart of Cairns.

In 1968 the building was extended to create a second courtroom and a Magistrate's Court. The building continued to be used as the City Courthouse until replaced by a new and larger police station and courthouse complex in Sheridan Street in 1992. After six years, a new era began with the reincarnation of the building as a pub.

CAIRNS COURTHOUSE HOTEL

ADDRESS
38 Abbott St, Cairns

TELEPHONE
(07) 4081 7777

WEBSITE
www.courthousehotelcairns.com.au

HOURS
Daily 10am–late.

GRUB
Open daily for lunch 12–3pm and dinner 5–9pm.

TOP DROP
The hotel is the biggest seller of Corona in Australia, and has 12 beers on tap including Carlton Draught, Pure Blonde, VB and Fosters.

WHERE TO STAY
Hotel Cairns is a family-owned Queenslander-style hotel with white plantation shutters, verandahs and latticework screens, 2 blocks from the Courthouse Hotel. It has 92 rooms and suites, from around $195. www.thehotelcairns.com

NEARBY ATTRACTIONS
Apart from daytripping to the Great Barrier Reef or islands, there are plenty of attractions in Cairns, including the Tjapukai Aboriginal Cultural Park, Skyrail Rainforest Cableway (a great way to also see the rainforest village of Kuranda) and the Cairns Wildlife Dome, on the roof of the Reef Hotel Casino.

MORE INFO
www.cairnsgreatbarrierreef.org
www.queenslandholidays.com.au

Some of that courthouse feel remains in the hotel, particularly in the two stylish Chamber rooms, at the front of the hotel near the main bar, which have elegant buttoned-leather lounge suites and plasma screens (just some of the 50 throughout the hotel).

Cairns Courthouse Hotel bar

The front beer garden has neatly trimmed box hedges and lawns, custom-built bench tables and chairs and one of the largest outdoor screens in Cairns, with state-of-the-art in-ground speakers for better sound throughout the garden. At weekends, all the big sporting matches are played on the plasma screens inside and outside the hotel, and there's live entertainment to kick back and enjoy every night from Thursday to Sunday.

The Watch House Restaurant is on the deck under a shady sail to keep off the worst of the north Queensland tropical sun, directly back from the beer garden, and can seat 120 people. The atmosphere is relaxed and the menu is founded on traditional Italian flavours, presenting classic dishes with a modern twist. Turn up for lunch or dinner on Tuesdays for special deals including T-bone steaks or pasta dishes for $10.

On Wednesdays, there's great family fun entertainment with a quintessentially Queensland flavour: live mud crab races in the front beer garden from 6.30pm. 'It's a bit different, a bit corny, but people love it,' says hotel owner Claud Mangifesta. 'We get between 150 and 200 people here for the crab races, up to 500 when it's the height of the tourist season. The crabs are raffled off at the end, and we give away prizes like skydiving or reef trips.'

During the week, you're likely to find business people having lunch at the pub, but at night and weekends the locals are joined by tourists. It's very much a family pub too, says Mangifesta. 'We're family-owned and -run, and we encourage families to come here; we're definitely not a backpacker-style pub. We offer good food, a safe environment and value for money, and people love that.'

All this is happening just a block from the Cairns Esplanade, which fronts Trinity Bay. There's no beach in Cairns, but the great – and hugely popular – alternative for cooling off is the saltwater lagoon and artificial beach set in a park on the waterfront. You're also not far from the Reef Fleet Terminal, which is the departure point for all the daily cruise boats to the outer Great Barrier Reef.

RAVENSWOOD

PUSHING OPEN THE saloon doors to the front bar of the Imperial Hotel in the tiny Queensland settlement of Ravenswood is like passing into a different era. Even the grand Edwardian exterior of the pub gives no hint of the opulence inside (or perhaps the rusting old truck bodies next to it keep expectations in check).

Built in 1902, near the end of Ravenswood's heyday when miners had 30 hotels to choose from, this is a pub that has changed little over the years: elaborate arches, turned columns, leadlighting, brass and cut-glass door handles, and an extraordinary carved bar elicit gasps from newcomers. The 'wow' factor is high.

John and Dianne Schulter bought the Imperial in 1998 and have run it off and on themselves since then. 'We've had other licensees here, but we need to get it back to where it should be, with service and quality as our number one and two priorities,' says John, a former schoolteacher who has lived and worked in north Queensland for many years.

Now a National Trust–classified town, Ravenswood is about 90 kilometres south of Townsville. 'We get a steady flow of travellers on weekends from Cairns, Charters Towers, Townsville and Bowen and

Imperial Hotel, Ravenswood

This is a pub that has changed little over the years: elaborate arches, turned columns, leadlighting, brass and cut-glass door handles, and an extraordinary carved bar elicit gasps from newcomers.

Front bar, Imperial Hotel

Mackay,' says Schulter. 'Our overnight guests are usually either tourists or mining contractors. My philosophy is to give them plenty of top food, plenty to drink and let them make their own fun.'

There's a jukebox in the bar, and a pool table in a large room behind the bar, where the late Eddie Charlton once played about a decade ago. Bar food is served at any time of day – rib-eye fillet, crumbed calamari, steak sandwiches, basic pub grub.

Two flights of elegantly carved cedar and oak stairs lead to the 15 guest rooms, which run off a startlingly green-painted hallway – 'yes, it's bilious, isn't it?' says Schulter – that is apparently much photographed for its novelty value. Antique beds, washstands and ornaments adorn the rooms. There are no ensuites but the three shared bathrooms have all been upgraded.

The name that's still above the front door is J. M. Delaney, the first licensee. Jim Delaney was the founder of Ravenswood's Donnybrook reef mine and used part of his great wealth to build the hotel, importing the carved bar with its stained glass from England and the leadlight tulip panels from France. He died in Sydney at the age of 28 a short time later, and his two sisters ran the Imperial for many years before selling to a consortium of local graziers.

Mining was the lifeblood of Ravenswood, which was the first major mining settlement to develop in north Queensland after the discovery of gold there in 1868, in what was already a successful farming area. The town was named after one of the district's early stations. Crushing machinery was brought to Ravenswood to process the ore in 1870 and by 1871 there were 2000–3000 miners on the field and Ravenswood had become Queensland's first large inland settlement. By 1872, the extraction of gold was becoming difficult and the discovery of gold at nearby Charters Towers saw many miners leave to try their luck there. Those who stayed were able to mine around 300 kilograms of gold from the area each year and when silver was discovered in 1880 the town managed to struggle on. New equipment meant deep mining began in 1901 and two years later the population of Ravenswood peaked at about 4700.

But it was not to last. An industrial strike in 1912–13 saw the town decline and this continued during World War I as the men of Ravenswood joined the armed forces.

THE SPOTTED COW

TOOWOOMBA

WHEN IS A sports bar not a sports bar? When it's the Spotted Cow. The Coorey family may be 'mad Rabbitohs fans' but when they took over an old pub in Toowoomba in December 1995 they made sure that this was a bar where supporters of any code are welcome and even the footy-challenged can feel at home.

With its traffic-stopping exterior, painted with wandering cows, it's easy to see that this might be a pub with a difference. And it is. In the Jersey Bar, its walls hung with framed and sometimes autographed rugby jumpers, it's easy to wonder whether the name refers to the decor or to the cows. And that, says Phil Coorey, is the point. 'It's deliberately ambiguous,' he says, 'because it's a great conversation starter.'

The rugby jerseys have come from all over, some from famous players, others from locals who have embraced the idea and donated family members' jumpers, sometimes as a memorial. 'There's a real old-school connection with our customers,' says Coorey. 'I actually don't think about them as customers; most of them are our friends, and they are wonderful people.'

The Spotted Cow, Toowoomba

With its traffic-stopping exterior, painted with wandering cows, it's easy to see that this might be a pub with a difference.

The family connection to Toowoomba goes back a long way. Dianne and Michael Coorey spent the early days of their marriage in the Darling Downs city and Phil was born there. The family later moved to Sydney, but on returning the connections were still there through Dianne's nine siblings, most of whom still lived in the area.

Three major renovations over the years – the latest and largest at the end of 2009 – have transformed the former Lucona Hotel, which stands on the corner of Ruthven and Campbell streets, just north of Toowoomba's CBD, and was first licensed in 1892. The name was changed after the first renovation in 1990. Michael and Dianne Coorey, who already had 15 years of catering experience, bought the Spotted Cow in 1995 and now run it as a family business with their son Phillip.

The cow murals might attract the curious, but in Toowoomba the Spotted Cow is well known as the best pub in town to watch sport. Once famed only as a rugby pub, big screens now show a whole range of events, from Aussie Rules live on Friday nights to

THE SPOTTED COW

ADDRESS
296 Ruthven St, Toowoomba

TELEPHONE
(07) 4639 3264

WEBSITE
www.spottedcow.com.au

HOURS
Daily 11am–late.

GRUB
Open daily for lunch 12–2.30pm and dinner 6–9.30pm.

TOP DROP
Belgian beers, including Leffe, are a specialty here, but there are 21 beers on tap.

WHERE TO STAY
Vacy Hall is a beautiful heritage-listed B&B built in 1899 with 12 rooms and suites, set in park-like grounds but only a few minutes' walk from Toowoomba's main street. Rates start from $98 midweek or $115 at weekends. www.vacyhall.com.au

NEARBY ATTRACTIONS
Russell St is known as 'heritage street' and has some of the city's finest architecture. The Cobb & Co Museum houses Australia's largest collection of horse-drawn vehicles, and the magnificently restored Art Deco Empire Theatre has regular concerts and performances. One of the best times of year to visit Toowoomba is Sept, during the annual Carnival of Flowers.

MORE INFO
www.toowoombaholidays.info
www.queenslandholidays.com.au

Spotted cows are everywhere

every major UFC fight, all rugby league and rugby union games not carried by free-to-air TV (including every Super 15 game), basketball, baseball and American gridiron football (a big night being an all-American theme for the annual Superbowl party).

The pub sponsors 'the best rugby union team in town', the Toowoomba Rangers, and also holds a major fundraiser each year for a local charity. In 2011 that was a flood-relief effort which raised $12 000 to help local farmers and businesses get back on their feet.

An extension at the back of the original hotel building has created the spacious light-filled (and cow-themed) dining room that now seats around 150 people. The servings are generous and the menu offers something for everyone. Specialties include the Big Cow T-bone, the Rugby Club Sandwich and the new lunchtime shank.

The kitchen's signature dish is black mussels from Spring Bay, Tasmania, served in a Belgian mussel pot with dunking bread. A 1 kilogram pot costs $25 and you can choose your flavour from provencale (tomato, herbs and coriander), Bangalow (ginger, garlic, chilli and basil), traditional laksa with coriander and coconut cream, Hoegaarden (Hoegaarden beer, citrus, chilli, garlic and ginger) or St Germain (white wine, chives, saffron and creamy garlic sauce). If you have a sweet tooth, the daily dessert board lists favourites like apple pie and Belgian chocolate waffles, all made by Dianne Coorey.

Special events are run throughout the year, including yabbie races on Australia Day and a traditional Oktoberfest celebration. The first Milking the Cow Beer Festival, held over the Queen's Birthday long weekend in June 2011, was a roaring success with thousands of people coming through the doors and it has become an annual event showcasing about 50 beers. 'After the flood, we really needed to give people from Brisbane, the Gold Coast and the south-east region a reason to come back to Toowoomba,' says Coorey. 'And they did. It will only get bigger and bigger in coming years.'

ILFRACOMBE

Wellshot Hotel, Ilfracombe

IT'S A CLASSIC tale: Jo Scott loved the pub so much she bought it. Born and bred in Ilfracombe, a village on the outskirts of Longreach in western Queensland, Jo started working in the Wellshot Hotel as a kitchen hand when she was 16. Today, she's the proud owner of the pub she practically grew up in.

Jo Scott loved the pub so much she bought it. Jo started working in the Wellshot Hotel as a kitchen hand when she was 16. Today, she's the proud owner of the pub she practically grew up in.

'After I left and went away to college, I would come back on the train, get off and go straight to the pub to work behind the bar,' she laughs. 'I just love it; it has never been just a job for me, even though it is hard work.'

Ilfracome's only pub, the Wellshot Hotel started life on a small railway siding west of Anakie called Withersfield, but as the railway line was being built, the pub's enterprising owner Paddy Finn decided to move it west along the line as it progressed. He dismantled it and moved it to Barcaldine, where the building stood for about ten years before once again coming down and being shifted by bullock cart to Ilfracombe, where it became the Wellshot.

That was in 1890. There were five pubs in the town at that time, but the Wellshot is the only survivor. The pub is named after Wellshot Station, the largest sheep station in the

Guest rooms open onto a verandah

View of the bar from the pool room

world at the time. And strangely, despite being 650 kilometres from the Queensland coast, Ilfracombe was named after a little seaside village in England.

The train still comes through the town, these days Queensland Rail's *Spirit of the Outback* makes its run from Brisbane and Rockhampton to Longreach twice a week in each direction, stopping at Ilfracombe to pick up or drop off passengers. It's a brief stop, not like past days when Jo recalls that the passengers would hop off for a quick beer while the train was in the station.

Fireplace in the lounge

By road, the approach to Ilfracombe is also very different. The locals call it 'the Machinery Mile', as the road through the town is lined with outdoor machinery – tractors, wool wagons, steam engines, horse-drawn sulkies, wool balers, earthmoving machinery, harvesters – that show the evolution of transport and farming machinery in Queensland's outback.

The accommodation wing at the rear of the building was built in 1891 and rebuilt in 1956, but the rest of the hotel is the same as it was more than a century ago. 'The only real modifications have been inside,' says Jo. 'It used to be a little bit of a maze inside, but some of the rooms have been opened up.' The main feature

Money and hats hang from the ceiling

of the pub is the bar, made from an opened-out old timber wool press. There is a wool-press table filled with fine merino wool, early photographs and other memorabilia are on display, there's money hanging from the ceiling, and a big collection of hats around the top of the bar. Take a minute or two to read 'The Wellshot and the Bush Pub's Hall of Fame', a poem inscribed on one of the walls.

Country-style pub meals are served daily, and for those who'd like to stay, there are seven air-conditioned hotel rooms (single, double, twin and family options) that all open onto a bush verandah. Two of the rooms – one with a queen-sized bed, the other with three singles – have a connecting door, making them an ideal choice for families. Guests share bathrooms – men's and women's – and there's also a guest laundry.

'Ilfracombe's a nice place to stop,' says Jo, speaking of the travellers who break their journeys here. 'It's a pretty, well-kept little town and everyone who lives here cares about it.'

With a population of about 200, Ilfracombe is only 27 kilometres from Longreach, making it a great alternative place to stay for those who want a quieter pace. The caravan and camping ground across the road from the pub is always busy.

'From here, you can make easy trips to Isisford, Barcaldine and Aramac as well as Longreach,' says Jo. 'Tourism is really massive in this area and there's a lot to see.'

WELLSHOT HOTEL

ADDRESS
Landsborough Hwy, Ilfracombe

TELEPHONE
(07) 4658 2106

WEBSITE
www.wellshothotel.com.au

RATES
From $40 per person to $100 for a family of 4.

HOURS
Daily 11am–late.

GRUB
Daily for lunch 12–2pm and dinner 6–8pm.

TOP DROP
XXXX Gold, VB and Carlton Midstrength are on tap.

NEARBY ATTRACTIONS
Apart from the machinery display run by the Ilfracombe Historical Society, another look back in time is at Langenbaker House, a tribute to pioneering families. Longreach has the major attractions of the Australian Stockman's Hall of Fame & Outback Heritage Centre and the Qantas Founders Museum. In Barcaldine (80 km E) there's the Australian Workers' Heritage Museum and the Tree of Knowledge Memorial.

MORE INFO
www.ilfracombe.com.au
www.queenslandholidays.com.au

Tasmania

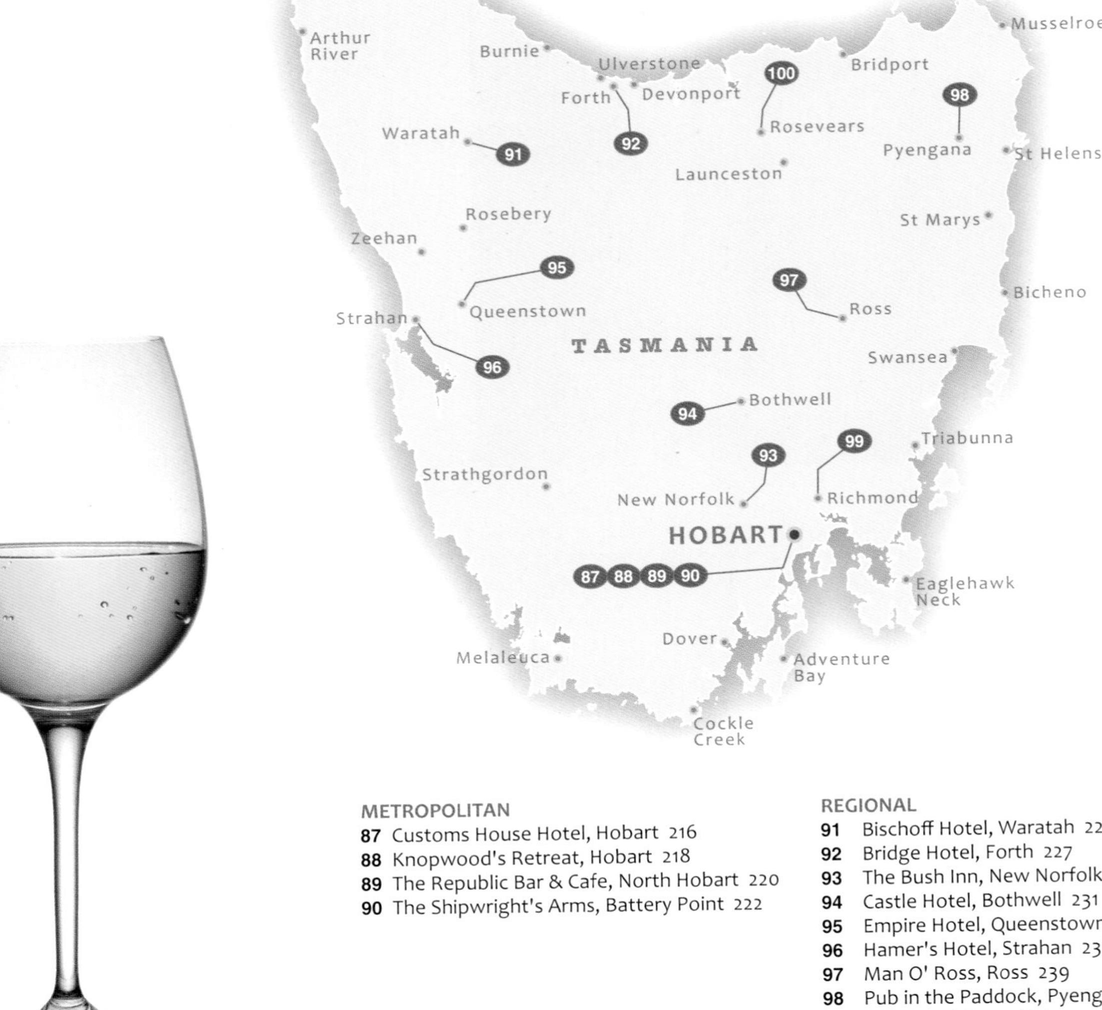

Opposite (clockwise from top): Empire Hotel, Queenstown; The Shipwright's Arms, Battery Point; Empire Hotel, Queenstown; Rosevears Waterfront Tavern, Rosevears.

METROPOLITAN

REGIONAL

EMPIRE
HOTEL
EMPIRE
HOTEL
OASIS

BEER
EVERYBODY NEEDS A HOBBY!

CUSTOMS HOUSE *Hotel*

HOBART

Sailors have always played a part in the history of the hotel and this tradition continues today, particularly when the Sydney-to-Hobart yacht race fleet comes into port.

Customs House Hotel, Hobart

IN THE EARLY days of the Customs House Hotel it was known as a 'chop house', which meant a good square meal could be found inside. Today, owners Paul and Karen Jubb hope the same can be said about their spacious restaurant overlooking the Hobart waterfront. Sailors have always played a part in the history of the hotel, located in the heart of Hobart's marine precinct, and this tradition continues today, particularly when the Sydney-to-Hobart yacht race fleet comes into port between Boxing Day and New Year.

Built by Charles Gaylor and licensed in 1846, the hotel took its name from its location opposite the then Customs House, now Tasmania's Parliament House. Gaylor was one of Hobart's early settlers and his name is cut into the front coping stone of the building, which is one of Hobart's oldest hotels.

In more recent years the hotel has expanded into the next-door shop and the former Marine Hotel, and in 2003 it underwent a major transformation when it merged with the adjacent ship chandlers' warehouse in Morrison Street. Both buildings are listed on the Tasmanian Heritage Register.

The latest renovation resulted in a main bar, a new 100-seat restaurant, a function area called Vue and 12 additional guest rooms, taking the total to 23 rooms, six with water views. Bar meals – seafood baskets, steak sandwiches, crumbed scallops, chicken schnitzel, burgers, parmigianas, game sausages with garlic mash, and other pub grub – are available in the main bar and there's live music from Wednesday to Saturday nights.

The pub has waterfront views

The cocktail and tapas lounge, Vue, has an extensive wine and cocktail list and is open Wednesday to Saturday. It has open fires during the colder months and access to an outdoor area in the warmer ones.

The Waterfront Restaurant specialises in fresh local seafood, with Spring Bay scallops, Barilla Bay oysters and seafood chowder among the dishes on offer. All the fish is bought from the fishermen on Constitution Dock. There are regular specials: mussels are half price on Mondays and oysters are half price on Tuesdays. Try the Spring Bay mussels with tomato and chilli provencale, or with a garlic, white wine and cream sauce. But those who prefer something other than seafood are well catered for too, as are vegetarians. The hotel has an extensive wine list of Tasmanian wines and there's a choice from a large range of beers.

Entrance to the bar

Guest rooms include double, twin and queen rooms, and a family room that sleeps five with a queen and three single beds. Most rooms have scenic views of the Tamar River and the docks, Salamanca Place and the gardens of Parliament House. All rooms have ensuites, television, a small fridge, tea- and coffee-making facilities, a hairdryer and internet access. Some rooms are above the bar, which can be noisy, but a good rate is usually available on them.

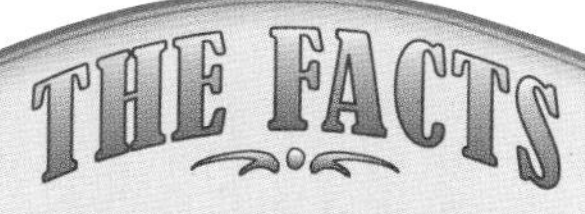

CUSTOMS HOUSE HOTEL

ADDRESS
1 Murray St, Hobart

TELEPHONE
(03) 6234 6645

WEBSITE
www.customshousehotel.com

RATES
Standard double room $135, standard twin $140, waterfront queen room $150, waterfront twin $155, family room $240. Extra person rate $40. Rates include a cooked breakfast.

HOURS
Sun–Thurs 11–12am and Fri–Sat 11–1.30am.

GRUB
Open for breakfast weekdays 7–10am, weekends and public holidays 8–10am; lunch daily 12–2.30pm; dinner Sun–Thurs 6–9pm, Fri–Sat 6–9.30pm. Closed Christmas Day.

TOP DROP
Beer on tap includes Cascade Draught, Cascade Pale Ale, Cascade Premium Light Ale, Carlton Pure Blonde, Carlton Draught, VB, Tooheys Extra Dry, Fat Yak and Guinness, and Bulmer's cider.

NEARBY ATTRACTIONS
Salamanca Pl and Salamanca Markets.

MORE INFO
www.hobarttravelcentre.com.au
www.discovertasmania.com.au

KNOPWOOD'S RETREAT

HOBART

Friday-afternoon crowds spill outside Knopwood's Retreat, Hobart

IN COLONIAL DAYS, when Hobart was a wild and bawdy town, there was none who liked a drink and a good time better than Reverend Bobby Knopwood. A far-from-reverend chap, by all accounts, Knopwood was the chaplain to the colony and a magistrate for its first two decades.

In 1829, he opened the pub he called the Whaler's Return and which now bears his name in the sandstone building on what is now Salamanca Place. It's likely he would approve highly of Knopwood's Retreat, still one of Hobart's most popular watering holes. The cosy pub has gone through several incarnations – at one point being the Lord Nelson, at another the Nautilus – and it was not until the 1980s that it took the name of the man who began it all.

One of Hobart's most famous attractions, the Salamanca Market, is held every Saturday on this land, right outside the door of Knopwood's Retreat.

To get an idea of the story, take a close look at the stained-glass panels around the top of the curved wooden bar. Each one tells part of the story of Hobart, from its Aboriginal heritage through the convict and colonial times, with scenes of whaling, a portrait of Lady Jane Franklin, the governor's wife who 'adopted' an Aboriginal child as her servant, and nudes that depict the days when the hotel's back rooms were a brothel. More startling than anything, perhaps, is coming face to face with a replica of Bobby Knopwood's death mask.

Knoppies, as the locals call it, is a welcoming place and it's easy to see why the small bar is usually crowded (but don't be put off). There's a large open wood fire, some striking works by Tasmanian artists, and the whole place has a warm and intimate atmosphere.

'We really try to keep it as traditional as possible, and that is part of its charm when a lot of other pubs have modernised,' says licensee Kate Cawthorn. And Knoppies seems to appeal to everyone, from fishermen and politicians (State Parliament is just a stone's throw away) to university types and tourists.

The curved wooden bar and its stained-glass panels

The combination of excellent coffee, food, beer, wine and the cosy atmosphere makes this pub a hot favourite at almost any time. During the day, it's usually busy with a lunch crowd but there are no bookings taken – so prop up at the bar and wait for a table to become free. The menu changes daily and is written up on a blackboard, with nothing more than $15.

On Friday nights the bar practically bursts at the seams with the after-work crowd, spilling out onto Salamanca Place, where there are more tables and chairs (and umbrellas for the sunny days). It's a big night, Friday, with two happy hours – from 7–8pm, when chicken wings and chips are served on the bar, and another at 9–10pm (without free food). On Saturdays happy hour is 6–9pm, with free nibbles served during the first hour.

Beers on tap vary, with darker ales served in winter. If you can't decide which to try, there's a beer sampler (the paddles are made of Tassie woods) of six, for $12. You'll also find Tasmanian whisky from Lark Distillery (just down the road in Davey Street) and Strait vodka from northern Tasmania. In winter there's gluhwein and hot soup, in summer sangria and cocktails are the go.

During summer, the Friday afternoon crowd often moves outside and overflows onto a nearby grassy patch in search of some shade under the trees. This is reclaimed land – look carefully from the front of the hotel and you will find a brass plaque that marks the original waterline of Sullivan's Cove in the early 1800s.

One of Hobart's most famous attractions, the Salamanca Market, is held every Saturday on this land, right outside the door of Knopwood's Retreat. Christmas Eve and New Year's Eve draw huge crowds to the area, as do the final days of the Sydney-to-Hobart yacht race as the boats come in.

And what became of Reverend Knopwood, the first official resident of Battery Point (previously known as Knopwoods Point)? Well, he didn't avoid trouble and he fell out with Governor George Arthur before dying in 1838 aged 75. Check out the brass plaque on the outside of Knopwood's Retreat that tells his version of the feud. But still, he urges the reader to 'pass under the portals of this fine house of refreshment and drink a toast to Bobby who once loved to stand here and praise God for the beauty and abundance towards us his humble servants in this most beautiful island'.

KNOPWOOD'S RETREAT

ADDRESS
39 Salamanca Pl, Hobart

TELEPHONE
(03) 6223 5808

EMAIL
knopwoods@bigpond.com

HOURS
Sun–Fri 11–12.30am,
Sat 10–12.30am.

GRUB
Weekdays lunch 12–2pm and Wed dinner 6–9pm. Bookings taken for dinner but not for lunch.

TOP DROP
There are 14 beers on tap, including Van Dieman's Land Stout, Boag's, Cascade, Coopers, Asahi and the Tasmanian ginger beer, Gillespie's.

WHERE TO STAY
Salamanca Inn is a modern apartment complex with 60 suites and apartments, a short walk from Salamanca Pl and Knopwood's Retreat, with rates from around $170 per night.
www.salamancainn.com.au

NEARBY ATTRACTIONS
Head to the Tasmanian Museum and Art Gallery on Macquarie St to find out more about the island state's heritage, culture and natural history. The collection includes the original death mask of Rev. Knopwood. www.tmag.tas.gov.au
Many of Hobart's other attractions are within walking distance of Knopwood's Retreat.

MORE INFO
www.discovertasmania.com

THE REPUBLIC
BAR & CAFE

NORTH HOBART

The Republic Bar & Cafe, North Hobart

IS IT A pub? Is it a gallery? Is it a cafe? The Republic is all three – and the combination works to make it one of the most popular pubs in Hobart, with a large and loyal following for its live music and its art. Supporting the arts is a vital part of what makes the Republic tick, and there's music here every night as well as changing exhibitions on the red wall that gives the gallery its name, all in a cool, casual atmosphere.

Originally the Rose Hotel, the pub opened in 1831 and the name was later changed to the Rose and Crown. By 1938 it had been substantially rebuilt as an Art Deco brick building standing on the corner of Elizabeth and Burnett streets in North Hobart and was then called the Empire Hotel. In 1997 the pub was taken over by Tony Heath and Peter McDonald, who decided to put an emphasis on live music and renamed it the Republic Bar & Cafe.

> The Republic is one of the most popular pubs in Hobart, with a large and loyal following for its live music and its art.

Part of the pub is given over to the Red Wall Gallery: the Republic has regularly exhibited artworks since it opened. The colourful major exhibition wall of the gallery, which gives it its name, brings warmth to the whole place and is designed to encourage people to spend more time looking at the exhibitions, as they eat, drink, debate and discuss.

'The Red Wall really came about because we had a bartender called Kim Duggan whose wife was an artist and we arranged to show her work. Then we had another artist, and it just started from there, holding regular exhibitions,' says manager Jeremy Heath. The exhibitions now change every four or six weeks, showcasing the work of emerging Hobart artists; the organisation of the venue is directed by local artists Nicole O'Loughlin and Rory Dick.

'The whole idea was to bring art to the people, rather than people to art,' says Jeremy Heath. 'It's about having the art displayed in a space that's being used by people.'

The Red Wall Gallery

When it's an opening night, the crowd is there for the art; at other times, the art is there for the people who come along to the bar. And the music can be anything from jazz and blues to acoustic, hip-hop or world music. Sessions start at 10pm on Friday and Saturday nights and at 8.30pm or 9pm on other nights. From time to time there are special events, such as Hot August Jazz, which starts at lunchtime.

The music attracts young and old. 'We've had a group of old footballers in their eighties in recently, and a family celebrating their child's second birthday, so there's no single demographic, it's for old and young. Who comes along often depends on what the music is that night,' says Jeremy.

The commitment to the arts also extends to poetry readings on the first Sunday of each month, and in true pub tradition there's also a quiz night twice a month, on the second and last Mondays – except in the busiest months of December and January.

The Republic's mood is cafe-style, relaxed and modern, with log fires inside and a beer garden with barbecue area out the back. An extensive cafe-type menu caters for all tastes and budgets, and there is also a specials board which changes regularly.

Nearly everything on the menu is sourced locally – no frozen fish here, it is all caught in Australian waters, with the squid and octopus from Tasmania and almost all other seafood being local. Beef, lamb and pork come from a Tasmanian butcher, and chicken dishes are made with chemical- and hormone-free birds (and the eggs are free range). The kitchen makes all its stocks, sauces and desserts in-house.

You'll find snacks, burgers, pizzas, nachos, salads and platters on the menu, along with delights like hand-rolled roast duck spring rolls, and more substantial fare in the fresh Tasmanian mussel pot, Moroccan lamb shanks or steaks from the chargrill, such as the 300 gram Australian grain-fed scotch fillet marinated in the Republic's own Jack Daniels whiskey marinade.

THE REPUBLIC BAR & CAFE

ADDRESS
299 Elizabeth St, North Hobart

TELEPHONE
(03) 6234 6954

WEBSITE
www.republicbar.com

HOURS
Mon–Tues 3pm–2am;
Wed–Sun 12pm–2am.

GRUB
Open for lunch Wed–Sun 12–2pm and for dinner daily 6–9pm.

TOP DROP
There are 10 beers on tap; the most popular is Carlton Draught.

WHERE TO STAY
The Lodge on Elizabeth, at 249 Elizabeth St, North Hobart, is one of the oldest buildings in Tasmania. It has 13 rooms with four-poster beds and ensuites, and a self-contained Convict's Cottage. Rooms: $130 single, $150–$170 double; cottage $170–$195 (minimum 2-night stay). Rates include breakfast. www.thelodge.com.au

NEARBY ATTRACTIONS
Hobart's newest and most talked-about attraction is the Museum of Old and New Art (MONA), at Berriedale, about 15 min drive from the CBD. This is Australia's largest privately owned art gallery, designed to intrigue and provoke. The collection ranges from antiquities from Egypt, Greece, Italy, Africa and Mesoamerica to contemporary art from around the world. www.mona.net.au

MORE INFO
www.discovertasmania.com

The SHIPWRIGHT'S Arms

BATTERY POINT

The Shipwright's Arms, Battery Point

THE SHIPWRIGHT'S ARMS is the sort of pub where anything might happen to liven up an already warm and lively scene. The sort of place where a woman might take off her pink high heels after a day at the races and hang them over the beer taps on the bar – and nobody will mind at all. Or where a bloke might take off his shirt to show someone a particular tattoo and attract a small group of interested observers along the bar.

A friendly ghost called Max has startled more than one publican as he clanks around with the pots and pans in the kitchen.

There's no pokies, no keno, no live music, no pool table ... but there's plenty happening if you keep your eyes and yours ears open, and Shippies (as the locals affectionately call it) has probably seen it all. A popular haunt for boaties and yachties and sea-going folk of all kinds, this Hobart institution has been around since 1846 but is as popular today as it always has been.

It's a pub that's more often frequented by regulars than by tourists but strangers are always welcome for a beer and a yarn. And if you're a visitor who's exploring the quaint Georgian village of Battery Point, one of Hobart's loveliest locales, then it's a great place to stop for some refreshment.

Shippies is a favourite with crews from the Sydney-to-Hobart yacht race, run every December, and its walls are hung with many photographs of the spectacular boats, a 7-metre-long photo-mural telling the story of the race and a display of every line-honours winner since the first in 1945.

The race starts in Sydney Harbour on Boxing Day and ends 630 nautical miles later in Hobart. It has become one of the great blue-water classics as sailors pit their skills and nerve against the fury of Bass Strait. On New Year's Day, after it's all over, the bar is packed with yachties bemoaning their fates in the race and swapping stories.

The Shipwright's Arms is a traditional old English-style corner pub filled with history and tradition. Apart from the Sydney-to-Hobart, it also has a unique collection of

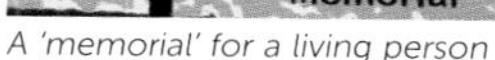

A 'memorial' for a living person

A maritime theme prevails

Tasmanian and maritime memorabilia, while the dining rooms display photographs of Old Hobart and Battery Point. The front bar, built by a shipwright, features Tasmanian timbers – and log fires that keep it cosy in winter. At the back is a sail-shaded beer garden that's perfect in summer.

Shippies has comfortable guest rooms upstairs, offering budget accommodation in single, double and triple-share (a double bed and one single) rooms. There are separate shared bathrooms for men and women down the hall. Newer, larger double rooms have ensuites, a flat-screen television and air conditioning (and some have views of the Derwent River). A self-serve continental breakfast is included in the room rate and there are tea- and coffee-making facilities in the guest kitchen at any time (along with a fridge and ironing facilities).

The small, sunny guest lounge also has a television, or you can just relax in an armchair with a book. It's a pleasant spot at any time of day, and has lovely views of the yachts on the beautiful Derwent River.

If you plan to dine in, be sure to make a booking for the bistro, because as one of Hobart's most famous hotels and with a reputation for good food, it can get busy – although there is another, more lively option of eating in the bar. The bistro menu is extensive and each main course is accompanied by a suggestion for a matching wine or beer. For instance, you might like to try a Cascade Premium Lager with your mustard and herb–crusted lamb rack, or Pepperjack Shiraz with the 300 gram yearling scotch fillet.

THE SHIPWRIGHT'S ARMS

ADDRESS
29 Trumpeter St, Battery Point

TELEPHONE
(03) 6223 5551

WEBSITE
www.shipwrightsarms.com.au

RATES
$75 single; $80 double for budget rooms with shared bathrooms; $150 single and $180 double for ensuite rooms. All rates include self-serve continental breakfast.

HOURS
Mon–Thurs 11am–11pm; Fri–Sat 11–12am; Sun 12–9pm.

GRUB
Open daily for lunch 12–2pm and dinner 6–8pm.

TOP DROP
Cascade beer is on tap – Premium Lager, Premium Light, Pale Ale and Draught.

NEARBY ATTRACTIONS
The Shipwright's Arms is a short walk from the Hobart CBD, bustling Salamanca Pl, State Houses of Parliament, the law courts and the waterfront.

MORE INFO
www.hobarttravelcentre.com.au
www.discovertasmania.com

It's 'Shippies' to the locals

The Shipwright's Arms has many fascinating features, including a series of unique hand-painted stained-glass windows. These are, as you'd expect, all on nautical themes – with one notable exception: Australia's only memorial window to a living person. The subject is Max Eiszele, a long-time regular patron at Shippies, who will happily have a beer 'with any mug'.

There's another Max who hangs around at Shippies too. A friendly ghost called Max has startled more than one publican or staff member as he clanks around with the pots and pans in the kitchen. With long white hair and a beard, and wearing a blue cap and overalls, Max is believed to be a whaler. The authors (and Shippies regulars) Charles Wooley and Michael Tatlow delved into the story of Max for their guide *A Walk in Old Hobart* and say his distinctive smell of vanilla is believed to be ambergris, excreted by sperm whales and used in candles made of whale oil.

The pub sign

But while Max may make his presence felt in the kitchen and in the publican's quarters upstairs, overnight guests can rest easy, as he has never been seen or heard in the guest rooms.

Bischoff Hotel

WARATAH

EVERYONE FROM BOLLYWOOD film-makers to *BRW* Rich List-ers have passed through the doors of the Bischoff Hotel in the eight years since Bev and Lew Rout have owned the pub. They're not in the least bit surprised really because, as Lew says, 'Where else can you wake up and see a waterfall from your bed?'

Winter snowfall at the Bischoff Hotel, Waratah

The Bischoff is in Waratah, a town of a few hundred people in Tasmania's Tarkine Wilderness area, about 4.5 hours from Hobart and less than an hour from Cradle Mountain. In the summer the streets are packed with cars, campervans and caravans – 'It's a bit like Pitt Street in Sydney,' jokes Lew – all keen for a look at the impressive Waratah Falls. 'It's the only waterfall where you don't have to even get out of your car to have a look.' That would be a waste, of course, and most people make the effort to take a closer look, either from outside the pub, looking across to the falls, or by walking to the bottom.

Several of the pub's guest rooms have views of the falls and because the rooms are away from the bar areas, you are likely to fall asleep – and wake up – to the sounds of the waterfall.

Several of the pub's guest rooms have views of the falls and you are likely to fall asleep – and wake up – to the sounds of the waterfall.

Waratah was founded on the back of the world's richest tin discovery in December 1871, made at Mt Bischoff by prospector James 'Philospher' Smith. The discovery triggered a mining boom at a time when Tasmania's economy was in difficulties after the ceasing of convict transportation in the 1850s. The Mount Bischoff Tin Mining Company was formed in August 1873 and mining began that December. When the mine closed in 1947 it had produced 81 000 tonnes of tin and provided a dividend equal to £200 for every £1 initially invested.

At its peak the town had a population of more than 5000. The first rail line on the Tasmania's west coast opened in July 1884, connecting Waratah to Emu Bay (now Burnie). One of Tasmania's first hydro-electric power stations opened in 1907 to supply power to the crushing mills and electric tram and cable cars that brought ore from the mine to the mills.

BISCHOFF HOTEL

ADDRESS
20 Main St, Waratah

TELEPHONE
(03) 6439 1188

WEBSITE
www.bischoffhotel.com.au

RATES
$45 single, $70 standard double or twin room, $80 double with waterfall view, $95 queen room with ensuite, $105 budget family room, $125 spa suite.

HOURS
Daily 12–10pm Dec–Easter, and 3.30–10pm at other times.

GRUB
Daily for lunch 12–2pm (Dec–Easter) and year-round for dinner 6–8pm.

TOP DROP
Beer on tap includes Boag's Draught, Boag's Classic Blonde, Boag's XXX Ale, Tooheys Old and XXXX Gold.

NEARBY ATTRACTIONS
A walk around Waratah will take you to St James Church (1880), Philosopher Smith's hut, the Waratah museum, the Athenaeum Hall (1887) and the Kenworthy Stamper Mill, an operating display of ore crushing. A 2 hr return walking trail to the old Hydro Power House starts opposite the Bischoff Hotel.

MORE INFO
www.wowtas.com.au
www.discovertasmania.com

The Bischoff Hotel opened in 1881. The current Queen Anne–style building dates from 1909 and still has much of its old-world charm, with high ceilings of pressed tin, an open log fire, huon pine mantles, king billy pine solid doors and blackwood banisters on the stairs.

Waratah Falls

The town is built around the shoreline of Lake Waratah. It is an ideal base to explore the west coast, while the lake is a great spot to catch trout; you need a licence to fish, and can buy one at the hotel.

Waratah remained largely isolated by road from the rest of Tasmania until the early 1960s. Apart from the train line serving the mine, the only access was on an unsealed track until a connecting road was finally completed in 1963. Today, motorcyclists relish the Hellyer Gorge and Savage River roads, on either side of Waratah (they are also stages for Targa Tasmania and Rally Tasmania).

The Bischoff Hotel has 19 rooms; only three have ensuites, one including a spa, while the others have shared bathrooms. All have televisions, electric blankets and heating, and there is wi-fi in most rooms. A central guest lounge and kitchen area has board games and a library, as well as tea- and coffee-making facilities.

The public bar, with its blackheart sassafras timber bar, can be crowded with tourists in the summer months, but in winter you're more likely to find miners and geologists from the still-working mine. In the dining room, the Bischoff burger is the signature dish, made to the cook's own recipe using premium steak mince and special herbs and seasoning. Huge T-bone or scotch fillet steaks are from local farms, served with a choice of homemade pepper or mushroom sauce. The mixed grill has 'a bit of everything' and there are also vegetarian dishes, and children's meals.

In the hotel lobby a battered aeroplane propeller takes pride of place, a relic from a locally famous plane crash in 1937. Two RAAF Hawker Demon fighters en route from Laverton Airbase in Victoria to Hobart went off course and emerged from fog over Waratah. Both circled then disappeared over Mt Bischoff. One crashed in the forest; the other returned to the town and crash-landed on Camp Road, and it is the propeller of this plane that is mounted in the foyer. 'No-one was killed in the crash,' says Lew, 'but it was possibly the first air–land rescue in Tasmania.'

To delve deeper into the history of Waratah, and to experience the Tarkine Wilderness first hand, you can retrace the steps of 'Philosopher' Smith and discover the waterfall named in his honour. It should only be attempted by the fit: the track to Philosopher Falls is a demanding walk of about two hours each way.

BRIDGE HOTEL

FORTH

A GHOSTLY JILTED bride, tales of murder, fires, flood and more ... for such a quiet and peaceful spot, the Bridge Hotel at Forth has seen – and survived – a lot.

Established in 1872, the hotel has been a favourite meeting place for all types and is a good stopping point between Devonport and Cradle Mountain on the old coastal highway. Set on the banks of the lovely Forth River, it also has a reputation as one of Tasmania's top live music venues. And then there are its famous meat pies ...

The Bridge Hotel, Forth

Owners Chris and Maureen Bramich, who have had the pub since 2000, are well aware that they are the custodians of a rich and vivid history that goes beyond the bricks and mortar of the twin-gabled heritage-listed hotel. Because here, it really is a case of 'if walls could talk'.

In 1998 Chris and Maureen started the annual Forth Valley Blues Festival, which now attracts up to 5000 people every March and which has earned Maureen the moniker Washboard Maud.

Forth was the second settlement in the County of Devon in the 1840s, and the pub has outlasted most of the town's oldest buildings. The hotel was first licensed and opened in January 1872 by John Liddle, who quickly set high standards and provided such good service to the community and travelling public that the pub became the centre for meetings, inquests and special gatherings. He ran the Bridge Hotel until 1881.

Forth was a busy shipping port with small ships and punts coming up to a shipping shed opposite the hotel at high tide. Produce boats would line up at the wharf and the main patrons of the hotel were seamen, who shared the bar with the timber cutters who were clearing the forests and shipping timber to the mainland. Later, road workers would quench their thirst when road building began. River transport in these times was often faster as the roads were boggy and impassable in winter and dry and rutted in summer.

At the 1879 parliamentary elections, the hotel was the local polling booth – and the scene of riots when Edward Braddon was elected to the House of Assembly to represent

West Devon. Armed police had to intervene when fights broke out using sticks and stones as weapons. When it was over, however, there were drinks all round.

In 1972, the then owner of the hotel, Ernie Morrison, prepared to celebrate its centenary, but all did not go well. Fire raged through the upper storey in September and Morrison saved the lives of two guests before the flames were put out. A week later Morrison's dog – named Hey You – was poisoned in his kennel, after which Morrison was shot and killed. Papers from the hotel safe were found in a rabbit burrow nearby but the takings were missing. A man was later convicted and sentenced to prison for life.

It is said that at night, Ernie Morrison roams the upper storey of the Bridge; there are the sounds of doors closing, quiet footsteps, objects being moved, and the soft whine of a dog. This sad tale has been immortalised in the song 'The River Ran Red' by blues artist Brian Fraser, after a night's stay in the hotel.

And that ghostly bride? The figure of a grief-stricken woman wearing a white wedding dress standing at the upstairs dormer windows became common knowledge at the turn of the 20th century. She was, it was said, gazing across to the bridge waiting for her bridegroom who had promised to return in time for their wedding. This 'friendly ghost' inhabits the upstairs section of the hotel and is perhaps responsible for the unexplained footsteps and ghostly figure in the hallway sometimes late at night.

Today, travellers to Cradle Mountain or the coast patronise the hotel. Forth is a few kilometres east of Ulverstone, 13 kilometres west of Devonport and 111 km north-west of Launceston, off the Bass Highway. A quiet drink, family gatherings or social events without the intrusive din of poker machines is what patrons are looking for – and what they find, according to Chris Bramich.

In 1998 Chris and Maureen started the annual Forth Valley Blues Festival, which now attracts up to 5000 people to the village every March and which has earned Maureen the moniker Washboard Maud. 'She's played with some of the greats when they come here, and I've been known to get up there with the bongo,' says Chris. There is live music at the pub almost every weekend, specialising in blues on Sundays. Other entertainment includes Poetry at the Pub, held about four times a year, when people come from miles around to hear readings. Happy Hour runs every Friday from 5–7pm, and on Thursday night from 5–6pm you can toss a coin with the barman for a free drink.

Meals are country-style with generous servings (half serves available) including a roast of the day and old-fashioned desserts such as golden syrup dumplings. But the most famous dish on the menu is the Forth Pub pie, which sells for $4 with sauce or homemade relish. It's a secret recipe which has been bringing those in the know to the village for years. 'When we bought the pub, we also bought the recipe from the old lady – now departed – who used to make them,' says Chris.

BRIDGE HOTEL

ADDRESS
Cnr Leith and Forth rds, Forth

TELEPHONE
(03) 6428 2239

WEBSITE
www.forthpub.com.au

RATES
The hotel has 4 rooms: double room is $50, twins are $45 and a single is $30.

HOURS
The bar is open 11–12am Sun–Wed and 11–2am Thurs–Sat.

GRUB
The Bar and Grill open for lunch Wed–Sun 12–2pm and for dinner Thurs–Sat 6–8.30pm.

TOP DROP
Four beers are on tap: Carlton Draught, Cascade Premium Light, Pure Blonde and Boag's Draught.

MORE INFO
www.discovertasmania.com.au

Carlton Draught, available bottled or on tap

THE BUSH INN

NEW NORFOLK

THERE IS NO debate about the history of this Tasmanian treasure. When Ann Bridger opened the Bush Inn at New Norfolk in 1825, she became the first in a long, unbroken line of licensees. The Bush Inn is officially the hotel that has traded longest from within the same building in Australia.

The Melba Room at the Bush Inn, New Norfolk

New Norfolk had been settled in 1808 by a small band of free farmers and convicts who were transferred from Norfolk Island to the Derwent Valley. It was the third planned settlement in Tasmania, after Hobart and Launceston. The Bush Inn was built in 1815, designed by and named after D. W. Bush, the clerk to the colony's first chaplain Reverend Bobby Knopwood (who has a pub named after him in Hobart).

The original building is still intact, with its solid Tasmanian blackwood floors, and in the cellar, with its sandstone floors, the original skittle alley is now used as a storeroom.

In lots of ways, not much has changed since Ann Bridger opened the doors more than 185 years ago. Even some of the furniture that Mrs Bridger brought to her new business remains in the hotel, including about a dozen leather dining chairs. The original building is still intact, with its solid Tasmanian blackwood floors, some of which (including that in the main entrance hall) were uncovered and repolished in 1991. Some of the brick walls are supported on roughly squared logs, and in the cellar, with its sandstone floors, the original skittle alley is now used as a storeroom. The Bush Inn is listed on the Tasmanian Heritage Register and is classified by the National Trust.

THE BUSH INN

ADDRESS
49–51 Montague St, New Norfolk

TELEPHONE
(03) 6261 2256

WEBSITE
www.thebushinn.info

RATES
$40 per person per night.

HOURS
Daily 11am–late.

GRUB
Open daily for lunch 12–2pm and dinner 6–8pm.

TOP DROP
Cascade Draught, Cascade Premium Light, Cascade Pale Ale and Guinness are on tap.

NEARBY ATTRACTIONS
If you are into history, check out one of Australia's oldest churches, the Anglican church of St Matthew, opposite Arthur Sq, built 1823. For more active adventures, take a 20 km jet-boat ride on the Derwent River and experience the thrill of the rapids and a few 360-degree spins with Tasmanian Devil Jet. www.deviljet.com.au

MORE INFO
www.discovertasmania.com.au
www.newnorfolk.org

Other fascinating and curious reminders of the pub's history remain on display. These include a huon pine christening font which sits in the hotel foyer. In the 1830s, Methodist clergymen visiting from Hobart preached in the taproom of the pub until New Norfolk's St Paul's Church was built in 1835. They left the font behind.

Records above the fireplace

Another claim to fame is the fact that the first telephone 'trunk call' in Australia was made from the Bush Inn by the then licensee, Captain Octavius Blockey, in 1888. At the other end of the line was the Hobart Post Office. The telephone used to make the call is mounted on the wall in the lobby beside the christening font. The first call to London from Tasmania was also made from the hotel, in February 1939. The hotel's telephone number was New Norfolk 1 until the 1970s, when the town exchange was automated.

There have been notable visitors too. The Irish-born composer William Vincent Wallace reputedly wrote the three-act opera *Maritana* in 1838 while staying in the hotel. Broadcasting history was made at the hotel on 29 June 1932 when for the first time, *Maritana* was produced and broadcast from the spot where it was composed, over the ABC's national network through station 7ZL Hobart. The records made of the broadcast remain in the dining room, framed and mounted over the fireplace.

Now known as the Melba Room, the dining room also boasts a piano and a large portrait of Dame Nellie Melba, who stayed at the hotel on her last Tasmanian visit in 1924 (and sang part of the lyrics from *Maritana* while she was there). Live music is still an occasional part of the scene at the Bush Inn, usually on a Friday night every few months, and the perfect place for it is the huge deck off the glassed-in dining room, overlooking the Derwent River.

The Bush Inn has three bars, five open fireplaces, a billiards room and the Melba Room restaurant, which delivers hearty pub food, most dishes for less than $20. Half serves are offered for most main courses, including the roast of the day. There's a snack menu of burgers, chips, steak sandwiches and the like, and a kids' menu for under-12s, where everything is $6.

Upstairs are 20 guest rooms – single, twin, double or family rooms – with shared bathrooms. They do have antique furniture, fireplaces, small fan heaters and electric blankets, but are simple and basic – and they have no televisions or telephones.

New Norfolk is about 30 minutes' drive west of Hobart, and is a good base for exploring the Derwent Valley.

CASTLE HOTEL

BOTHWELL

WHEN YOU ORDER the smoked trout niçoise salad at the Castle Hotel in Bothwell, you should know that the fish has been caught and smoked by the licensee, Dennis Bell. Bothwell's setting, on the picturesque Clyde River at the foothills of the central Tasmanian highlands, is a drawcard for fishermen, and Bell is not immune to the river's lure.

The Castle Hotel, Bothwell

Such hands-on attention is part of the charm of this historic pub, about an hour's drive north of Hobart. Built in 1829, just six years after Bothwell was settled by Scottish colonists, it is the only remaining hotel in the town from an original four and is the third-oldest continuously licensed hotel in Australia.

Bell, a former Sydney banker, and his partner Julie Tay bought the hotel in 2003 and have done much to restore and renovate it, while still keeping the charm that imbues much of Bothwell. Like many of the 52 buildings in town that have either been classified or registered by the National Trust it is made from sandstone, with a brick addition on the side.

'When the upstairs guest rooms were being renovated we uncovered the original ornate Georgian wall stencilling, and we have left a section of it in two rooms so guests can still see it,' says Bell.

When you order the smoked trout niçoise salad at the Castle Hotel you should know that the fish has been caught and smoked by the licensee, Dennis Bell.

The hotel was built by settler and alleged sly grogger John Vincent and was originally called the Norwood Inn. Vincent later went on to build the London Inn in Spring Hill and the recently re-opened Callington Mill at Oatlands.

Today, the pub has a reputation for excellent food. 'We think we offer something that is varied and different to the usual pub meals,' says Bell. The Cascade stout pie is a favourite, a beef pie filled with a rich stew thickened with the stout and served in a ramekin dish. Other dishes include Moroccan lamb shanks, and pub standards like garlic prawns and surf'n'turf 'but with our own sauces'. Lunch is served every day but dinner is

CASTLE HOTEL

ADDRESS
14 Patrick St, Bothwell

TELEPHONE
(03) 6259 5502

EMAIL
info@castlehotelbothwell.com.au

RATES
$105 double, including continental breakfast.

HOURS
Mon–Thurs 11am–10pm; Fri 11am–11pm; Sat 10am–11pm; Sun 12–8pm.

GRUB
Lunch daily 12–2pm, dinner Fri–Sat 6–8pm, pizza on Wed nights.

TOP DROP
Cascade Draught, Boag's Draught and Bundaberg rum on tap.

NEARBY ATTRACTIONS
Drop into the Australasian Golf Museum and the local information centre on Market Pl, just up the street from the Castle Hotel. While you're there, pick up a brochure for a self-guided tour of Bothwell's many historic buildings. Most were built by convict labour and feature plaques explaining some history about each.

MORE INFO
www.discovertasmania.com
www.ausgolfmuseum.com

limited to weekends, while Wednesday is pizza night. House guests will be catered for any night of the week.

In the bar you are likely to meet some colourful local characters, perhaps from the local football club or Landcare group, or fishermen with tall tales to tell. The hotel is the major sponsor of the Bothwell Football Club, the only remaining football club in Tasmania's Central Highlands area. Other sporting types are likely to be golfers, as Bothwell's major claim to fame is as the home of Ratho, Australia's oldest golf course, established the same year as the pub. Ratho is a public course and green fees are only $15.

A great stop for self-drive tourists

Ratho is also the name of one of the three guest rooms upstairs, which have names instead of numbers. The other two are Clyde (for the river) and Saxon (for the merino wool that comes from the area). The rooms are furnished in period style, but with mod cons like bar fridges, televisions and DVD players, and an iron and ironing board; all three rooms also have access to a verandah. One room has an ensuite bathroom; the other two have private bathrooms, but as they are down the hallway fluffy bathrobes are provided. The rooms have oil heaters, there are electric blankets on the beds and the bathrooms also have heating.

With so much history, Bothwell (population about 400) has much to offer. Queens Park in the centre of town is a striking village green with views along many of Bothwell's historic streetscapes. If your tastes don't run to fishing or golf, you might want to take a look at the whisky distillery at nearby Nant Estate, built in 1821. Today, it offers whisky tours, tastings, dinners and the option to buy a 100-litre barrel of whisky with bespoke bottling and labelling. Tours run daily 10am–4pm, but bookings are essential.

The original sandstone part of the pub

EMPIRE HOTEL

QUEENSTOWN

AT THE TOP of the imposing staircase at the heart of the Empire Hotel a shadowy figure is reflected in the mirror on the landing. Captured on camera, the ghost that haunts this historic hotel may look like a woman but is believed to be that of a regular patron who departed this world – and his favourite table in the restaurant – in 1919. Whether you believe in ghosts or not, more than one person has seen what is believed to be the spectre of John Keating and the ghost story lives on.

The Empire Hotel, in the Tasmanian mining town of Queenstown, dates back to 1901 when the region's mining wealth was at its peak. This 'grand old lady of the West Coast' has a prominent place in the town's streetscape.

Inside, the ornate National Trust–listed staircase made from Tasmanian blackwood has a history of its own. The raw timber was shipped to England, carved and sent back to Queenstown to be assembled and installed in the hotel in 1904. The staircase features hand-carved acorns on the newel posts. Dame Nellie Melba graced these stairs, as did union leader (and later parliamentarian) King O'Malley, who started the Labour movement in Queenstown.

Queenstown's Empire Hotel and war memorial

The ornate staircase made from Tasmanian blackwood has a history of its own. The raw timber was shipped to England, carved and sent back to be assembled and installed in the hotel in 1904.

The richly furnished dining room

So palatial was the Empire in its heyday that – even though it was just one of 14 hotels in town at the time – more than one famous name saw fit to visit. On the wall of the dining room is the original menu from a 1909 occasion when Australia's second Prime Minister, Alfred Deakin, dined here. The seven-course luncheon included boiled trumpeter with egg sauce, roast lamb with redcurrant jelly (among a choice of meats) and plum pudding with brandy sauce.

The restaurant – still really a large traditional dining room – retains its grandeur and is richly furnished with heavy drapes, antiques and other reminders of the past. In winter, the open fire is lit. These days, the kitchen produces reputedly the best food in town, including chargrilled steaks, all prime Tasmanian Cape Grim beef. There are regular specials, too: Monday night is $18 T-bone

Part of the bar at the Empire Hotel

night, Wednesday is the day for an $8 pie at lunchtime, and on Sunday a $16 two-course roast dinner is served.

Elaborate cornices, plasterwork, archways and pressed-metal ceilings add to the hotel's atmosphere, and Queen Victoria looks down from above the door to the front bar, which has more memorabilia and a pool table.

The ornate blackwood staircase

Upstairs, modest but clean and comfortable rooms are ready for guests – but it is best not to expect anything like the style and comfort the stairs might suggest! The somewhat startling salmon-pink paint on the walls of the accommodation level is part of the hotel's heritage and unlikely to change. All rooms are off a long hallway, as are the male and female toilets and bathrooms – two showers and a deep old bathtub in each. There are 20 standard rooms (four with ensuites) and all have electric blankets on the bed, but not all have heating. There is also a family room with an ensuite, and three double 'backpacker-style' rooms (each with a television and heater) share a bathroom.

The standard single rooms have a basin, chair, heater, wardrobe and a view of Mt Owen. A backpacker four-share room also has its own lounge room with a television, microwave and fridge – and a mountain view.

Mt Owen and Mt Lyell are the two largest mountains of the many that surround Queenstown. At sunset their summits blaze orange and pink, but by day they show a cratered moonscape. For a 360-degree view of the town, walk up the Spion Kop hillock.

The Iron Blow on Gormanston Hill was the first local goldmine that made a fortune – not from gold but from the copper in the ore that continues to be Queenstown's largest product. To get a feel for the mining heritage of the town, take an underground tour into one of Australia's largest hard-rock mines, 6 kilometres beneath the surface.

A mining town for more than a century, Queenstown is now a heritage town that is a popular tourist destination for its 19th-century pubs (the Empire is just one of them) and for the West Coast Wilderness Railway. The railway, directly opposite the Empire, runs restored steam locomotives through some of Tasmania's most spectacular rainforest and gorges.

From Queenstown it is 250 kilometres to Hobart or 240 kilometres to Launceston, making it an easy choice to take in the West Coast and see another side of Tasmania.

EMPIRE HOTEL

ADDRESS
2 Orr St, Queenstown

TELEPHONE
(03) 6471 1699

WEBSITE
www.empirehotel.net.au

RATES
Standard single room $30; standard double or twin room $50; double with ensuite $75; extra person rate $15. Quad-share backpacker rooms $25 per person. Standard rooms share a bathroom.

HOURS
Bar open 11–1am.

GRUB
Restaurant open daily for lunch from 12pm and for dinner 6–8pm.

TOP DROP
There is a large range of beers, Tasmanian and mainland wines, as well as Guinness and Kilkenny on tap.

NEARBY ATTRACTIONS
Across the street from the hotel is the beautifully restored West Coast Wilderness Railway (www.puretasmania.com) that runs daily between Queenstown and Strahan (in both directions). Queenstown is also noted for its moonscape, the result of many years of mining in the area. There is a public golf course with a couple of 'special' rules for poor weather conditions! The area is popular for walking, local fishing and 4WD tracks.

MORE INFO
www.westernwilderness.com.au
www.discovertasmania.com.au

STRAHAN

Hamer's Hotel, Strahan

STUDY THE WALLS of the bar in Hamer's Hotel and you'll learn a lot about this small town perched on the edge of the Tasmanian wilderness. You'll realise, fairly quickly, that perhaps Strahan is not the tourist town you thought it was. That's an easy assumption to make, because much of this West Coast hamlet's focus is on tourism and many touring options are prominent along the Strahan waterfront – the cruise boats and the cafes, the accommodation and the buses. But it doesn't take much to scratch the surface and find the real Strahan.

It's as easy, really, as spending time in the pub. The first hotel on this waterfront site at Risby Cove was at the turn of last century, when a three-storey hotel called Clark's Hotel was built. It was later called the Macquarie Harbour Hotel, but in 1936 the current brick hotel was built for Mrs Mary Jane Hamer, who ran it until the end of World War II, when her youngest daughter, Mrs Vera Wilson, took it over. It was sold in the 1950s and has had a string of owners since then.

The rooms are spacious enough for a small Huon pine dining table and chairs, for those who want to dine in with a view of the harbour.

During the 1990s, Tasmanian tourism entrepreneur Simon Currant redeveloped the hotel, along with much of Strahan village including the replica cottages alongside the hotel, based on photos of the history of the area. Hamer's Hotel is now owned by Federal Hotels.

Memories on the bar wall

But all that is history, and what really tells the story of the pub and the community is the different sections around the Memory Wall of the bar. First, you may be attracted by the photographic memories of celebrity visitors, among them Prince Charles and Jack Halligan 'The Kalgoorlie Kid', the World Number One pool player who came to play with the locals.

But then, starting near the windows that look out to the harbour, you will get the real story. 'Our Losses' is a wall of images of townspeople – some of them too young – who have died in recent years. A special mention is there for the late Jack 'Soldier' McDermott, who came in to light the fire in the pub every morning. Then you come to 'Our Boats', including piners' punts and the first cruise boat in Strahan, and 'Our Landscape' shots. 'Our Town' records events of note, such as the stranding of beached whales, the work of the Whale First Response Team and of Wildcare, and the exploits of local sporting teams. 'Our Fish' boasts the big ones that didn't get away.

There's a dartboard, a television, two pool tables (a local eight-ball competition runs on Thursday nights in winter) and lots more historic photos of the town. Happy hour, with hot food on offer, is 6–7.30pm on Wednesday and Friday evenings. Settling in by the open log fire for a beer or a glass of Tasmanian wine is very appealing. The tiny bottleshop has very good specials, especially on Tasmanian wines and beers.

Next to the bar, Hamer's Grill offers steaks, seafood, chicken, pasta and daily seasonal specials. There's a lunch and dinner menu – with many of the same top choices on both. For lunch there's also some lighter fare, like a 'cheesy' steak sandwich (porterhouse,

HAMER'S HOTEL

ADDRESS
41 The Esplanade, Strahan

TELEPHONE
(03) 6471 4335

WEBSITE
www.puretasmania.com.au

RATES
$270 double in high season, but 50% or more off in low season.

HOURS
Daily 11am–11pm.

GRUB
Open for lunch 12–2pm and dinner 5.30–9pm daily (except Christmas Day).

TOP DROP
Boag's, Pure Blonde, Carlton Draught and XXXX Gold on tap.

NEARBY ATTRACTIONS
River cruises depart from Strahan for the fabulous Gordon River, also stopping at the former convict settlement on Sarah Is. Evening cruises also head to the tiny Bonnet Is, with its lighthouse and penguin colony. The West Coast Wilderness Railway links Strahan and Queenstown (with bus transfers for the return journey) and is a great day out. For an insight into the history of the Tasmanian timber and mining industries take the interesting Piners & Miners day tour.

MORE INFO
www.westernwilderness.com.au
www.discovertasmania.com.au

Hamer's Grill and lounge bar

onions, bacon and cream cheese sauce on Turkish bread, served with chips) or Macquarie Harbour smoked salmon with wild rocket and citrus salad and wasabi crème fraiche.

Dinner offers some heartier dishes, such as rosemary, thyme and garlic roasted chicken breast with red wine jus and baked vegetables. Be warned: the steaks are huge, including a 400 gram Cape Grim rump for $26.

Upstairs are four guest rooms. The old backpacker rooms are now motel-style double rooms with ensuite, television, fridge, toaster, tea- and coffee-making facilities and electric blankets on the beds. The rooms are also spacious enough for a small Huon pine dining table and chairs, for those who want to dine in with a view of the harbour. All rooms have doors to the balcony, with privacy screens between each, and a small table and chairs outside.

If the rooms are booked out, there are plenty of other accommodation choices in Strahan, including the hotel's sister property, which has 140 rooms on the hill overlooking the harbour, and the 11 reproduction cottages along the main street.

Strahan (pronounced 'strawn') is not the rugged town it once was, the home of fishermen, piners, miners and railwaymen. But the fishing boats still head out from Macquarie Harbour to the wild Southern Ocean every day and trains (albeit for tourists) still run on the rainforest tracks.

Pub sign

For an insight into the history of the town – and a fun night out – head along to the nightly performance of *The Ship That Never Was*, a two-hander play by local writer/historian Richard Davey in a small theatre almost opposite the pub. The hour-long play – with lots of audience participation (but of the kind that won't make you cringe) – claims to be the longest running in Australia, with daily performances since 1993.

Strahan is about four hours' drive from Hobart. It's a place where you'll find history at every turn.

MAN O' ROSS

ROSS

Man O' Ross

The elm-lined streets, once shared by red-coated soldiers and convicts in chains, are now walked by tourists wielding cameras to capture the sandstone Georgian buildings with their cottage gardens.

FOUR HISTORIC BUILDINGS stand on the main crossroads in the town of Ross, on Tasmania's Heritage Highway. They are known as 'Temptation', 'Salvation', 'Recreation' and 'Damnation'. It's not hard to work out which one is the Man O' Ross, the town's oldest licensed hotel.

As you enter the town from the north – after an hour's drive from Launceston – you will come to the junction of Church and Bridge streets. On your left is the Man O' Ross – which is, of course, Temptation. Facing it across Church Street is the Catholic church (Salvation), diagonally opposite is the town hall (Recreation) and across Bridge Street is the old Ross gaol (Damnation), now a private home.

All are sandstone buildings, dating back to the first years of Ross, which was established as a garrison town in 1812 at a strategically important crossing point on the Macquarie River – one of several such towns built between Launceston and Hobart by the 1820s, largely using convict labour. Today it remains one of Tasmania's best preserved and most picturesque historic villages, just 121 kilometres north of Hobart or 78 kilometres south of Launceston.

MAN O' ROSS

ADDRESS
35 Church St, Ross

TELEPHONE
(03) 6381 5445

WEBSITE
www.manoross.com

RATES
$75 single; $90 double; $125 family room. Rates include continental breakfast.

HOURS
Daily 11am–late.

GRUB
Open daily for lunch 12–2pm and dinner 6–8pm.

TOP DROP
Beers on tap include Boag's Premium Light, Cascade Premium Light, Guinness and XXXX.

NEARBY ATTRACTIONS
The Tasmanian Wool Centre, 48 Church St, details the growth of the region and the wool industry since settlement; it celebrates the importance of wool to Tasmania and highlights the historical significance of Ross as one of Tasmania's earliest rural settlements. The Centre is one of Tasmania's main tourist attractions, receiving more than 75 000 visitors annually.

MORE INFO
www.visitross.com.au

The elm-lined streets, once shared by red-coated soldiers and convicts in chains, are now walked by tourists wielding cameras to capture the sandstone Georgian buildings with their cottage gardens, or intent on exploring the antique and craft shops, museums and coffee shops.

The Man O' Ross hotel, built in 1835 by William Saddler, is constructed from local hand-cut sandstone and has timbered gables. It is quaint looking, with a cottage garden, a large dining room and a beer garden out the back, and traditional pub accommodation upstairs.

Country-style meals are served in the pleasant dining room, which has a fire burning in winter. Lunch can be served in the beer garden if the weather permits. The menu always has specials on offer – dishes like game pie, Tasmanian rainbow trout or a lamb T-bone, usually for less than $20. Kids' meals are around $6.50, and are smaller versions of adult meals, like bangers and mash and spaghetti bolognaise – but there's a pizza option that's strictly for young ones.

Upstairs, the hotel has seven rooms, with shared bathroom facilities. Some rooms have double queen-sized beds or twin beds, and there is a family room with a double bed and two single beds. All have sash windows and have been refurbished with a colonial-style decor. For those chilly Tasmanian nights, all the rooms have heating and electric blankets on the beds.

The main attraction in the town is the stunning stone bridge over the Macquarie River. Ross Bridge, the third oldest in Australia, was built in 1836 and is decorated with Celtic symbols, animals, and faces of notable people of the time. It is illuminated at night, and the best views of it are from the river's north bank. The Macquarie River and surrounding lakes are world renowned for their rainbow and brown trout.

Ross is an integral part of driving Tasmania's Heritage Highway. By the mid-19th century, convict labor had produced what was considered to be the finest highway of its time in Australia. Today, many of the towns along the Heritage Highway have magnificent examples of Georgian and Victorian architecture. It takes about two hours to drive between Launceston and Hobart on this route but you could easily spend several days exploring as you go.

Ross Bridge

PUB *in the* PADDOCK

PYENGANA

The Pub in the Paddock, Pyengana

Priscilla and Pinky are patient pigs. They wait contentedly in their pens in the garden of the Pub in the Paddock, secure in the knowledge that before long someone will bring them a beer.

PRISCILLA AND PINKY are patient pigs. They wait contentedly in their pens in the garden of the Pub in the Paddock, just beyond the tractor shed, secure in the knowledge that before long someone will bring them a beer.

And someone always does. But – in case you are worried about their welfare – never more than 12 stubbies a day, and even then it is really only water with a tiny splash of beer in the bottom to add a bit of flavour. To give them a drink, you have to ask the barman, who has a special supply ready for them, and when the pigs' dozen is gone, there's no more on offer.

The beer-drinking pigs at the Pub in the Paddock have become famous over the years, despite their relative isolation. This bucolic part of north-east Tasmania is a beguiling part of the world, and the hamlet of Pyengana (from an Aboriginal word meaning 'meeting of two rivers') is tucked in a beautiful valley of lush dairy farmland, 27 kilometres from the coastal town of St Helens.

Priscilla and Pinky reside behind a fence that bears a sign: 'Geez I'm dry, I'd luv a beer'. The sign looks like it's been there longer than they have – and it probably has, because these two pigs are the latest in a line that began when former publican Chris Mundy started the gimmick in the 1990s. Previous visitors may recall the original pig, Slops, then there was Grog ('a nasty bugger', confides a local at the bar), a few Babes and at least two earlier Priscillas.

Driveway sign and the pub's letterbox

The Pub in the Paddock is one of Tasmania's oldest country pubs, licensed since about 1880, and is well worth the short detour off the main road. It was built as a homestead for the Terry family, who had 15 children (some of the boys reputedly more interested in drinking than in farming). Once licensed, their home became St Columba Falls Hotel, named for the cascading waterfall a little further down the valley. The pub was the social hub of the valley, with the barn becoming a dance hall and later a picture theatre on Saturday nights.

In 1963, during a major flood, a stranded tourist was helped and hosted by the then publican, Griff Parry. When the grateful traveller got home again, he sent a postcard of thanks, but being unable to remember the name of the pub, addressed it simply to: 'The Pub in the Paddock, North East Tasmania'. The postcard arrived and the name stuck – and has now been officially changed.

Hospitality is still paramount, and in winter the three-way fireplace to the dining room and bar areas – and another in the front bar – keeps the Tasmanian chill out. Meals are hearty, with roasts and specials on the menu. And, in case you were wondering, the pigs may come and go, but they are never going to appear on the menu, assures current licensee Kristine Millwood.

'We're just an old-fashioned pub, with good traditional counter meals,' says Kristine, who grew up in the area and turns out the meals in the kitchen herself.

The menu is typical pub fare with some interesting twists. Entrees include deep-fried crumbed camembert with cranberry sauce, mini spring rolls with sweet chilli sauce

and chargrilled meatballs with barbecue sauce. The speciality main course is Pub Chicken, a breast of chicken sautéed with bacon, onion, green peppercorns and a white wine and cream sauce. There's also homemade 'roo patties, served with gravy and vegetables, and the classic Reef & Beef (scotch fillet steak topped with prawn cutlets and sweet chilli sauce), at $27.50 the most expensive item on the menu.

Pigs are everywhere

Seven guest rooms run off a corridor on the far side of the dining room, with men's and women's bathrooms at the end of the hall. Kristine and her partner Tom also have plans to establish a free camping area for caravans and campervans.

Live music and talent nights provide entertainment from time to time, but even without that, it's an easy place to sit and chat for hours with the locals. There are plenty of stories from the Pyengana Valley to hear – and Kristine has one of the best.

When she took over the pub, she found among the newspaper clippings and photos on the bar wall that tell the story of the village, one concerning her great-aunt Anne Beechey. In 1908, Anne got lost in the bush while out looking for the cows. After nine days, she emerged and asked a farmer to direct her home. She lost her toes on both feet to frostbite, and told of how for the last two days she had been stalked by two Tasmanian tigers as they waited for her to die. But still, she didn't want to put the farmer to any trouble and declined his offer of a lift home ... she was happy to walk.

Priscilla quenches her thirst

The last reported sighting of a Tassie tiger here was in 1995, although the species was officially declared extinct nearly a decade earlier. Keep your eyes peeled when you take a walk in the Pyengana area!

The Pub in the Paddock – and its pigs – is well worth a detour.

THE PUB IN THE PADDOCK

ADDRESS
250 St Columba Falls Rd, Pyengana

TELEPHONE
(03) 6373 6121

EMAIL
pubinthepaddock@harboursat.com.au

RATES
$55 single, $75 double, $80 twin, $115 family room (sleeps 4). Continental breakfast $9.

HOURS
Daily 10.30–12am.

GRUB
Daily for lunch and dinner.

TOP DROP
Beer on tap includes Boag's, VB and Cascade Light.

NEARBY ATTRACTIONS
A few minutes' walk down the road is the Pyengana Dairy Company, where you can taste award-winning, traditionally made cheddar cheeses or delicious ice-cream while you watch the cows being milked. Don't miss the spectacular St Columba Falls, plunging nearly 90 m from the Mt Victoria foothills to the South George River valley. The falls are 6 km past the pub.

MORE INFO
www.discovertasmania.com

Richmond Arms

RICHMOND

The Richmond Arms

ONCE A KEY military post and convict station, Richmond was established strategically between Hobart and the Port Arthur penal settlement in the 1820s. With its attractive buildings made from convict-hewn sandstone and bricks, it is a delightful tourist destination. Richmond is also a key point on Tasmania's historic Convict Trail and in it you will find Australia's oldest gaol – even older than Port Arthur – as well as the oldest bridge, Catholic church, primary school and post office.

Richmond is regarded as one of the best – if not *the* best – preserved Georgian village in Australia. Set in the Coal River Valley, it is surrounded by hillside vineyards.

A hotel has stood on Bridge Street since 1827 but the name of the Richmond Arms was only bestowed on the existing building in 1972. Before that, the pub was called the Commercial Hotel, built in 1888 to replace the Lennox Arms, which had been destroyed by fire.

The Lennox Arms was built by Richmond's first major 'developer', James Kestell Buscombe, who was also responsible for building the granary and post office, Tower Windmill and Cottage (1831 and 1837) and his home, Prospect House, which still stands on the outskirts of the village. His brother Henry was a builder, known to have built Oak Lodge and St John's Church, and probably the Lennox Arms. The two-storey inn had an upstairs assembly room used for meetings, including those of the Royal Agricultural Society, and election results were announced from its verandah to the often drunken crowd below.

In 1886 the Commercial Hotel in turn also burnt down. The fire destroyed most of the original building – the only part still left is the old stables, now accommodation. The current Georgian-style building replaced it two years later. In the 1980s, when the tourist trade to the town began to boom, the hotel was renamed the Richmond Arms.

Outdoor dining

Only 20 minutes' drive from Hobart, Richmond is regarded as one of the best – if not *the* best – preserved Georgian village in Australia. Set in the Coal River Valley, it is surrounded by hillside vineyards, and the sandstone cottages and elegant houses that line the streets – some of them now shops and galleries – make it postcard-perfect.

The Richmond Arms today is very much a family pub: a basket of toys sits on the floor in the Bistro Lounge. Beyond the bistro is the Saloon Bar. You can order meals in either, or dine in the formal dining room on the other side of the main entrance. On sunny days, the tables outside in the front garden bar are a great spot (and there's a photo opportunity the kids will like with the old convict stocks outside too).

The Saloon Bar and Bistro Lounge offer light snacks and hearty meals along with seafood and cheese platters – all made with local produce. There's also a children's menu and daily specials such as beer-battered prawns or a king pork chop with apple cider sauce.

Old convict stocks

Some of Tasmania's finest pinots, cabernets, chardonnays and rieslings come from the 30 vineyards in the Coal Valley, and many of them are featured on the wine list here. The main bar has TAB, keno, a pool table, jukebox and live entertainment, or you can just relax in front of the open fire.

The only surviving part of the old Lennox Arms was the sandstone stables, which still stand. Built in 1827, they have been renovated to preserve their original character and now form the hotel's accommodation wing. There are four rooms – single, double and twin, as well as a family room that sleeps up to six – all with ensuite bathrooms and a television.

RICHMOND ARMS

ADDRESS
42 Bridge St, Richmond

TELEPHONE
(03) 6260 2109

WEBSITE
www.richmondarmshotel.com.au

RATES
$99 single, $120 double, plus $15 per extra person, including continental breakfast.

HOURS
Mon–Tues 11am–9pm; Wed 11am–10pm; Thurs–Sat 11am–11.30pm; Sun 11am–8.30pm.

GRUB
Open daily for lunch 12–2pm and dinner 5–8pm.

TOP DROP
Featured brews are from Cascade: Amber Ale, Pale Ale, Blonde and Stout. There's also an extensive range of local and Australian wines and beer.

NEARBY ATTRACTIONS
The historic Richmond Bridge is a short walk from the hotel, as is the Old Richmond Gaol. There are also a number of walking tracks and wildlife parks to explore.

MORE INFO
www.richmondvillage.com.au
www.discovertasmania.com

ROSEVEARS WATERFRONT TAVERN

ROSEVEARS

Rosevears Waterfront Tavern

EVERY DAY FOR nine years publican Clive Porter dropped what he was doing to walk out onto the front steps of his tavern and wave to the cruise boat as it went by on its trip down the Tamar River. Clive became a familiar sight to those on the river and was known for this small friendly gesture – but as his retirement approached in 2011, he wondered if a new licensee would keep the tradition going.

Rosevears Waterfront Tavern is the only substantial building in the pretty village of Rosevears, in the Tamar Valley 18 kilometres north of Launceston. The tavern, built in 1831, has wonderful views of the West Tamar River and across the valley, so try for a table by the window – or in the garden bar if the weather is fine – to watch the boats and the birds go by.

The pub was first licensed on 24 September 1831 as the Rose Inn, making it one of the oldest continuously licensed hotels in Australia. But the man whose name it now takes – William Henry Rosevear – was probably not the man who built it, according to Clive Porter, who says much of the history of the pub is unknown.

The wisteria-covered beer garden runs off the main bar, and is a lovely spot to sit in the sun while you watch the pelicans glide over the river.

What is known, however, is that Rosevear had arrived in Tasmania from the colony at Swan River (now Perth, Western Australia) with his wife and children in 1829. He had been a farmer in England, and soon took up 256 hectares in the West Tamar region (later expanding with another 172 hectares) for farming and orchards. And he certainly had a connection with the pub. Records show he had held the licence of the Half Way House between 1833 and 1834, and was listed as the licensee of the Rose Inn in 1835 and again between 1848 and 1851. He died in 1860, aged 73.

'There's also a story that Mrs Rosevear is the ghost that haunts the pub – apparently she fell down the stairs,' says Porter. 'But I don't believe the Rosevears ever lived here.'

Plenty of labels to choose from

The village of Rosevears was the site of early shipbuilding on the Tamar. The area and the shipyards were also known as Battery Point and Cimitieres Point (after Colonel Gilbert Cimitiere, Commandant of Port Dalrymple between 1818 and 1822). Among the shipbuilders was sea captain George Plummer, who arrived in Tasmania in the late 1820s. The Plummers' shipyard built *Rebecca*, in which John Batman sailed to Port Phillip in 1835, which resulted in the founding of Melbourne. There is a plaque on the water's edge where *Rebecca* was launched.

Inside the tavern there are still sections of the original brickwork. There are several areas to eat in: the main bistro overlooking the water or a larger, more formal dining area behind it, as well as cosy booths off the main bar where there's a stone fireplace and wooden mantle in which patrons have carved their names over the years.

There's a bar menu – for ordering only in the bar or the beer garden – with about five choices, all priced at $16, such as fish and chips, a fish burger, steak sandwich, roast of the day and baglaki (marinated beef strips, salad and yoghurt in a warm bun). The à la carte menu has the usual pub grub, including a Rosevears chicken parmigiana, steaks, roast, pasta and a vegetarian chilli. There are also daily specials, meals like lamb shanks, beef curry and pork porterhouse.

The wisteria-covered beer garden runs off the main bar, and is a lovely spot to sit in the sun while you watch the pelicans glide over the river. It's very family-friendly and there are high chairs if you need one.

Within walking distance of the tavern are vineyards with cellar doors, and the village has an art gallery and antique shop. But one of the nicest things to do is simply walk (or drive) along the waterfront. There is lots of birdlife, and for a fabulous view of the Tamar Valley head up to Bradys Lookout (named for the bushranger Matthew Brady who used this spot to look for potential victims).

ROSEVEARS WATERFRONT TAVERN

ADDRESS
215 Rosevears Dr, Rosevears

TELEPHONE
(03) 6394 4074

HOURS
Daily 11am–late.

GRUB
Open for lunch daily 12–2pm and dinner Sun–Thurs 6–7.15pm, Fri–Sat 6–8pm.

TOP DROP
Boag's Draught and Boag's Premium Light on tap.

WHERE TO STAY
Rosevears Vineyard Retreat has 20 stylish eco-chalets, a combination of studio, 1-bedroom and 2-bedroom apartments, from $164. www.rosevears.com.au

NEARBY ATTRACTIONS
To take a river cruise for a look at Rosevears from the water, join Tamar River Cruises in Launceston. A 2.5 hr afternoon cruise runs Oct–April. www.tamarrivercruises.com.au

MORE INFO
www.discovertasmania.com.au
www.tamarvalley.com.au

Index

About the author

LEE MYLNE propped up at bars all over Australia as she gathered stories for *Great Australian Pubs* and learned a lot about the places she visited through the eyes of the locals. Based in Melbourne, Lee began her career as a newspaper journalist but itchy feet found her specialising in travel writing. She is the author of seven guidebooks and a contributor to travel anthologies and many leading publications. She is a Life Member and past president of the Australian Society of Travel Writers. When Lee is not travelling or writing, she's usually planning the next adventure.

Acknowledgements

Many people – friends and strangers, too numerous to mention individually here – shared their favourite pubs with me in the course of researching this book. Not all their suggestions made it to these pages, but most of them got checked out and I'm grateful for all the tips. I would like to thank the owners, licensees and staff at the 100 hotels in this book who took time to share their stories, and the stories of their pubs, with me. In particular, the following people and organisations gave invaluable practical assistance during my travels around Australia: Philip Engelberts, Gaynor Stanley and the South Australian Tourism Commission; Largs Pier Hotel, Largs Bay; the Stirling Hotel, Stirling; Jane and Ross Fargher of Prairie Hotel, Parachilna; Moya and Peter Buckley of Moonshadow Villas in Darwin, who went above and beyond to help; Airborne Solutions and pilot David Paech, who found a seat for me on one of their pub heli-tours out of Darwin, allowing me to cover a lot of ground in a short time; Caves House Hotel, Yallingup; Soniya Fernandez and *Spirit of Tasmania*, for taking me and my car to Tasmania; Pure Tasmania for hospitality and generous help on the West Coast.

For breaking the loneliness of life on the road for several months, I thank the following people for their hospitality, their fine company in the bars and dining rooms of pubs around the country, their friendship and their love: Jessica Mylne; Kris Madden and Tony Meagher; Christine Salins; Lyn Singer; Mike Bingham; Andrew Bain; Stuart Innes; Annette Brimson; Len Zell; Ewen Bell; Virginia Cairns; Graeme Willingham; Tommy Campion; Pamela Wright.

Acknowledgements

Publications manager
Astrid Browne

Managing editor
Melissa Krafchek

Project manager and editor
Clare Coney

Editorial assistance
Janet Austin

Cover design
Steve Smedley of tontodesign

Internal page design
Peter Dyson at desertpony

Layout
Megan Ellis

Cartography
Bruce McGurty, Paul de Leur, Emily Maffei

Index
Max McMaster

Pre-press
PageSet Digital Print & Pre-press

Photography credits

Main cover image
Sail & Anchor Hotel at dusk, Fremantle, Western Australia (© photolibrary. All rights reserved.)

Cover and title page images
Guest lounge at the Australian Hotel, The Rocks, New South Wales (Courtesy the Australian Hotel); Dog lounging on the floor of the Imperial Hotel, Ravenswood, Queensland (Len Zell); Flaming steak on the grill at Breakfast Creek Hotel, Albion, Queensland (Courtesy Breakfast Creek Hotel)

Back cover
Prairie Hotel, Parachilna, South Australia (Australian Geographic); Bar stools at Fortune of War, The Rocks, New South Wales (Courtesy Fortune of War); Statue in German Arms Hotel, Hahndorf, South Australia (Lee Mylne); Pie with mushy peas at the Lord Nelson Brewery Hotel, The Rocks, New South Wales (Courtesy the Lord Nelson Brewery Hotel)

Half-title page
Middle Park Hotel, Middle Park, Victoria (Courtesy Middle Park Hotel)

Title page
Exterior of Young & Jackson, Melbourne, Victoria (David Hannah/ Lonely Planet Images)

Generic images used throughout
Shutterstock.com (Alexey Pustoshilov, Graphic design, Ragnarock, Julian Rovagnati, Vadim Kolobanov, Evgeny Karandaev, bogdan ionesc, Imageman, WITTY234, Pixelbliss, Aaron Amat, Tarasyuk Igor)

Page 3
Courtesy Wig & Pen, Canberra

Author's photo (page 251)
Ewen Bell

All other images are © Lee Mylne except for the following:

New South Wales and the Australian Capital Territory
Page 5 Top courtesy the Newport Arms Hotel, below left courtesy Wig & Pen, below centre courtesy the Australian Hotel, below right courtesy Lord Nelson Brewery Hotel; 6 Top courtesy the Australian Hotel; 7 Top and below courtesy the Australian Hotel; 8 Top and below right courtesy the Australian Hotel, below left courtesy Little Creatures Brewing; 9 Courtesy Fortune of War; 10 Top right courtesy Russell Hotel; 15 Top and below left courtesy the Lord Nelson Brewery Hotel; 16 Top and below courtesy the Lord Nelson Brewery Hotel; 17 Top courtesy the Newport Arms; 18 Courtesy the Newport Arms; 26 Esther La Rovere; 27 Top Esther La Rovere; 39 Below courtesy Castlemaine Perkins (Lion Nathan); 40 Courtesy Tourism New South Wales (Hamilton Lund, Destination NSW); 45 Top courtesy Australian Capital Tourism; 46 Courtesy Australian Capital Tourism; 47 Top and below courtesy Wig & Pen, Canberra; 48 Top and below right courtesy Wig & Pen; 49 Courtesy Wig & Pen

Victoria
Page 51 Top courtesy Middle Park Hotel, below left courtesy Tourism Victoria, below centre courtesy Grand Pacific Hotel, below right courtesy Holgate Brewhouse; 53 Top and below centre courtesy the Esplanade Hotel; 54 Top and below courtesy the Esplanade Hotel; 55 Top courtesy Hotel Lincoln; 56 Top and below courtesy Hotel Lincoln; 57 Top courtesy Middle Park Hotel; 58 Top and below centre courtesy Middle Park Hotel; 59 Top and below courtesy Middle Park Hotel; 64 Top courtesy Young & Jackson; 65 Top and below courtesy Young & Jackson; 66 Top and below centre courtesy Young & Jackson; 71 Top and below courtesy Tourism Victoria; 73 Top courtesy Tourism Victoria; 74 Courtesy the Farmers Arms; 77 Top courtesy Healesville Hotel 78 Courtesy Healesville Hotel; 79 Top courtesy Tourism Victoria; 80 Top courtesy Holgate Brewhouse, below courtesy Tourism Victoria; 81 Top courtesy Hotel Shamrock; 82 Courtesy Tourism Victoria; 83 Top courtesy Mildura Grand Hotel; 84 Top and below right courtesy Mildura Grand Hotel; 85 Top and below courtesy Mildura Grand Hotel; 88 Top courtesy Tourism Victoria; 89 Courtesy Royal Mail Hotel; 91 Top courtesy Tourism Victoria; 92 Top courtesy Walhalla's Star Hotel; 93 Top and below courtesy Walhalla's Star Hotel

South Australia
Page 95 Top courtesy Australian Geographic, below centre courtesy the Edinburgh Hotel, below right courtesy Largs Pier Hotel; 97 Courtesy the Edinburgh Hotel; 98 Top courtesy Largs Pier Hotel; 99 Top and below courtesy Largs Pier Hotel; 100 Top courtesy Largs Pier Hotel; 101 Courtesy Walkers Arms; 102 Top and below courtesy Walkers Arms; 103 Top and below courtesy Walkers Arms; 113 Top courtesy Innamincka Hotel; 114 Courtesy Innamincka Hotel; 126 Courtesy the Stirling Hotel; 127 Top and centre courtesy the Stirling Hotel; 128 Top courtesy South Australian Tourism Commission; 129 Courtesy Coopers Brewery

Western Australia
Page 131 Below left courtesy Sail & Anchor Hotel, below right courtesy the Esplanade Hotel; 132 Top courtesy the Brass Monkey; 133 Top and below courtesy Lonely Planet Images (Orien Harvey); 137 Top courtesy Sail & Anchor Hotel; 138 Top and below courtesy Sail & Anchor Hotel, Fremantle; 139 Top and below left courtesy Sail & Anchor Hotel; 142 Top courtesy Caves House Hotel; 143 Courtesy Caves House Hotel; 144 Top courtesy the Esplanade Hotel; 145 Below courtesy the Esplanade Hotel; 146 Top and below right courtesy the Esplanade Hotel; 147 Top courtesy Margaret River Hotel; 148 Courtesy Margaret River Hotel; 151 Top courtesy the New Norcia Hotel; 152 Top and below courtesy the New Norcia Hotel

Northern Territory
Page 161 Top and below left courtesy Tourism NT; 163 Courtesy Tourism NT

Queensland
Page 173 Top courtesy Tourism Queensland, below centre courtesy Breakfast Creek Hotel; 174 Top courtesy Breakfast Creek Hotel; 175 Top and below centre courtesy Breakfast Creek Hotel; 176 Top and below courtesy Breakfast Creek Hotel; 179 Courtesy the Norman Hotel; 180 Courtesy the Norman Hotel; 181 Top courtesy the Plough Inn; 182 Courtesy the Plough Inn; 183 Top courtesy the Regatta Hotel; 184 Top and below courtesy the Regatta Hotel; 185 Top courtesy Story Bridge Hotel; 186 Top left and right courtesy Story Bridge Hotel; 187 Top and below courtesy Story Bridge Hotel; 190 Top courtesy Tourism Queensland; 191 Courtesy Tourism Queensland; 195 Top courtesy Corones Hotel; 196 Courtesy Tourism Queensland; 197 Top courtesy Cairns Courthouse Hotel; 198 Courtesy Cairns Courthouse Hotel; 199 Len Zell; 200 Len Zell; 201 Below Len Zell; 204 Top courtesy St Bernards Hotel; 205 Courtesy St Bernards Hotel; 206 Top and below right courtesy St Bernards Hotel; 207 Top courtesy travelstories.com.au (Lee Atkinson); 208 Courtesy Tourism Queensland; 211 Top courtesy Wellshot Hotel; 212 Top left, right and below centre courtesy Wellshot Hotel; 213 Courtesy Wellshot Hotel

Tasmania
Page 217 Top courtesy Customs House Hotel; 218 Top courtesy Lonely Planet Images (Grant Dixon); 219 Courtesy Knopwood's Retreat; 220 Top courtesy the Republic Bar & Cafe; 221 Courtesy the Republic Bar & Cafe; 223 Below courtesy Cascade Brewery; 225 Top courtesy Bischoff Hotel; 226 Courtesy Bischoff Hotel; 228 Courtesy Fosters Group; 231 Top courtesy Castle Hotel; 232 Top courtesy Castle Hotel; 239 Top courtesy Tourism Tasmania; 240 Courtesy Tourism Tasmania

Explore Australia Publishing Pty Ltd
Ground Floor, Building 1, 658 Church Street,
Richmond, VIC 3121

Explore Australia Publishing Pty Ltd is a division of Hardie Grant Publishing Pty Ltd

Published by Explore Australia Publishing Pty Ltd, 2012

National Library of Australia Cataloguing-in-Publication entry

Author:	Mylne, Lee
Title:	Great Australian pubs / Lee Mylne.
Edition:	1st ed.
ISBN:	9781741173680 (pbk.)
Notes:	Includes index.
Subjects:	Bars (Drinking establishments)--Australia. Hotels--Australia.
Dewey Number:	647.9594

ISBN-13 9781741173680

10 9 8 7 6 5 4 3 2 1

Printed and bound in China by 1010 Printing International Ltd